PHR® and SPHR®

Human Resources
Certification Complete

Review Guide

2018 Exams

James J. Galluzzo III, SPHR

SYBEX®
A Wiley Brand

Senior Acquisitions Editor: Kenyon Brown
Development Editor: James Compton
Copy Editor: Kim Wimpsett
Editorial Manager: Pete Gaughan
Production Manager: Kathleen Wisor
Executive Editor: Jim Minatel
Proofreader: Amy Schneider
Indexer: Johnna VanHoose Dinse
Project Coordinator, Cover: Brent Savage
Cover Designer: Wiley
Cover Image: © Getty Images, Inc./Jeremy Woodhouse

Copyright © 2018 by John Wiley & Sons, Inc., Indianapolis, Indiana

Published by John Wiley & Sons, Inc. Indianapolis, Indiana

Published simultaneously in Canada

ISBN: 9781-119-42652-3
ISBN: 978-1-119-42641-7 (ebk.)
ISBN: 978-1-119-42667-7 (ebk.)

Manufactured in the United States of America

For general information on our other products and services or to obtain technical support, please contact our Customer Care Department within the U.S. at (877) 762-2974, outside the U.S. at (317) 572-3993 or fax (317) 572-4002.

Wiley publishes in a variety of print and electronic formats and by print-on-demand. Some material included with standard print versions of this book may not be included in e-books or in print-on-demand. If this book refers to media such as a CD or DVD that is not included in the version you purchased, you may download this material at http://booksupport.wiley.com. For more information about Wiley products, visit www.wiley.com.

Library of Congress Control Number: 2018951985

To Melissa, Catharine, Kim, and Judy. Thank you for all your love and inspiration.

About the Author

James J. Galluzzo III, SPHR®, is a strategic human resources professional and leader with nearly 25 years of experience. He is a Senior Professional in Human Resources (SPHR) certified by the HR Certification Institute. He served as an Adjutant General's Corps officer in the United States Army, where he held several HR positions of increasing responsibility during his tenure, finally culminating as chief of leadership development for the 40,000 Army HR professionals around the world before his retirement in 2014.

He was instrumental in establishing the partnership between the HR Certification Institute and the Army to help military HR professionals seeking civilian credentials as they transitioned from service into civilian work. He is a former HR director of South Carolina's State Housing Finance and Development Authority and is currently the corporate HR director for John Harris Body Shops, an automotive collision repair company in South Carolina and Georgia.

J. earned a bachelor's degree in electrical engineering from Clarkson University and an MBA from National University in California. He continues to volunteer for projects that strengthen the HR profession.

You can reach J. through LinkedIn (linkedin.com/in/james-galluzzo-sphr-62b44a69).

Acknowledgments

The writing of a review guide, especially one of this scope, is not an individual achievement sport, and as such there are many individuals to whom I owe a great deal of thanks and acknowledgment for their contribution and support. First, the outstanding editors, Jim Compton and Katie Wisor, did a fantastic job in helping me bring out my best to present to the readers, along with all the other folks at Sybex and Wiley who made this book possible.

Additionally, I wish to thank Kenyon Brown, senior acquisitions editor, for giving me the opportunity to develop and write this review guide. I am also very fortunate that I had a chance meeting with Sandy Reed, SPHR, who thought to recommend me to Ken for this project.

As many HR professionals would agree, experience is the best teacher. To this, I thank the many leaders, soldiers, family members, and civilian professionals with whom I had the privilege to serve over a 20-year career in the United States Army and all the wonderful experiences and lessons I learned.

Enid Conner, Ron Frye, and Kim Pruitt, my fabulous HR team from SC Housing, and Claire Wessinger from John Harris Body Shops are the epitome of dedicated HR professionals who work tirelessly each day to meet the demands of the employees they serve. My transition to the civilian HR world would not have been successful or possible without their support and teamwork.

Finally, a great deal of thanks to my family, friends, and professional colleagues who encouraged me to complete this endeavor and for all their love and commitment over the years.

Contents

Introduction

Congratulations on your choice to prepare and sit for the Professional in Human Resources (PHR®) or Senior Professional in Human Resources (SPHR®) exam. These accredited exams are the gold standard of HR credentialing and represent decades of professional rigor and stringent practice analysis study conducted by the HR Certification Institute (HRCI®). HR professionals who are working to earn these most recognized HR credentials will see changes in the areas of responsibility and knowledge that are the results of a 2017 detailed study of the current state of HR practice in the United States.

This book is meant for anyone seeking either the PHR® or SPHR® certification with the new exams based on the changes to the exam content outlines effective August 1, 2018. It is also an ideal review for any HR practitioner who wants to increase their knowledge and professional depth of HR practices. If you are preparing for other HRCI® exams in the PHR/SPHR family, this book may also be useful to review for additional context across the HR field of study for those exams.

This review guide has been designed to work along with the *PHR and SPHR Human Resources Complete Certification Exam Study Guide*, also from Sybex. The study guide provides more depth and review of the functional areas covered by the exam content outlines and more real-world examples. This review guide helps solidify the required experience-based knowledge to help you successfully prepare and pass the PHR® or SPHR® exam.

Book Structure

This book has been laid out in a comprehensive and systematic way that follows the exam content outlines for the PHR® and SPHR® exams. The individual chapters cover distinct functional areas of human resources. The book has two parts. The first part consists of Chapters 1–5 and is designed to prepare individuals who want to sit for the Professional in Human Resources (PHR®) certification exam. The second part consists of Chapters 6–10 and is designed to prepare individuals who want to sit for the Senior Professional in Human Resources (SPHR®) certification exam. It is not necessary to review the entire book, as each part covers the necessary exam content outline for that particular exam.

Part One: PHR®

- Business Management
- Talent Planning and Acquisition
- Learning and Development
- Total Rewards
- Employee and Labor Relations

Part Two: SPHR®

- Leadership and Strategy
- Talent Planning and Acquisition
- Learning and Development
- Total Rewards
- Employee Relations and Engagement

While the exam content outlines list the responsibilities before the required knowledge, this review guide covers the knowledge first. The reasoning is that an HR practitioner cannot assume responsibilities and take proper action without first understanding the key knowledge for a particular area. Also, this book does not cover each responsibility or knowledge point in order in the chapter text but elects to group key concepts together as they would likely be handled by function in a professional HR setting. I have kept the numbering convention the same at the beginning of each chapter; so the responsibilities start at "1" for each new functional area, but the required knowledge continues from the previous chapter for both parts. I believe this structure will make it easy for you to learn the information in the shortest time with the highest possible retention.

How to Use This Book

Several learning tools are included in the book. These tools will help you retain vital exam content as well as prepare to sit for the actual exams.

Objective Map and Opening List of Objectives   At the beginning of the book you'll find a detailed exam objective map showing you where each of the exam objectives is covered. In addition, each chapter opens with a list of the exam objectives it covers. Use these resources to see exactly where each of the exam topics is covered.

Exam Essentials   Each chapter includes a number of exam essentials. These are the key points that you should take from the chapter, identifying topics on which you should focus when preparing for the exam.

Chapter Review Questions   To test your knowledge as you progress through the book, there are review questions at the end of each chapter. As you finish each chapter, answer the review questions and then check your answers—the correct answers appear in the appendix, "Answers to Review Questions." You can go back to reread the section that deals with any question you got wrong to ensure that you answer correctly the next time you're tested on the material.

Interactive Online Learning Environment and Test Bank

The interactive online learning environment that accompanies *PHR® and SPHR® Human Resources Certification Complete Review Guide: 2018 Exams* provides a test bank with study tools to help you prepare for the certification exam—and increase your chances of passing it the first time! The test bank includes the following:

Sample Tests   All the questions in this book are provided, including the chapter tests that include the review questions at the end of each chapter. In addition, there are two practice exams (one each for the PHR® and SPHR®) that have a variety of question formats that match the newly structured exams as of the fall of 2018. Use these questions to test your knowledge of the review guide material. The online test bank runs on multiple devices.

Flashcards   One set of questions is provided in digital flashcard format (a question followed by a single correct answer). You can use the flashcards to reinforce your learning and provide last-minute test prep before the exam.

Other Study Tools   A glossary of key terms from this book and their definitions is available as a fully searchable PDF.

Go to www.wiley.com/go/sybextestprep to register and gain access to this interactive online learning environment and test bank with study tools.

Overview of the HRCI® Credentials

HRCI® has several credentials in the HR field that serve HR professionals in the United States and international settings. They range from entry-level credentials for people transitioning to or beginning a career in HR to credentials for senior HR professionals responsible for strategic HR decisions and functions within an organization.

For more than 40 years, HRCI® has used rigorous standards and evaluations of current HR practices, along with experts from the field, to develop and validate an HR body of knowledge that is wide ranging and the gold standard for HR professionals. From this body of knowledge, exam content outlines are created for each certification that serve as the foundation for exam questions for each certification exam. At the time of this publication, HRCI® offers eight credentials. Here's a brief look at each:

Associate Professional in Human Resources (aPHR)™   HRCI's Associate Professional in Human Resources™ (aPHR™) is the perfect certification to help you with your career growth and provide you with the confidence to launch into the HR profession. The aPHR is specifically designed for professionals who are just beginning their HR career journey and proves your knowledge of foundational human resources.

Eligibility Requirements   To be eligible for the aPHR you must have a high school diploma or global equivalent. No HR experience is required since this is a knowledge-based credential.

Associate Professional in Human Resources—International (aPHRi)™   If you are new to HR and want to distinguish yourself in the field, the Associate Professional in Human Resources—International™ (aPHRi™) helps propel your career growth and provide you with the confidence to launch into the HR profession. *HR professionals in the United States are not eligible for this exam.*

Eligibility Requirements   To be eligible for the aPHRi, you must have a high school diploma or global equivalent. No HR experience is required since this is a knowledge-based credential.

Professional in Human Resources (PHR)®   This is the flagship HR credential from HRCI®. The most widely known certification, PHR demonstrates mastery of the technical and operational aspects of HR management, including U.S. laws and regulations. The PHR is for the HR professional who has experience with program implementation, has a tactical/logistical orientation, is accountable to another HR professional within the organization, and has responsibilities that focus on the HR department rather than the whole organization.

Eligibility Requirements   To be eligible for the PHR, you must meet one of the following conditions for education and experience:

- At least one year of experience in a professional-level HR position plus a master's degree or higher
- At least two years of experience in a professional-level HR position plus a bachelor's degree
- At least four years of experience in a professional-level HR position plus a high school diploma

Professional in Human Resources—California (PHRca)®   The PHRca demonstrates mastery of the laws, regulations, and HR management practices unique to the state of California. The PHRca is for professionals who either practice in California or are responsible for human resource management in California. You do not have to be located in California to earn a PHRca. Many certification holders add the PHRca to their other HRCI credentials.

Eligibility Requirements   To be eligible for the PHRca, you must meet one of the following conditions for education and experience:

- At least one year of experience in a professional-level HR position plus a master's degree or higher
- At least two years of experience in a professional-level HR position plus a bachelor's degree
- At least four years of experience in a professional-level HR position plus a high school diploma

Professional in Human Resources—International (PHRi)®   The PHRi (formerly the Human Resources Business Professional™, or HRBP™), for internationally based practitioners, validates professional-level competency, knowledge, and skills to help to propel your HR career forward. The PHRi demonstrates mastery of generally accepted technical and operational HR principles in a single international setting. *HR professionals in the United States are not eligible for this exam.*

Eligibility Requirements   To be eligible for the PHRi, you must meet one of the following conditions for education and experience:

- At least one year of experience in a professional-level HR position plus a master's degree or global equivalent

- At least two years of experience in a professional-level HR position plus a bachelor's degree or global equivalent

- At least four years of experience in a professional-level HR position plus a high school diploma or global equivalent

Senior Professional in Human Resources (SPHR)®   This credential is widely recognized as the industry leader for senior HR professionals. The SPHR demonstrates mastery of the strategic and policy-making aspects of HR management as practiced in the United States. The credential is designed for big-picture thinkers responsible for planning rather than implementing HR policy. SPHR professionals are responsible for HR department goals, for breadth and depth of knowledge in all HR disciplines, and for understanding business issues beyond the HR function.

Eligibility Requirements   To be eligible for the SPHR, you must meet one of the following conditions for education and experience:

- At least four years of experience in a professional-level HR position plus a master's degree or higher

- At least five years of experience in a professional-level HR position plus a bachelor's degree

- At least seven years of experience in a professional-level HR position plus a high school diploma

Senior Professional in Human Resources—International (SPHRi)®   The SPHRi (formerly the Human Resources Management Professional™, or HRMP™), for internationally based HR leaders, validates senior-level HR competency and mastery of generally accepted HR principles in strategy, policy development, and service delivery in a single international setting. The SPHRi requires documented knowledge of local employment laws. *HR professionals in the United States are not eligible for this exam.*

Eligibility Requirements   To be eligible for the SPHRi, you must meet one of the following conditions for education and experience*:

- At least four years of experience in a professional-level HR position plus a master's degree or global equivalent

- At least five years of experience in a professional-level HR position plus a bachelor's degree or global equivalent

- At least seven years of experience in a professional-level HR position plus a high school diploma or global equivalent

Global Professional in Human Resources (GPHR)®   The GPHR demonstrates your expertise of multinational HR responsibilities, including strategies of globalization development of HR policies and initiatives that support organizational global growth. It shows you have the knowledge and skills needed to manage HR challenges in a global marketplace.

Eligibility Requirements   To be eligible for the GPHR, you must meet one of the following conditions for education and experience:

- Have at least two years of experience* in a global professional-level HR position *and* a master's degree or higher

- Have at least three years of experience* in a professional-level HR position (at least two in global HR) *and* a bachelor's degree

- Have at least four years of experience* in a professional-level HR position (at least two in global HR) *and* a high school diploma

Note: Global HR experience is defined as having direct, cross-border HR responsibilities for two or more countries or regions.

For more information on credentials offered by the HR Certification Institute, visit https://www.hrci.org/our-programs/our-certifications.

Day of the Exam

After you gain the necessary prerequisites to sit for the exam, the PHR® or SPHR® exam serves as the final measure to earning your certification. You are already well ahead of the game in preparing for the exam when you purchase this book. Your commitment to the preparation will help you arrive with confidence on the day of the exam. Throughout the course of this book, you will find sections that offer tips on what to do on the day of the exam. While you are not allowed to take any materials or exam aids into the testing area, you are given scratch paper to work with during your exam. One important point to realize is that employment laws change constantly. Candidates are responsible for knowing the HR laws and regulations that are in effect at the time of their exam. Therefore, it may be helpful to jot some notes about any recent changes of major laws related to HR.

Additionally, be sure to follow all the basic-test taking advice, such as getting a good night's sleep, eating a good breakfast, and going through breathing and focus exercises before the exam. Please consider the following items during the exam as well:

- Take the time to read through each question slowly and completely. Fully understanding what is being asked in the question can contribute greatly to getting the right answer.

- Don't get stuck on any one question; you can mark an answer you are unsure of to return to later. However, remember not to leave it blank, just in case you run out of time and are unable to return to the answer.

- Try not to overthink the question with personal experience. Some companies have different practices, and some may be, unknowingly, not following best practices. A question about how your company in particular does business may require a different answer than the generic correct rule or procedure.

For more information from HRCI® on preparing for the exam, be sure you check out https://www.hrci.org/how-to-get-certified/taking-the-exam for more valuable resources.

Objective Map

Use the following summary of the PHR® and SPHR® Exam Content Outlines to find where each functional area and each specific topic is covered so you can focus on the areas you most need to review.

PHR® Exam Content Outline

The PHR® exam is created using the PHR® Exam Content Outline. Created by HR subject-matter experts in the field, it is a comprehensive outline of responsibilities of and knowledge needed by today's HR professional. The outline is grouped into five functional areas. The following are the official PHR® exam objectives, as specified by HRCI®.

Business Management

The following responsibilities and knowledge make up the Business Management functional area and are covered in Chapter 1 of this book:

Responsibilities:

- Interpret and apply information related to general business environment and industry best practices.

- Reinforce the organization's core values, ethical and behavioral expectations through modeling, communication, and coaching.

- Understand the role of cross-functional stakeholders in the organization and establish relationships to influence decision making.

- Recommend and implement best practices to mitigate risk (for example: lawsuits, internal/external threats).

- Determine the significance of data for recommending organizational strategies (for example: attrition rates, diversity in hiring, time to hire, time to fill, ROI, success of training).

Knowledge of:

- Vision, mission, values, and structure of the organization
- Legislative and regulatory knowledge and procedures
- Corporate governance procedures and compliance
- Employee communications
- Ethical and professional standards
- Business elements of an organization (for example: other functions and departments, products, competition, customers, technology, demographics, culture, processes, safety and security)
- Existing HRIS, reporting tools, and other systems for effective data reporting and analysis
- Change management theory, methods, and application
- Risk management
- Qualitative and quantitative methods and tools for analytics
- Dealing with situations that are uncertain, unclear, or chaotic

Talent Planning and Acquisition

The following responsibilities and knowledge make up the Talent Planning and Acquisition functional area and are covered in Chapter 2 of this book:

Responsibilities:

- Understand federal laws and organizational policies to adhere to legal and ethical requirements in hiring (for example: Title VII, nepotism, disparate impact, FLSA, independent contractors).
- Develop and implement sourcing methods and techniques (for example: employee referrals, diversity groups, social media).
- Execute the talent acquisition life cycle (for example: interviews, extending offers, background checks, negotiation).

Knowledge of:

- Applicable federal laws and regulations related to talent planning and acquisition activities
- Planning concepts and terms (for example: succession planning, forecasting)
- Current market situation and talent pool availability
- Staffing alternatives (for example: outsourcing, temporary employment)
- Interviewing and selection techniques, concepts, and terms
- Applicant tracking systems and/or methods

- Impact of total rewards on recruitment and retention
- Candidate/employee testing processes and procedures
- Verbal and written offers/contract techniques
- New hire employee orientation processes and procedures
- Internal workforce assessments (for example: skills testing, workforce demographics, analysis)
- Transition techniques for corporate restructuring, mergers and acquisitions, due diligence processes, offshoring, and divestitures
- Metrics to assess past and future staffing effectiveness (for example: cost per hire, selection ratios, adverse impact)

Learning and Development

The following responsibilities and knowledge make up the Learning and Development functional area and are covered in Chapter 3 of this book:

Responsibilities:

- Provide consultation to managers and employees on professional growth and development opportunities.
- Implement and evaluate career development and training programs (for example: career pathing, management training, mentorship).
- Contribute to succession planning discussions with management by providing relevant data.

Knowledge of:

- Applicable federal laws and regulations related to learning and development activities
- Learning and development theories and applications
- Training program facilitation, techniques, and delivery
- Adult learning processes
- Instructional design principles and processes (for example: needs analysis, process flow mapping)
- Techniques to assess training program effectiveness, including use of applicable metrics
- Organizational development (OD) methods, motivation methods, and problem-solving techniques
- Task/process analysis
- Coaching and mentoring techniques
- Employee retention concepts and applications
- Techniques to encourage creativity and innovation

Total Rewards

The following responsibilities and knowledge make up the Total Rewards functional area and are covered in Chapter 4 of this book:

Responsibilities:

- Manage compensation-related information and support payroll issue resolution.
- Implement and promote awareness of noncash rewards (for example: paid volunteer time, tuition assistance, workplace amenities, and employee recognition programs).
- Implement benefit programs (for example: health plan, retirement plan, employee assistance plan, other insurance).
- Administer federally compliant compensation and benefit programs.

Knowledge of:

- Applicable federal laws and regulations related to total rewards
- Compensation policies, processes, and analysis
- Budgeting, payroll, and accounting practices related to compensation and benefits
- Job analysis and evaluation concepts and methods
- Job pricing and pay structures
- Noncash compensation
- Methods to align and benchmark compensation and benefits
- Benefits programs policies, processes, and analysis

Employee and Labor Relations

The following responsibilities and knowledge make up the Employee and Labor Relations functional area and are covered in Chapter 5 of this book:

Responsibilities:

- Analyze functional effectiveness at each stage of the employee life cycle (for example: hiring, onboarding, development, retention, exit process, alumni program) and identify alternate approaches as needed.
- Collect, analyze, summarize, and communicate employee engagement data.
- Understand organizational culture, theories, and practices; identify opportunities and make recommendations.
- Understand and apply knowledge of programs, federal laws, and regulations to promote outreach, diversity, and inclusion (for example: affirmative action, employee resource groups, community outreach, corporate responsibility).
- Implement and support workplace programs relative to health, safety, security, and privacy following federal laws and regulations (for example: OSHA, workers' compensation, emergency response, workplace violence, substance abuse, legal postings).

- Promote organizational policies and procedures (for example: employee handbook, SOPs, time and attendance, expenses).

- Manage complaints or concerns involving employment practices, behavior, or working conditions, and escalate by providing information to appropriate stakeholders.

- Promote techniques and tools for facilitating positive employee and labor relations with knowledge of applicable federal laws affecting union and nonunion workplaces (for example: dispute/conflict resolution, anti-discrimination policies, sexual harassment).

- Support and consult with management in performance management process (for example: employee reviews, promotions, recognition programs).

- Support performance activities (for example: coaching, performance improvement plans, involuntary separations) and employment activities (for example: job eliminations, reductions in force) by managing corresponding legal risks.

Knowledge of:

- General employee relations activities and analysis (for example, conducting investigations, researching grievances, working conditions, reports, etc.)

- Applicable federal laws and procedures affecting employment, labor relations, safety, and security

- Human relations, culture and values concepts, and applications to employees and organizations

- Review and analysis process for assessing employee attitudes, opinions, and satisfaction

- Diversity and inclusion

- Recordkeeping requirements

- Occupational injury and illness prevention techniques

- Workplace safety and security risks

- Emergency response, business continuity, and disaster recovery process

- Internal investigation, monitoring, and surveillance techniques

- Data security and privacy

- The collective bargaining process, terms, and concepts (for example: contract negotiation, costing, administration)

- Performance management process, procedures, and analysis

- Termination approaches, concepts, and terms

SPHR® Exam Content Outline

The SPHR® exam is created using the SPHR® Exam Content Outline. Created by HR subject-matter experts in the field, it is a comprehensive outline of responsibilities of and knowledge needed by today's Senior HR professional. Like the PHR®, the SPHR® outline is grouped into five functional areas. Three of the functional areas have the same heading but slightly different focus on the exam content outline. The following are the official SPHR® exam objectives, as specified by HRCI®.

Leadership and Strategy

The following responsibilities and knowledge make up the Leadership and Strategy functional area and are covered in Chapter 6 of this book:

Responsibilities:

- Develop and execute HR plans that are aligned to the organization's strategic plan (for example: HR strategic plans, budgets, business plans, service delivery plans, HRIS, technology).
- Evaluate the applicability of federal laws and regulations to organizational strategy (for example: policies, programs, practices, business expansion/reduction).
- Analyze and assess organizational practices that impact operations and people management to decide on the best available risk management strategy (for example: avoidance, mitigation, acceptance).
- Interpret and use business metrics to assess and drive achievement of strategic goals and objectives (for example: key performance indicators, financial statements, budgets).
- Design and evaluate HR data indicators to inform strategic actions within the organization (for example: turnover rates, cost per hire, retention rates).
- Evaluate credibility and relevance of external information to make decisions and recommendations (for example: salary data, management trends, published surveys and studies, legal/regulatory analysis).
- Contribute to the development of the organizational strategy and planning (for example: vision, mission, values, ethical conduct).
- Develop and manage workplace practices that are aligned with the organization's statements of vision, values, and ethics to shape and reinforce organizational culture.
- Design and manage effective change strategies to align organizational performance with the organization's strategic goals.
- Establish and manage effective relationships with key stakeholders to influence organizational behavior and outcomes.

Knowledge of:

- Vision, mission, and values of an organization and applicable legal and regulatory requirements
- Strategic planning process
- Management functions, including planning, organizing, directing, and controlling
- Corporate governance procedures and compliance

- Business elements of an organization (for example: products, competition, customers, technology, demographics, culture, processes, safety and security)

- Third-party or vendor selection, contract negotiation, and management, including development of requests for proposals (RFPs)

- Project management (for example: goals, timetables, deliverables, and procedures)

- Technology to support HR activities

- Budgeting, accounting, and financial concepts (for example: evaluating financial statements, budgets, accounting terms, and cost management)

- Techniques and methods for organizational design (for example: outsourcing, shared services, organizational structures)

- Methods of gathering data for strategic planning purposes (for example: Strengths, Weaknesses, Opportunities, and Threats [SWOT], and Political, Economic, Social, and Technological [PEST])

- Qualitative and quantitative methods and tools used for analysis, interpretation, and decision-making purposes

- Change management processes and techniques

- Techniques for forecasting, planning, and predicting the impact of HR activities and programs across functional areas

- Risk management

- How to deal with situations that are uncertain, unclear, or chaotic

Talent Planning and Acquisition

The following responsibilities and knowledge make up the Talent Planning and Acquisition functional area and are covered in Chapter 7 of this book:

Responsibilities:

- Evaluate and forecast organizational needs throughout the business cycle to create or develop workforce plans (for example: corporate restructuring, workforce expansion, or reduction).

- Develop, monitor, and assess recruitment strategies to attract desired talent (for example: labor market analysis, compensation strategies, selection process, onboarding, sourcing and branding strategy).

- Develop and evaluate strategies for engaging new employees and managing cultural integrations (for example: new employee acculturation, downsizing, restructuring, mergers and acquisitions, divestitures, global expansion).

Knowledge of:

- Planning techniques (for example: succession planning, forecasting)

- Talent management practices and techniques (for example: selecting and assessing employees)

- Recruitment sources and strategies
- Staffing alternatives (for example: outsourcing, temporary employment)
- Interviewing and selection techniques and strategies
- Impact of total rewards on recruitment and retention
- Termination approaches and strategies
- Employee engagement strategies
- Employer marketing and branding techniques
- Negotiation skills and techniques
- Due diligence processes (for example: mergers and acquisitions, divestitures)
- Transition techniques for corporate restructuring, mergers and acquisitions, offshoring, and divestitures
- Methods to assess past and future staffing effectiveness (for example: cost per hire, selection ratios, adverse impact)

Learning and Development

The following responsibilities and knowledge make up the Learning and Development functional area and are covered in Chapter 8 of this book:

Responsibilities:

- Develop and evaluate training strategies (for example: modes of delivery, timing, content) to increase individual and organizational effectiveness.
- Analyze business needs to develop a succession plan for key roles (for example: identify talent, outline career progression, coaching and development) to promote business continuity.
- Develop and evaluate employee retention strategies and practices (for example: assessing talent, developing career paths, managing job movement within the organization).

Knowledge of:

- Training program design and development
- Adult learning processes
- Training and facilitation techniques
- Instructional design principles and processes (for example: needs analysis, content chunking, process flow mapping)
- Techniques to assess training program effectiveness, including use of applicable metrics
- Career and leadership development theories and applications
- Organizational development (OD) methods, motivation methods, and problem-solving techniques

- Coaching and mentoring techniques
- Effective communication skills and strategies (for example: presentation, collaboration, sensitivity)
- Employee retention strategies
- Techniques to encourage creativity and innovation

Total Rewards

The following responsibilities and knowledge make up the Total Rewards functional area and are covered in Chapter 9 of this book:

Responsibilities:

- Analyze and evaluate compensation strategies (for example: philosophy, classification, direct, indirect, incentives, bonuses, equity, executive compensation) that attract, reward, and retain talent.
- Analyze and evaluate benefit strategies (for example: health, welfare, retirement, recognition programs, work-life balance, wellness) that attract, reward, and retain talent.

Knowledge of:

- Compensation strategies and philosophy
- Job analysis and evaluation methods
- Job pricing and pay structures
- External labor markets and economic factors
- Executive compensation methods
- Noncash compensation methods
- Benefits program strategies
- Fiduciary responsibilities
- Motivation concepts and applications
- Benchmarking techniques

Employee Relations and Engagement

The following responsibilities and knowledge make up the Employee Relations and Engagement functional area and are covered in Chapter 10 of this book:

Responsibilities:

- Design and evaluate strategies for employee satisfaction (for example: recognition, career path) and performance management (for example: performance evaluation, corrective action, coaching).
- Analyze and evaluate strategies to promote diversity and inclusion.

- Evaluate employee safety and security strategies (for example: emergency response plan, building access, data security/privacy).
- Develop and evaluate labor strategies (for example: collective bargaining, grievance program, concerted activity, staying union free, strategically aligning with labor).

Knowledge of:

- Strategies to facilitate positive employee relations
- Methods for assessing employee attitudes, opinions, and satisfaction
- Performance management strategies
- Human relations concepts and applications
- Ethical and professional standards
- Diversity and inclusion concepts and applications
- Occupational injury and illness prevention techniques
- Workplace safety and security risks and strategies
- Emergency response, business continuity, and disaster recovery strategies
- Internal investigation, monitoring, and surveillance techniques

PHR®

PART

I

What This Part Covers

The first five chapters of this book are dedicated to the PHR® exam and cover all the topics and information needed to successfully sit for the exam. These chapters stand alone as the only content portion of the book needed. The second half of the book is not required reading if you intend to take the PHR® exam only. If you are undecided as to which exam you should take, you can compare the chapter outlines for the content differences. You will notice that certain material may overlap, but the level of focus is different, varying from the tactical day-to-day HR functions to the higher-level strategic HR practices.

Chapter

1

Business Management

THE PHR® EXAM CONTENT FROM THE BUSINESS MANAGEMENT FUNCTIONAL AREA COVERED IN THIS CHAPTER CONSISTS OF THE FOLLOWING RESPONSIBILITIES AND KNOWLEDGE AREAS. RESPONSIBILITIES:

✓ **01** Interpret and apply information related to general business environment and industry best practices

✓ **02** Reinforce the organization's core values, ethical and behavioral expectations through modeling, communication, and coaching

✓ **03** Understand the role of cross-functional stakeholders in the organization and establish relationships to influence decision making

✓ **04** Recommend and implement best practices to mitigate risk (for example: lawsuits, internal/external threats)

✓ **05** Determine the significance of data for recommending organizational strategies (for example: attrition rates, diversity in hiring, time to hire, time to fill, ROI, success of training)

IN ADDITION TO THE PRECEDING RESPONSIBILITIES, AN INDIVIDUAL TAKING THE PHR® EXAM SHOULD HAVE WORKING KNOWLEDGE OF THE FOLLOWING AREAS, USUALLY DERIVED THROUGH PRACTICAL EXPERIENCE:

✓ **01** Vision, mission, values, and structure of the organization

✓ **02** Legislative and regulatory knowledge and procedures

✓ 03 Corporate governance procedures and compliance

✓ 04 Employee communications

✓ 05 Ethical and professional standards

✓ 06 Business elements of an organization (for example: other functions and departments, products, competition, customers, technology, demographics, culture, processes, safety and security)

✓ 07 Existing HRIS, reporting tools, and other systems for effective data reporting and analysis

✓ 08 Change management theory, methods, and application

✓ 09 Risk management

✓ 10 Qualitative and quantitative methods and tools for analytics

✓ 11 Dealing with situations that are uncertain, unclear, or chaotic

This chapter looks at the important functions and roles that human resources (HR) professionals play in an organization with respect to the overall business environment. As a general rule, the HR team uses information about the organization and the business environment to reinforce expectations of stakeholders, influence decision makers, and avoid risk.

This function is tremendously important for HR professionals to master and understand. This portion is weighted as 20 percent of the PHR® exam. Often many HR professionals operate in smaller organizations as the sole subject-matter expert of the company and have a great deal of responsibility to support the key executives who rely on their experience and qualifications. HR professionals who understand and execute these responsibilities well will set themselves apart from their peers.

Required Knowledge

Smart people learn from their mistakes. Wise people learn from other people's mistakes. Knowledge comes from either personal experience or the study of the experiences and lessons taught to us by others. HR professionals preparing for this exam must possess certain knowledge acquired from experience or study. In this chapter, the knowledge portion reviews business management practiced at the operational level of the organization, which includes topics such as corporate governance and procedures, employee communications, business elements, and the underlying mission, vision, and values of the company.

Mission, Vision, and Values

HR professionals must know the mission, vision, and values of the company. In many of their tasks discussed later in the chapter, they function as the champions, interpreters, or arbitrators of these concepts to the employees. The mission of the company is usually expressed as a short statement sentence describing the purpose of the company's existence. It should be overarching and usually is an infinitive statement to do something. It answers the question, "Why?"

The vision of a company looks at the future and paints a vivid picture of what the organization will look like as it grows, develops, or changes over time. The vision considers where the organization is at present and describes where it wants to go. A vision must be able to be consistently repeated by employees to be effective. In other words, they are all able to describe the same picture. Vision statements should be simple to be effective and, in some instances, consist of only a phrase or a couple of words. Table 1.1 shows some mission and vision statements from familiar organizations.

TABLE 1.1   Sample mission and vision statements

Statement	Company
"The Walt Disney Company's objective is to be one of the world's leading producers and providers of entertainment and information, using its portfolio of brands to differentiate its content, services and consumer products." https://thewaltdisneycompany.com/about/	Walt Disney Company
"As a leader in the global steel industry, we are dedicated to delivering high-quality products to our customers and building value for all of our stakeholders." https://www.ussteel.com	U.S. Steel
"Empower every person and organization on the planet to achieve more." https://www.microsoft.com/en-us/about/default.aspx	Microsoft
"The mission of Southwest Airlines is dedication to the highest quality of customer service delivered with a sense of warmth, friendliness, individual pride, and company spirit." http://investors.southwest.com/our-company/purpose-vision-values-and-mission	Southwest Airlines

Values are the foundation of how a company is going to perform its mission and achieve its vision. From the HR perspective, a goal is to ensure that employee behaviors are aligned with the values of the organization. When behaviors are not aligned, the resulting issues and negative outcomes can impact performance management, employee relations, and HR development, all of which are reviewed in later chapters. Values must be communicated and modeled consistently throughout the organization to be effective. It is always the values that are practiced, not the ones that are written, that define how the organization conducts itself.

Types of Organizational Structures

Structure is essential for a company, and the HR professional must understand how a company is organized to perform critical tasks essential to operations. Often the HR professional must know the various departments or teams and how they are interconnected to establish policies over personnel transfers, evaluations, promotions, and other routine HR actions. Each organization is different, so there may be slight variations in how the organizational structure develops as a company expands. Knowing the choices that a company has about how to lead and control operations enables the HR professional to advise the corporate executives who are making structural decisions.

Two common approaches to organizational structure are the matrix and hierarchy methods. In a hierarchy, the structure resembles a pyramid. The chief decision-maker, such as a chief executive officer, president, or chairperson, is the ultimate head of the organization responsible for all actions and the accomplishment of the mission, vision, and values of the company. Below the organizational head might be division heads and then lower management and finally the teams of employees. In this kind of structure, there is a general stovepipe of information, and the flow tends to go up and down with little contact across. Figure 1.1 shows an example of an organizational hierarchy.

FIGURE 1.1   A hierarchical organizational structure

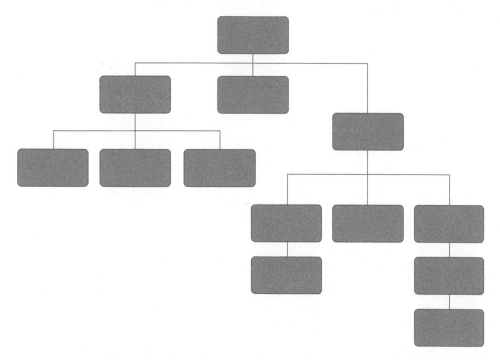

The other common structure is a matrix. This example is often shown as a series of groups or equal parts all sharing responsibilities for the execution of the company mission. In these environments, information can flow across as well as up and down. While it may seem that this would be a preferred method given the more open communication, it has its own unique challenges; there can be too much information sharing, as well as conflicting guidance based on different priorities or interpretations of the needs. Employees who work in a matrix environment must be more disciplined when resolving problems because their access means they can impact a far greater portion of the company with each decision. In

Figure 1.2, you can see the differences in structure compared to the hierarchical organization shown in Figure 1.1.

FIGURE 1.2   A matrix organizational structure

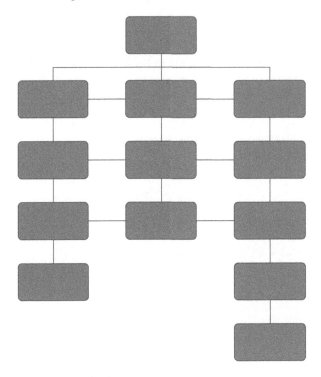

Legislative and Regulatory Processes

HR professionals must know how laws and regulations are created to prepare an organization effectively for their implementation. Some laws or regulations can have wide impact on the operations of a company. For example, in 2016, the Department of Labor announced a major rule change to the administrative exemption to the overtime provision of the Fair Labor Standards Act (FLSA). This proposed rule change would have raised the minimum salary for exempted professionals significantly, thereby dramatically increasing the number of nonexempt workers in the United States. However, almost immediately several groups filed lawsuits in federal court, and an injunction was placed on the rule's implementation. In that same year, the elections in November saw a change in political parties in the executive branch and a change in governing priorities, further delaying any changes to the rule. Without the knowledge of how and when an organization must follow rule changes and the legal and regulatory processes that accompany them, companies could go back and forth changing their employees' status with respect to the exemption standard, creating confusion and costing money in added payroll costs.

Figure 1.3 highlights the regulatory process. It starts with a proposed rule or rule change by the executive agency tasked by law with establishing those rules. For example, the Department of Labor establishes rules related to the Fair Labor Standards Act. Next, the proposed rule will have a public comment period. This period is the time during which groups and individuals impacted by the rule can submit concerns or recommend changes to the rule and offer insight as to how the new standard would impact them. Finally, all the submissions are reviewed, and, if necessary, changes are made before the final rule is published. The final rule will have an effective date when all organizations subject to the rule must be in compliance. Knowing how the Department of Labor issues a rule change, and the period of time that is allowed to adopt the changes into practice within your organization, will allow you to prepare key leaders, change policies and procedures, and inform employees to facilitate the changes to the organization effectively.

FIGURE 1.3   U.S. federal regulatory process

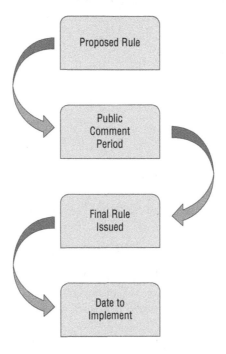

HR functions within the realm of regulations. Since the late 1800s our modern HR practices can be tied to laws in the United States and globally that protect workers, establish working conditions, create rules for corporate governance, and perform other such functions that will be discussed throughout this book. It is imperative that as an HR professional you understand not just that rules change but how and when.

It is also important to know that from state to state and locally there may be differences in rules and laws that impact a company, especially one that operates in multiple locations. Laws in states that mandate minimum wages to be higher than the federal minimum are just one of a myriad of examples that affect HR operations. These concepts will be discussed further in other chapters.

Ethical and Professional Standards

HR professionals have access to a wide variety of sensitive and personal information in the conduct of their jobs. An HR professional must maintain the highest ethical and professional standards. The HR Certification Institute certification process requires all applicants to adhere to a code of ethics to maintain their credential. In general, HR professionals must not use their position and privilege for their own personal benefit. They must strive to protect sensitive HR-related information about others in the organization and avoid conflicts of interest. Those holding the PHR® must acknowledge the ethical and professional responsibilities in these six areas:

- Professional responsibility
- Professional development
- Ethical leadership
- Fairness and justice
- Conflicts of interest
- Use of information

I recommend that any applicant preparing for the certification exam review the code of ethics and professional responsibility at https://www.hrci.org/docs/default-source/web-files/code-of-ethical-and-professional-responsibility(1)-pdf.pdf.

Corporate Governance and Compliance

The knowledge of rules and regulations an HR professional needs also includes corporate governance procedures and compliance. HR professionals are responsible for knowing current reporting requirements with respect to laws such as the Sarbanes-Oxley Act.

The Sarbanes-Oxley Act of 2002

The Sarbanes-Oxley Act of 2002, or SOX, was enacted following several public corporate and accounting scandals that occurred in the early 2000s. It set standards of corporate governance, oversight, auditing independence, and enhanced financial disclosure. To review the law, you can visit www.sec.gov/about/laws/soa2002.pdf.

Corporate governance procedures vary based on the type of company (private, public, not-for-profit) and the number of employees. In addition to federal statutes, the organization may be subject to state provisions depending on which states the company does business in. Also, international corporations have added compliance requirements throughout the globe, especially throughout Europe and Asia.

These are elements of corporate governance to review:

- Board composition and election of officers
- Corporate responsibility statements and ethics
- Conflict-of-interest policies and procedures
- Internal and external auditing practices
- Financial disclosure statements
- Whistleblower protection

An organization's HR department should have working knowledge of the activities surrounding these elements and the input that is required. For example, it is not necessary to know how to do a full audit of the organization. However, HR professionals will provide documents such as payroll records and personnel files to verify or validate parts of the audited reports. HR professionals must know how their functional activities are tied to others within the organization.

Business Elements

The functional areas that form the core of a company are called *business elements*. Operations, sales, marketing, finance, information technology, and procurement all work together, along with human resources, to drive business processes and achieve the company's goals. While it is not a requirement to perform their functions, HR professionals who understand how the other elements operate will have a decided advantage over their peers. A 2016 survey conducted by the HR Certification Institute, available at https://www.hrci.org/about-hrci/why-choose-hrci, shows why corporate executives value HR professionals who possess this knowledge and how it impacts a company.

Operations

Operations is the part of the organization that delivers the product or services to the consumer. It is the profit center of the company and is the purpose of the organization's existence. All other elements of the company support the operations and daily activities of this division. The chief operating officer (COO) is the C-suite executive tasked with overseeing this element that ensures the day-to-day execution of the plans and vision of the company's leadership team.

Operations will track production, quality, conversion rates, materials, and other resources used in producing a good or service. Managers will be the most technically knowledgeable in the company and along with the workers are the largest division.

Sales

The sales team is responsible for identifying, attracting, and retaining customers that demand the goods or services the company produces. They coordinate heavily with operations so that the total production meets the demands to ensure a steady flow. They forecast demand and study trends to determine which product or service will be needed and when. The sales team is usually the external face of the company and is sometimes also referred to as *business development*, especially when the role of sales is to find new customers. This division is also responsible for handling any concerns or complaints by these external business partners that are buying the goods.

Marketing

Marketing determines what the consumers need and then works with the capabilities of the company to create the good or service that meets that need. The marketing team evaluates public demand but also looks across other businesses to determine the competition that may already be meeting a specific need. It compares the costs of entering this demand space against the potential revenue that can be generated by delivering a new business line.

Marketing uses analytics to help determine a price point, develops promotional material or a campaign to draw consumers or alert them to something the company creates, and explains the details or features about a good or service the company provides that differentiates them from competitors offering similar items.

Finance

Finance is the division that plans and controls the execution of budgets, accounting, and auditing all financial resources and activities for an organization. They prepare the financial statements using generally accepted accounting principles (GAAP). GAAP accounting practices are rules or guidelines companies follow when preparing statements.

Different organizations may follow different practices in accounting based on the type of organization they are. For example, in the United States, governmental accounting practices are different from corporate accounting practices. It is not important for an HR professional to know the details of the accounting rules, but awareness of the type of accounting will assist in knowing the information that is generally provided for audits and record keeping.

Information Technology

With the ever-growing dependence on technology in companies, the information technology (IT) division has become increasingly critical to the success of an organization. IT is responsible for the infrastructure of the technology to include hardware, software, development, and maintenance. Data storage, security, and classification are also areas where the IT team plays a key role. IT may have application development, web design, or other subfunctions that tie directly to the flow of electronic information throughout the company. The team ensures availability and accessibility to data for internal and external consumers with an authorized need for it.

Procurement

Even for small companies, there is a need to buy supplies, establish contracts and vendors, and conduct supply chain management. Therefore, the procurement team has buyers who solicit vendors and prepare invitations for bid, also referred to as *requests for proposals*. Procurement also maintains inventory controls, develops specifications for purchases, and negotiates the prices for those purchases. Procurement is closely connected to operations, as business lines may not be able to function properly without certain supplies, putting the organization at risk of failing to deliver its intended good or service.

Products, Competition, and Culture

HR professionals must also have situational awareness of the product lines of a company and the competitive environment. Competitors will also compete for human capital as well as market share. HR professionals should understand how having a competitive advantage helps the business achieve its goals. The operating environment will have impact on wages and the availability of skilled labor especially. How the company establishes its corporate culture will address many operational issues, including processes, safety, and security, and the use of technology throughout the organization. Another key business element is the overall demographics of the stakeholders. As Chapters 2 and 3 discuss, diversity improves an organization. The demographics of a company will have some bearing on how training and development, planning, and acquisition are done within the company and how employees are able to meet the goals and objectives of the company.

Technology to Support HR Activities

A variety of technology tools can support HR professionals in accomplishing the tasks to be performed. In general, a human resources information system (HRIS) is the electronic hub to store, access, and analyze HR data about employees in the organization and effectively provide accurate reports to decision-makers. There are many vendors and programs that can be used to accomplish this, and the choice largely depends on the size and type of organization. These systems range from storing basic personal data all the way to massive databases with thousands of fields. Obviously, the more complex a system, the more training involved for the system users, and the greater need to ensure data accuracy. Many systems have a self-service function that allows the individual employee to update certain elements to increase the timeliness and accuracy of the data being stored. It presumes that an employee entering information such as home address is more likely to be accurate with their own information than someone performing data entry from written information on a paper form that must be transposed and uploaded to a digital record.

The data that is stored is used to provide reports and analysis on the current status of the human capital and to make projections about needs in the future. HR professionals must know how to use these systems to compile data and prepare the information for executives and managers to use effectively in making decisions. Routine reports are created that can show trends and forecast demands. Effective data reporting and analysis is a key skill to possess.

Qualitative and Quantitative Methods and Tools

Qualitative and quantitative methods and tools are needed for analysis, interpretation, and decision-making purposes. A simplified way of understanding these concepts is that qualitative information answers the question "How well?" and quantitative answers "How much or how many?" Two important questions for HR to understand are the following:

Are we doing the right (proper) things?

Are we doing things right (correctly)?

To answer these questions, HR professionals have a variety of tools and measures they can use. They establish metrics with benchmarks to measure performance and effectiveness in core competencies throughout the organization. They use methods such as cost-benefit analysis, discussed later in this chapter, to determine whether a course of action will provide sufficient return on investment (ROI) to overcome any possible negative consequences to that same decision. Finally, HR professionals can examine and understand financial statements to measure recruiting costs, payroll expenses, benefits, and other costs that impact the profitability of the company and make recommendations or adjustments to improve the financial position of the organization.

Quantitative methods include mathematical sets such as statistical averages, regression analysis, or standard deviations. These formulas are tools for HR professionals to determine average salaries in a pay group, the relationship of variables such as education level to starting salary in statistical modeling, and the range and distribution of salaries in a pay group.

Communication Skills and Strategies

Communication is a critical skill in HR. HR professionals must be well versed in the variety of strategies available to send and receive information and provide feedback. Communications consist of verbal and nonverbal cues that individuals interpret through the filter of their experience and can sometimes distort through prejudices or biases that may exist in the receiver. How the communicator presents the information can also have a profound impact on the reception. For example, a message sent by email is received differently than one communicated by telephone or in person because of a lack of nonverbal and visual cues that are not conveyed in text. There is often no emotion or timbre in a written communication that is more apparent in direct visual or auditory communication. The following are some other considerations for communication:

- Collaboration (communicating with a group and sharing complex ideas across a multitude of media)
- Presentation styles (how mannerisms, voice inflection, tonality, and wit or humor can affect the message being delivered)
- Sensitivity (delicate topics require a different approach and understanding of how the audience will be impacted by the subject matter)
- Language barriers (especially in multinational or multilingual environments)
- Speaking style (being clear and concise)

Employee Communications

Getting information to the employee is a continual challenge for HR professionals. HRISs often have a communication feature such as email notification, but that is not a complete solution. A company must make a deliberate effort to reach their employees and provide current information on the current state of the business. One effective method is the use of employee newsletters. A newsletter can be digital or hard copy, but the important factor is that relevant information is presented in a timely manner to the employees. These are some topics that may be of interest:

- Upcoming events
- Welcoming new employees
- Announcing rewards and recognitions such as promotions or awards for performance or contributions
- Changes or clarification to policies or procedures
- Information on benefits programs such as open enrollment
- Employee assistance program information to help improve the resiliency of employees

Change Management Theory, Methods, and Application

Organizations must adapt to grow and therefore must change. Consider the last company to make horse-drawn carriages; they might very well have been the best maker of such transportation. However, with the creation of the automobile, their function became obsolete. Technology changed the needs and demands of the market, and any company that failed to change lost its business. It is easy to accept that things change; however, the reality is that managing change effectively is difficult. HR professionals must understand how to manage change as a process and function of the company.

There are numerous change management theories. Among them are Kotter's theory, Lewin's change management model, and nudge theory, to name a few. For some examples and explanations, refer to https://www.process.st/change-management-models/. It is not important or required to know the intricate details of all change management theories, but there are similarities among them that should be reviewed. In general, the organization recognizes a need for change and a desired end state once the change is implemented. Next the organization must prepare for the change and communicate the significance and importance of the change to the employees to gain support and momentum to adopt the change. Then the company implements the change and must include a process to evaluate how the change is being received and integrated into current operations. Finally, the company reaches a new stasis having fully accepted and assimilating the change. This process continues as the needs for change keep presenting themselves.

Uncertainty and Unclear Situations

You often may be in a volatile, uncertain, complex, or ambiguous (VUCA) environment. This VUCA world we live in requires flexibility and the ability to adapt to changing surroundings. Effective HR professionals will anticipate needs of the company, as they are able to sense environmental changes that will have strategic impact. One of the most significant skills required of HR professionals is to see gray areas and not so much black and white. Every decision about human capital will have lasting effects and potentially unintended consequences. As these will develop rapidly, HR professionals must be timely and responsive in even the most unclear situations to act decisively.

Risk Management Techniques

For the PHR® exam preparation, Chapter 5 discusses associated concepts of risk management as a function of HR; however, a core knowledge point is to understand the choices an organization has about risk in general. These risk management techniques define how an organization will proceed to address the risk once identified. The general choices are avoidance, mitigation, transference, and acceptance. Each of these choices seeks to address the risk in a manner that is acceptable by the company and is consistent with the organizational values.

In avoiding risk, the company elects not to pursue a goal or perform a task because the risk is too great and cannot otherwise be resolved. While this is an option, it comes with the loss of an opportunity to benefit from a positive outcome. Generally, however, the choice to avoid a risk may come after a risk-reward or cost-benefit analysis and a determination is made that the risks far outweigh the potential positive outcome, which is not assured. Mitigation is most often the choice agreed upon by an organization. The company seeks ways to reduce the identified risks through the implementation of controls and measures, while leaving a residual risk. It is impossible to remove all risk in this case, but with mitigation, the risk is now below the value of the positive result expected and can be supported in a business decision.

Transferring risk is not mitigation because the total risk is still present. However, the area exposed might be different and therefore have less impact to the overall organization. Insurance is an example of risk transference, in which a company hedges against loss by providing a premium to a provider that calculates the likelihood of loss. Workers' compensation insurance and employer group health coverage are examples of transferring risk to employees and the organization.

The final option is acceptance, which means that the executives responsible for decisions in the organization have underwritten the risk as a function of the work to be performed and are fully aware of the consequences of a negative outcome. Ultimately, any residual risk falls in this category regardless of the other three choices. It is imperative that HR professionals understand that they must identify risks to the organization related to HR actions, but that it is a function of the executive to choose to accept that risk. The largest danger is that they are often underwriting risk that they do not fully understand or are not aware of.

Exam Essentials

Know how the mission, vision, and values of a company interrelate.   Companies exist for a purpose, usually to deliver a product or service to a consumer. When the company is organized, the executive team charts the course of the company defining these three elements. Often, they come in the form of a statement or summary, but what is essential to understand is that the actions of the company are what define these concepts, not what it says on paper. You should review your company's mission, vision, and values as well as other organizations' and look at how each organization defines its own purpose.

Review core business concepts and functions.   One of the greatest criticisms of HR professionals is that they lack common business competencies and view HR in isolated terms. It is important to review each of the functions of business and how they impact HR and, more importantly, how HR impacts them. Pay particular attention to those functions in business such as accounting that have mirror processes or are closely related to HR functions. The more general business knowledge you possess, the more fluent you will be in terminology and concepts.

Responsibilities

The PHR® exam asks questions related to the responsibilities of an HR professional. These are the tasks that someone in human resources *does* each and every day. In Functional Area 01: Business Management, these tasks relate to the business environment and how to interpret and apply information related to industry best practices. HR professionals are expected to reinforce the core values of an organization and understand the needs of stakeholders. They implement best practices to reduce the risk profile of the company and help measure the success of the company by determining the significance of data related to organizational strategy.

Assess the General Business Environment

HR professionals have the responsibility to gather information about the general business environment and examine industry best practices and use that information to improve conditions within the organization through establishment of policies and procedures that effectively manage the human capital. They must use their knowledge to interpret the significance of available data and use critical thinking to apply the information to organizational practices.

Gathering Information from Internal Sources

As an HR professional, you are part of a network within the organization that optimally should be working to achieve the same goals at the strategic level. Each department within the organization should be integrated and collaborate to ensure that tasks performed by the individual support the team, department, division, and organizational goals. When the executive or C-suite is developing these goals, it is important to get input from all elements of the company.

The following departments and functions are potential sources of internal information:

- Information technology
- Marketing
- Finance and accounting
- Operations
- Business development
- Sales

The departments provide quarterly reports and forecasts, business projections, budgets, new product information or programs, and other internally generated data and metrics that are indicators that drive human resources decisions. Each division has different functions and will bring different viewpoints to the meeting, which can help the organization grow.

 Real World Scenario

Technology Improvements

A company has as one of its strategic goals to use modern technology to improve its operations. The executive director wants the company to offer telecommuting as a way to hire and retain top talent but is concerned about how the practice will work and the overall impact to operations. The organizational leadership works together to facilitate this change across the agency.

The information technology department must look at the security implications of remote users using a virtual private network (VPN) to access the network and the increased demand for laptops and other equipment the organization must provide to users who will be doing telework. This may require the procurement department to acquire new equipment that meets certain specifications. Finance will be involved as the change will have repercussions on the budget, and HR will develop policies for the agency to follow and training for managers on how to lead teams remotely to adapt to this new way of doing business.

Each area contributes and brings key pieces of the puzzle without which there could be unforeseen risks or gaps that could negatively affect the overall business. The outcome of an orchestrated plan supports the vision of the CEO or director and can be directly tied to a specific strategic objective or goal.

The information that a human resources professional has access to within an organization can be used to interpret data and make recommendations and decisions that affect the company. HR uses information gathered from reports produced by the finance department, marketing, sales, operations, information technology, legal, and others. HR experts must know how the different business units fit into the overall organization. By understanding these internal customers' needs and objectives, HR can provide timely and relevant support that enables the company to achieve its mission.

Gathering Information from External Sources

While an HR professional can use information gathered from internal sources, many factors are beyond the control of an organization and will over time greatly impact its success. These external factors come from a variety of sources, and as an HR professional, you are expected to know how to interpolate the data and make inferences about how it will inform practices and policies within the company.

A great example is to look at regulatory changes from the government. In 2016 the U.S. Department of Labor announced a final rule change to the administrative test for exemption to the overtime rule of the Fair Labor Standards Act. The previous rule had a salary threshold of $23,660, regardless of the type of work or position that would otherwise qualify an individual for exempt status under the rule. This regulatory change proposed to move the threshold to more than $47,000 and further benchmark the amount to 40 percent of the median wage of the United States, which would automatically place thousands of workers in a nonexempt status, thus making them eligible for overtime pay. This one regulatory change could have affected hundreds of companies across the country and would have ramifications on workforce planning, compensation and benefits, and policies and procedures, and it could alter strategic plans. If a company wanted to hire or expand operations as part of its strategic goals and objectives, this cost of labor change as a result of the regulation could impact that goal. While HR professionals do not have a crystal ball and cannot always know what external factors will change, they must be aware of and responsive to the potential for change. Staying informed and current on HR regulations, networking with other HR professionals, and following changes in industry practices will help ensure that such environmental changes don't disrupt the organization.

Here are environmental scan areas to consider:

- General business environment
- Industry practices (sometimes referred to as *best practices*)
- Technology changes
- Economic outlook
- Labor market
- Legal and regulatory environment

Communicate Values

Throughout this book, I will stress the importance of communication as a responsibility and obligation of HR professionals. At the strategic level, this means communicating values. HR professionals through word and action will communicate with employees and managers about the values espoused by the company. They must faithfully adhere to these values they present so as to provide a clear and consistent message to the intended recipient.

Communicating Core Values

A key responsibility of HR professionals is to facilitate the development and the communication of the organization's mission, vision, core values, and ethical behaviors. The modeling of these behaviors and the representation to the employees are critical requirements. Values and ethical behaviors must be consistently conveyed across the organization. The company values must be reflected in performance management systems, policies, and practices so that employees that exhibit desired behaviors are recognized and rewarded.

Values can be communicated through company internal communications such as employee newsletters. They are embedded in company training and onboarding practices. As part of the formalized decision-making process of the company, the company values should be considered to ensure that choices reflect the ethos of the organization.

Coaching and Modeling Core Values

Once the values of an organization have been communicated across all levels consistently, the HR team plays a key role in helping managers coach their employees and model the values of the company. Coaching is a different strategic capability and is defined by how effective a leader is at motivating, encouraging, and disciplining their followers to strive toward a common goal.

Table 1.2 shows a variety of methods of influencing individuals and groups to act or demonstrate behaviors. The proper choice is dependent on the situation, the leader, and the followers. Leaders must conduct themselves in a manner that properly reflects the behaviors they want their followers to exhibit.

TABLE 1.2   Motivational techniques

Motivational Types	Impact to Employees
Rewards and recognition	Provides money or other consideration when desired behaviors are demonstrated consistently over time.
Incentives	Formal or informal social contract where employees perform to achieve a desired benefit once a task is completed.
Promotion or increased responsibility	Opportunities are provided to employees that allow them to expand job duties or roles usually with an increase in salary or other tangible benefit.
Goals	Employees work as individuals or teams to achieve agreed-upon measurable standards within a specific time.

 **Real World Scenario**

Meeting Protocol

I once worked for a boss who had a particular pet peeve about cell phones going off in meetings. During discussions it was considered rude for a phone to ring loudly, as it would distract the group and divert attention from the issue under consideration. He began to institute the "Blue Coke" rule, which was his way of referring to an adult beverage like a beer to his younger children. Anyone whose cell phone rang in a meeting would be responsible for the next round of "Blue Cokes" at the next after-work pub call. Of course, we all had a great deal of fun when the boss himself once let his phone ring and then followed through by honoring the penalty. While it was a fun way to deal with an issue, at the heart was really a core value that said no one person was more important than the group and that to be considerate to the group, everyone's full attention was needed.

Establishing Key Business Relationships

Human resources is concerned with maintaining positive, productive relationships throughout a company's life cycle. From the employee to employer, or stakeholder to executive, or customer to company, the HR functions help build and maintain these relationships. Among the more critical relationships are those that are forged at the strategic level. These relationships serve a high-level purpose to provide insight, access, and ability for the HR professional to influence and shape the company's direction and maximize the human capital potential of the organization.

Influence Organizational Decision-Making

HR professionals must build and maintain strong relationships within the organization. Decision-makers rely on you to have discretion and maintain confidentiality with sensitive information. Access to key leaders is essential for exerting direct influence over the organizational decision-making process. Senior executives are more likely to share their thoughts with someone observed to be technically competent, honest, and trustworthy. Integrity is essential for any HR professional.

- Be approachable and open
- Maintain confidentiality
- Actively listen to concerns and issues
- Offer technically sound analysis
- Stay within your scope of responsibility and expertise
- Be professional

Successful HR professionals have a high degree of skill with interpersonal communications. They understand organizational behavior and can evaluate personal motivations and emotions of others. They have strong emotional intelligence. This is not to say that all HR professionals are "nice" or "people friendly." In fact, there are several parts of HR that are certainly not "nice" (like having to terminate an employee). What they are is empathetic to the situation.

HR professionals use referent or expert power to influence others. Managers and executives see them as subject-matter experts and rely on their judgment in situations involving the human capital of the organization.

Review the following observations to determine the strength of the relationship:

Access   Do you have access to the key individual(s) making decisions? If your information and analysis are going through a filter process and there are layers of bureaucracy or intermediaries between you and the key decision-maker, it is unlikely you exert a great deal of influence over their decisions.

Support   Do key leaders support your initiatives and decisions? Are recommendations made by you implemented? Or even better, are you given autonomy to implement certain decisions that have been delegated to you by executives? Good HR professionals will have great support from those making decisions. They will acknowledge your expertise and advise others to bring concerns and issues to you for advice and counsel. Your sphere of influence grows with more support by decision-makers.

Candor   Do you filter comments and advice to shape what you need to say because "the boss" isn't receptive to hearing it? HR professionals must speak their minds but tactfully. Dissent, in most cases, does not equate to disrespect. Sometimes HR must tell decision-makers the hard truth about the situation from the human capital perspective. If you feel you cannot be candid for fear of the reaction or response, your ability to influence the situation will be diminished. Otherwise, you will second-guess what information to provide and when; over time this will erode confidence in what you are saying.

Communication   Closely related to candor, communication refers to the means of and frequency of the flow of information. Are items expressed in formal communications with memorandums and carefully worded emails? Is there informal, more frequent dialog with influencers throughout the organization? What process is established to ensure feedback and accountability when information is transmitted?

Building Alliances and Networks

A key responsibility for an HR professional is to establish relationships with individuals and groups external to the organization. The field of human resources is complex and constantly changing. While certified professionals are expected to know much, they are not expected to know everything. Only through building relationships and alliances with others can you help the organization achieve its strategic goals.

Community Partnerships   Community partnerships are important for corporations, especially those that have a large impact to the economy, labor force, or environment. Even small companies can belong to a business coalition that seeks to improve a local community or neighborhood that supports and hosts those businesses.

These are types of community partnerships:

- *Civic*: Government leaders, law enforcement, civic groups, community organizations, local community colleges
- *Business*: Chamber of Commerce, business coalitions, job training centers, benefit providers (healthcare, retirement)
- *Nonprofit*: Charity organizations, religious centers of influence

Corporate Responsibility   Corporate responsibility is the self-control regulating mechanism by which modern businesses operate. There are many instances where although a corporation is permitted to (may) do something, its corporate responsibility dictates otherwise (should). There are several factors to consider including the spirit of a law or regulation, the ethics of a situation, or the impact to a social compact or the environment. A company with a strong sense of corporate responsibility views itself as part of the community and understands that business decisions do not occur in a vacuum. It serves as an internal control that allows a business to function within acceptable social norms.

Best Practices to Mitigate Risk

As a key advisor to the organization, HR professionals must identify and manage risks associated with human resources. It is helpful to understand enterprise risk management (ERM) and the process to identify risks, reduce hazards when possible, implement control measures, and evaluate the entire process.

The table for risk (Figure 1.4) shows criticality versus likelihood of occurrence. To show where risks are low, moderate, high, or very high, the risk is measured by how likely or often it may occur in a given situation and then if it occurs, how significant the loss to the organization would be. This is important because sometimes implementing a control might be more expensive than the cost of the loss if it happens.

FIGURE 1.4   The risk table

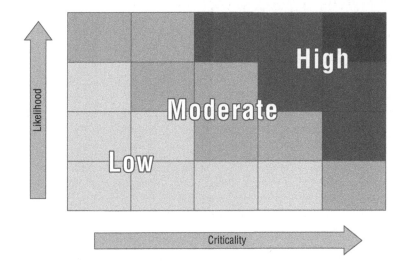

Human resources will develop policies that contribute to protecting the organization from potential risks. While some policies, like safety protocols, are more obvious when thinking about hazards and danger, ERM is not confined to physical hazards or Occupational Safety and Health Administration (OSHA) regulations. Any internal control might be protecting the company from loss or damage. Today, information and specifically personally identifiable information (PII) is valuable and highly susceptible to loss or theft from a company. Privacy policies that control access, storage, and transmission of data are forms of internal controls that mitigate risk.

As part of risk management, HR must establish practices and follow policies that are consistent and compliant with laws and regulations. This is to avoid possible litigation or at a minimum make such lawsuits unsuccessful. Lawsuits from former or current employees because of inadequate practices or flawed policies can pose a threat to the company's financial stability.

Risk can be internal to the company, such as insider action by employees or unwittingly facilitating access to sensitive information through negligent practices. Risk is also external through outside actors that intend to harm the company such as thieves, hackers, or corporate espionage for trade secrets. HR must have internal safeguards and measures to secure the company from both types of threats to the organization.

Data Analysis and Organizational Strategy

One responsibility of the HR professional is to determine the significance of data for recommending organizational strategies. The collection and analysis of the data was discussed previously, but once the data is collected, the HR professional will determine how this information is relevant and present the information in a concise manner so that executives can make decisions. Many metrics show an overall view of how effectively the company is maximizing its human capital potential.

For example, the attrition rate of the company, or how often employees separate and leave the organization, is useful to determine if the right individuals are being hired or if there is a training gap that causes managers to prematurely terminate an employee. Other metrics, such as diversity in hiring practices, are required by law but also provide insight into how the company selects its employees.

Time to hire and time to fill will allow the company to evaluate the timeliness of the recruiting process, which may be internal or external or a combination of both. Of course, once onboarded, employees will require training and the success of such can be evaluated as well.

Exam Essentials

Know how to gather information about the general business environment from internal and external sources.   Be familiar with the variety of sources of information and how to extract data and conduct analysis to provide a common business operating picture to executives. Be able to identify best practices in an industry and determine how those practices can be applied to your organization.

Know the importance of key business relationships.   Understand the significance of building and maintaining strong relationships both internally and externally to the company. Be able to influence decision-makers and assess the strength of business relationships. Also, know the importance of corporate responsibility and community involvement.

Know practices and methods to mitigate risk.   HR professionals should know sources of potential internal and external risk to a company and how to mitigate them. Be familiar with proper procedures to reduce a company's exposure to litigation related to HR practices. Protect personally identifiable information of employees from unauthorized disclosure.

Summary

Embrace the business; then embrace the job. Being an effective HR professional requires an understanding of basic concepts related to business and management. The PHR® exam will test your knowledge and experience in business matters. Mission, vision, and values are translated into strategic goals and objectives. These goals are the foundation for policy, programs, and processes throughout an organization, many directly tied to HR practices that will be discussed in the following chapters. As one of the organizational leaders, an HR professional must know and demonstrate the desired behaviors of the company reflective of the values it shares with employees. Finally, an HR professional constantly evaluates the effectiveness of the organization through metrics.

Test-Taking Tip

Review your company's mission or vision statement and any related information on company values. Look for links to HR policies and practices that are directly attributed to these statements or values and the overall impact to business management they have. However, when looking at questions during the exam, read the questions carefully. Many times, answers to a generic question may not be exactly how your company chooses to operate, so be careful of the variations.

Review Questions

1. Which of the following is *not* considered to be a management function?
    A. Planning
    B. Controlling
    C. Implementation
    D. Organizing

2. Human resources policies for a company should be aligned with the company's _____ .
    A. Mission
    B. Management style
    C. Processes
    D. Values

3. A government agency will sell bonds on the market to generate revenue for programs. Before these bonds are sold to investors, financial statements will be prepared to show the creditworthiness of the organization. To prepare these statements, the finance department uses _____ .
    A. GAAP
    B. FLSA
    C. FDIC
    D. FASB

4. A company that has a unique opportunity in manufacturing by relocating to a state that will offer tax incentives demonstrates an example of what?
    A. Competitive advantage
    B. Branding
    C. Strategic planning
    D. Cost-benefit analysis

5. Enterprise risk management takes into consideration _____ when making business decisions about corporate strategy.
    A. Frequency of occurrence
    B. Key performance indicators
    C. Severity of loss
    D. Both A and C

6. In establishing business relationships, it is important that you do which of the following?
    A. Be approachable and open yet maintain strict confidentiality to more effectively influence decision-makers
    B. Establish personal relationships beyond a professional rapport to get to know someone
    C. Restrict or limit the amount of communication between parties to respect privacy
    D. All of the above

7. During a proposed rule change at the federal level, in which phase do regulators gather information on the impact to small businesses?

   A. During the initial phase while the rule is being crafted

   B. During the public comment period

   C. After the final rule is published

   D. Only during court cases challenging the rule

8. A crucial skill for an HR professional when adapting to a changing business environment is _____ .

   A. Gathering all information but not making any decisions until the last possible moment to prevent making a bad decision

   B. Being comfortable dealing with volatile, uncertain, complex, and ambiguous situations and proactively reacting to changes

   C. Telling shareholders about the changes at an annual meeting

   D. Training managers to understand how the changes affects their job

9. The Sarbanes-Oxley Act of 2002 established rules governing _____ in response to the public corporation and accounting scandals that occurred around that time.

   A. Board composition and the election of officers

   B. Reporting conflicts of interest

   C. Financial disclosure statements

   D. All of the above

10. A new HRIS is needed by the company. An HR professional might provide input on the vendor selection process *except* which of the following?

   A. Evaluating proposals

   B. Developing an RFP

   C. Monitoring the performance of a vendor

   D. Determining how to fund the purchase

11. Audits and project management techniques are used primarily in which business management function?

   A. Planning

   B. Organizing

   C. Directing

   D. Controlling

12. When motivating employees, a manager can use what means at their level with little or no additional approvals from higher-level management?

   A. Goals

   B. Incentives

   C. Rewards

   D. Promotion

Chapter 2

Talent Planning and Acquisition (PHR® Only)

THIS CHAPTER COVERS THE PHR® EXAM CONTENT FROM THE TALENT PLANNING AND ACQUISITION FUNCTIONAL AREA AND CONSISTS OF THE FOLLOWING RESPONSIBILITIES AND REQUIRED KNOWLEDGE. FOR SPHR® EXAM CONTENT, REVIEW CHAPTER 7. RESPONSIBILITIES:

✓ 01 Understand federal laws and organizational policies to adhere to legal and ethical requirements in hiring (for example: Title VII, nepotism, disparate impact, FLSA, independent contractors)

✓ 02 Develop and implement sourcing methods and techniques (for example: employee referrals, diversity groups, social media)

✓ 03 Execute the talent acquisition life cycle (for example: interviews, extending offers, background checks, negotiation)

IN ADDITION TO THE PRECEDING RESPONSIBILITIES, AN INDIVIDUAL TAKING THE PHR® EXAM SHOULD HAVE WORKING KNOWLEDGE OF THE FOLLOWING AREAS, USUALLY DERIVED THROUGH PRACTICAL EXPERIENCE:

✓ 12 Applicable federal laws and regulations related to talent planning and acquisition activities

✓ 13 Planning concepts and terms (for example: succession planning, forecasting)

✓ 14   Current market situation and talent pool availability

✓ 15   Staffing alternatives (for example: outsourcing, temporary employment)

✓ 16   Interviewing and selection techniques, concepts, and terms

✓ 17   Applicant tracking systems and/or methods

✓ 18   Impact of total rewards on recruitment and retention

✓ 19   Candidate/employee testing processes and procedures

✓ 20   Verbal and written offers/contract techniques

✓ 21   New hire employee orientation processes and procedures

✓ 22   Internal workforce assessments (for example: skills testing, workforce demographics, analysis)

✓ 23   Transition techniques for corporate restructuring, mergers and acquisitions, due diligence processes, offshoring, and divestitures

✓ 24   Metrics to assess past and future staffing effectiveness (for example: cost per hire, selection ratios, adverse impact)

This chapter reviews the critical functions of talent planning and acquisition. This functional area covers 16 percent of the PHR® exam. Many of the responsibilities and tasks associated with this chapter are most closely related to day-to-day, transactional HR tasks in identifying, attracting, and employing talent. Additionally, this chapter discusses the required knowledge and responsibilities associated with following all federal laws related to the hiring process. This functional area covers recruiting, selecting, and retaining employees and the processes, procedures, and rules that govern the associated tasks. It also reviews the complete life cycle of talent acquisition from the initial interview, through a successfully negotiated offer, to the due diligence of candidate background and reference checks.

Required Knowledge

In current HR practice today, recruiting has become a specialty subset of the profession. Because this function is not necessarily a core competency of a business model, many organizations may, at least in part, outsource the responsibilities that are time-consuming and require specific knowledge. The required knowledge for an HR professional in the area of talent planning and acquisition will help an organization to build and maintain a strong team of employees even if some of the tasks are conducted outside the company. Knowing how these functions work will develop depth within the HR team.

Talent Planning Activities and Concepts

HR professionals must be fluent in the concepts and terms related to talent planning and acquisition. This includes an understanding of applicable federal laws and regulations that govern these activities. HR professionals should be familiar with examples of intricate processes and details such as forecasting and succession planning that represent the required knowledge for the PHR® exam.

Federal Laws and Regulations

This review guide is not a legal guide and is not intended to determine the legality of particular practices or policies within an organization. However, HR professionals should be familiar with the applicable laws and be able to analyze how those laws may impact the hiring and employment decisions for the company.

Having access to legal counsel familiar with employment law is important to an organization. The HR professional will work hand in hand with employment attorneys to mitigate risk associated with employment practices. Litigation that results from bad hiring decisions can be costly both financially and to the company's reputation. Even in cases where there is a settlement, it is still an expensive proposition. A proactive approach to strong, compliant employment policies is the best way to guard against lawsuits.

Title VII of the Civil Rights Act of 1964

The most significant legislation that governs antidiscrimination in hiring is the Civil Rights Act of 1964. Title VII of that act lays the groundwork to ensure equality in hiring, pay, training, and other employment matters. While some states have passed other laws, this law still serves as the foundation of employment hiring practices in the United States.

The law makes it illegal to discriminate on the basis of race, color, religion, gender, or national origin. Additional federal laws have also been passed that include age, pregnancy, physical disability, and veteran status as protected classes.

Gender Identity and Sexual Orientation as Protected Classes

While Title VII protects against gender discrimination, the laws on transgender and gender identity are still evolving in court cases at the state and federal levels. Also, some states have laws that protect individuals from discrimination on the basis of sexual orientation; but again, at the federal level, whether Title VII applies has not been determined by the courts. In all cases, it is always best for an HR professional to implement hiring practices that ensure a fair and neutral process and thus allow the strongest diversity among applicants.

The Americans with Disabilities Act and the ADA Amendments Act

This federal legislation prohibits discrimination on the basis of a disability. The term *disability* refers to any impairment that limits a basic life function. While physical disabilities may be easier to identify by employers, this law also covers mental disabilities. These disabilities are not required to be severe or permanent. The law also requires employers to provide reasonable accommodation to employees with a disability. Reasonable accommodation is provided following an interactive process whereby an employee may request accommodation and the company and employee work jointly to find a resolution that meets the employee's needs without undue burden or hardship caused to the employer.

🌐 Real World Scenario

A Standing Desk

An employee complains of chronic back pain and has been missing several days from work because of a repeated back ailment. She has a clerical job that requires working at a desk where she sits several hours a day. In discussing the continued pain and discomfort, the employee mentions to her supervisor and later HR that her doctor has recommended periods of standing to relieve pressure on the lower back. Under the Americans with Disabilities Act (ADA), even though the employee may not have said the words *reasonable accommodation*, this would trigger an interactive process.

The company was able to procure an adjustable desk platform that could be elevated and lowered so that the employee could stand for periods and continue to work and then sit as desired. In many cases such accommodations are inexpensive and provide a simple solution that meets the needs of the employee. As a result, there was a sharp reduction in the number of missed days because of illness and an increase in productivity of the employee. Other types of equipment accommodations might be a specialized chair, computer monitor, or keyboard. Even some software like voice recognition programs can help employers meet the needs of their employees with physical disabilities.

The Equal Employment Opportunity Act of 1972

This law further strengthened Title VII to cover a large portion of the employers in the United States and established the Equal Employment Opportunity Commission (EEOC) as the government office charged with administering and overseeing the rules and regulations, including interpretations of the law. The act applies to private companies that employ more than 15 people in full-time–equivalent positions; to federal, state, and local governments; and to educational organizations. The EEOC provides guidance to employers in the form of the Uniform Guidelines on Employee Selection Procedures that an HR professional should be familiar with to understand how to avoid bias or prohibited hiring practices that create disparate treatment or disparate impact to protected classes of employees.

The Immigration Reform and Control Act

This law has two major functions. The first is to prevent discrimination against employees based on national origin or citizenship by providing clear guidelines to employers on hiring foreign nationals and the proper documentation of foreign workers in the United States. The second imposes civil and criminal liability to employers for knowingly employing undocumented workers who are not eligible for employment in the United States. It is the responsibility of the employer to prove an employee's eligibility. This is done using the federal I-9 form to verify identity and right to work in the United States.

There are several choices for an employee to prove identity and
employment authorization on the I-9 form; however, the employer should
not state a preference or demand certain choices from employees as this
alone could be discriminatory and violate the law.

Planning Concepts and Terms

HR professionals must know the various techniques and methods of planning, marketing, and staffing the workforce of the organization. They must have working knowledge of
alternatives to direct hires and the sources of qualified candidates. Finally, they must understand how market forces and outside influences can impact the available talent pool and
how to use this knowledge to have a comprehensive recruiting strategy.

Planning Techniques: Succession Planning and Forecasting

Succession planning is not identifying a single person to take someone's job in the future
when the individual leaves or retires. It is a comprehensive career development model that
determines the required knowledge, skills, and abilities for a position and then plans how
employees within the organization can learn and develop them through education, training,
and experience. Ideally, the goal is to have a bench of potential successors to key jobs in the
organization. It also means, as a corollary, that the organization identifies the key jobs in
the company that either are low density and hard to fill or perform tasks deemed critical to
the organization's core competencies. Through this technique there is a deliberate process
to identify and groom quality employees with leadership potential. There is a risk, however,
as there is no guarantee that these employees remain in the organization or that anticipated
openings emerge when expected to allow timely promotions.

Forecasting looks at the demographics of the organization and determines things such
as years remaining before retirement eligibility and turnover rates to project losses to the
company. It uses skills inventories and surveys to determine the available talent to meet
company talent demands. It then compares the available talent pool, examining graduation rates, market salary studies, skills, and geographic limitations for jobs. A geographic
limitation might be something like the availability of affordable housing in the area for the
workforce. This would impact a company's ability to hire employees, especially from outside the area needing to relocate.

Staffing Alternatives

Staffing alternatives are means to employ a workforce that may not be organic to the
company. There are various techniques and resources that an organization can use to manage these available sources of talent. HR must assess alternatives and determine viability.
Companies can choose to hire a talent management firm to provide temporary workers
or temp-to-permanent hires in which an outside source is completely responsible for the
recruiting, selecting, hiring, and sometimes training before the employee works for the
company. In the case of staffing firms, even the management of payroll and benefits is
handled externally for a fee usually calculated as a premium on the salary wage.

Outsourcing is where the entire function is performed by a separate company, eliminating the need for the talent or skills within the company. This is a good technique when the tasks are not the core competencies of the company. *Job sharing* is where two part-time employees can fill one full-time–equivalent position, reducing cost by reducing eligibility for full-time benefits. In some cases, this benefits employees that need more flexibility in their schedule or are not available for full-time work. Another staffing technique for long-time workers of the company is a *phased retirement.* In these circumstances, a senior worker transitions over a predetermined time (usually a year) and goes from a full-time worker to a part-time worker but maintains eligibility for benefits or is provided with an incentive. This allows upward movement in the company for highly qualified workers while providing business continuity, stability, and predictability for workers transitioning to retirement.

Hiring Talent

When hiring for a company, HR professionals must know the current market situation and the availability of talent. They become knowledgeable about proper interview techniques and how to track applicants at each stage of the hiring process. Finally, they understand the impact of total rewards on recruitment and retention of strong talent that meets the mission and values of the company.

Market Conditions

The availability of talent is impacted by the current market situation, and an HR professional must be able to analyze and understand these trends to make good hiring decisions. If a company has a high demand for skilled labor, it is often more difficult to fill vacancies because of the requirement to find talent with the right knowledge, skills, and abilities for a position. Generally, as the economy improves, unemployment drops, decreasing the availability of surplus talent. Also, the number of voluntary quits as a percentage of separations increases because employees have more confidence that they can find suitable work with other employers and may demand increases in wages or benefits to be retained.

 Skilled trade positions are especially difficult as individuals require specialized training in their craft. For many years focus in the United States has been on white-collar jobs requiring a four-year degree. Vocational and technical schools are now seeing a resurgence as a result of increasing costs in higher education, an aging population of trade workers, and corporate focus on apprenticeships and internships to grow and develop talent from within.

Interview Techniques

One of the most important parts of the selection and hiring process is the interview. Ultimately, interacting with the candidate and understanding firsthand the qualities, knowledge, skills, abilities, and other attributes the individual is capable of bringing to the organization is a critical step. However, it is because of human fallibility that this one step is more fraught with the peril of error than any other. We too often bring our own lenses formed with the bias of experience into the process, so it is essential that HR professionals understand the limitations and restrictions that accompany this process.

Behavioral Interviews

These types of interviews are common in the workforce today and are intended to give insight into how an applicant might handle a hypothetical situation that may occur by linking past actions or results to the future job. These questions may be structured in the manner "Give me an example of a time when you . . . ," and the fill-in-the-blank would be related to the context of the new job, such as "had to deal with a difficult decision" or "made a mistake on the job" or "implemented a new program that employees needed help to understand."

While behavioral questions are popular, they have some challenges. First, most prepared applicants will have studied the types of behavior questions that will be asked and have prepared answers. These answers may or may not provide any more insight into the candidate's abilities. Next, since the questions are derived from a previous experience or hypothetical situation, they may not have relevance to the future position, and the employee may end up acting differently in that context.

Situational Interview

A situational interview is similar to the behavioral interview but does not look at past experience or actions; instead, it places the applicant in a scenario and asks them to describe the actions they might take if such an event were to occur. This allows the interviewer to perhaps set the stage of the conditions that the applicant might face in the job and how that individual might go about responding to the situation.

The shortcoming of this process is that the answer may be dependent on how well the scenario is described, and what facts are provided may affect the outcome of a decision. For example, if the situation called for handling a difficult employee who is being aggressive with co-workers, the applicant might respond with an answer to verbally reprimand the worker or choose some other disciplinary action. However, the situation changes if, in the scenario of handling this employee, other facts come to light such as a lack of training, development, or involvement by the supervisor that has contributed to such employee actions.

Group Interview

A group interview takes advantage of the multiple perspectives of different individuals evaluating the candidate at the same time. There are two types, panel and team interviews. In a team approach, all the members of the group are from the same work team and could be peers, subordinates, and supervisors. This is necessary because the team so heavily relies on cooperation among the group that input is needed from all levels. At the panel interview, there may be a representative group that comes from different departments in the organization. Each panel member may represent the areas that the position works with or may provide the subject-matter expert who can assess different competencies.

While group interviews allow everyone to get an understanding of the applicant, depending on the group size, the amount of time allotted might be split among the group members, limiting the amount of information that can be determined by any one individual in depth. The larger the panel, the more uncomfortable an applicant may be in answering questions. Finally, it is important to have a diverse panel if the intent is to gain more perspectives. Panels that are composed of all one gender, race, or ethnic group might inadvertently have bias to some candidates.

The Applicant Tracking System

Modern HR practices include hiring and recruiting through the Internet. Paper forms are replaced by digital applications completed online by the applicant. There are several commercial off-the-shelf applicant tracking systems (ATSs) widely available, depending on the size and scope of the organization, that allow HR to sort and screen applicants based on experience and skills. The system stores the information digitally and tracks the applicants through the entire process. Current employment law and regulations allow for the digital storage of applicant information, provided voluntarily by applicants, used to verify and validate compliance with antidiscrimination laws. By using digital databases, instead of cumbersome paper tracking, a company can more readily track, measure, and analyze trends to improve the quality and diversity of the workforce. For larger organizations, an ATS is critical to keep track of the potentially hundreds of applicants for each available job.

These systems can also be linked to third-party vendors for conducting reference and background checks by seamlessly transferring personal information needed to conduct these checks and provide the required notices to obtain consent by the applicant to conduct these reviews. It is important when reviewing references that HR obtain consent to disclose personal information and to provide the applicant with their rights concerning reference checks. Applicants must be afforded the opportunity to respond to any negative information from outside references.

Retaining Talent

Hiring quality employees is only a step in the life cycle of talent planning and employment. Once they are on board, it becomes the job of the HR professional to ensure that the organization is capable of retaining the necessary talent to meet their goals and objectives into the future. While employee engagement and human resources development will be discussed in later chapters, analyzing the talent and understanding how compensation and benefits can impact the workforce are covered here. You also will look at the variety of ways employees transition from the company and some of the reasons why that relate to company decisions on workforce size and scope.

The Impact of Total Rewards on Recruitment and Retention

To hire and maintain a quality workforce requires an effective pay strategy that considers the total rewards for the employee. While pay is often the strongest motivator, it is not the only reason employees seek employment nor is it the only reason employees stay with an organization. Chapter 4 discusses total rewards in depth, but it is worth noting here that a diverse workforce will have diverse motivations for working in a job.

Rewards and Recognition Programs

A consistent program that rewards employee behaviors that emulate the company's values will encourage employees to be retained in the organization if those rewards are valued by the employees. The rewards can be large or small but should demonstrate how the employer values the contribution made by the employee. For example, if an employee's action saves the company thousands of dollars, providing a $5 gift card to a coffee shop doesn't say that the employee's actions are highly valued.

Training and opportunities to grow and develop skills are also a means of recognizing the achievement and potential of employees. The employer should dedicate resources to helping manage the talent so that there is a pool of available individuals who can be moved into leadership or supervisory roles capable of performing those tasks and responsibilities successfully. Chapter 3, "Learning and Development," discusses in more depth ways to develop and deliver this training.

Integrating and Onboarding Talent

Finding the right talent to fit the organization is challenging. However, a new employee must quickly integrate into the company to perform their duties effectively and support the overall mission. A successful onboarding process and orientation has a significant impact on an employee's feelings of belonging and retention with the organization. The process is reinforced with each interaction between the company and the candidate and also includes testing, negotiations, and offers.

Candidate or Employee Testing

Testing serves a legitimate purpose in the evaluation of talent in the hiring process. It is critical that HR professionals have knowledge about proper testing procedures that assess what is needed to make a decision but avoid testing biases that could violate equal opportunity protections of candidates. In general, a company should ensure that testing procedures provide the following:

- Testing is conducted without regard to protected classes.
- Testing is properly validated and job-related.
- Alternative methods are used if possible, when there is a disparate impact to certain classes with the test results.
- Testing results are predictive of performance success.
- Testing decisions are deliberate and well-conceived by the organization to achieve a legitimate business outcome.

The EEOC lists several examples of employment tests including cognitive tests, personality tests, medical examinations, credit checks, and criminal background checks. For more information, you can review EEOC guidelines at https://www.eeoc.gov/policy/docs/factemployment_procedures.html.

Credit checks and criminal background checks are considered to be part of an assessment of a candidate's potential in a position. These important checks are a legitimate part of a company's due diligence process in vetting potential employees. However, restrictions and limitations have been placed on these background checks by the Fair Credit Reporting Act (FCRA) and by many state laws that attempt to reduce the potential disparate impact of certain protected classes. These candidates have a higher percentage of criminal history for infractions that are often not related to the duties and responsibilities of a potential job and may face discrimination in the hiring process.

Employment Offers

The employment offer is the verbal and written correspondence that outlines the agreement for terms of employment. It establishes the quid pro quo for what an employer provides in terms of compensation, benefits, and working conditions for the services to be provided by the employee and the manner in which those services are to be provided to be deemed acceptable.

It is best that an employment offer be provided in writing and accepted with a signature from the employee. A contingent offer is sometimes made if both parties agree to move forward pending the successful outcome of some subsequent action such as a background check, drug screening, or medical exam. In some cases, if a degree is required for a position, a contingent offer is made pending receipt of official transcripts.

An offer letter should have key pieces of information that clearly state the terms and conditions of employment:

- Proposed salary and benefits to include how they are to be paid or delivered
- Hours of work, place of duty, start date and time
- Any special conditions or requirements that must be met
- A time frame for which to consider the offer and to provide a response
- A clear statement that the employment is "at will" to avoid legal issues and expectations that are sometimes part of an employment contract.

An employment contract differs from an offer letter as it establishes an express agreement between the employer and employee and speaks to the nature of the employment. For example, some teachers are hired year to year under a contract where they teach for a given school or district and must complete satisfactory work for the entire school year. They are not allowed to transfer or change school districts without proper notice or acceptance from their current employer, or they may face censure and be unable to practice because teachers are regulated and require licensure. Other examples might be a veterinarian who signs a noncompete clause contract stating that if they leave a practice, they cannot go to work for a competitor for a period of time within a given radius.

Employment contracts are part of employment law, and HR practitioners should always consult an experienced employment attorney when navigating these topics.

Post–Employment Offer Activities

Once an employee has accepted an offer of employment, an HR professional must ensure that the new employee is integrated into the organization. There are critical legal requirements that must be completed immediately to verify employment eligibility. The I-9 form is a federal form that an employer must complete for every individual employed by the organization. It records information on citizenship and identification to help an employer determine a worker's status. These forms must be maintained for the entire period of employment and retained after employment in accordance with federal guidelines. E-Verify is the online web-based system that compares information on the I-9 with other government information to validate the information provided.

If an employment offer included relocation activities and cost, the HR department may have a role in that process, working with the new employee to help them move to the area. They ensure that all supporting documentation and receipts are submitted for reimbursable expenses and assist with providing information on the local area including schools, real estate agents, local cultural venues and attractions, and other similar life needs to help employees assimilate faster.

Orientation and Onboarding

All new employees must be properly welcomed to the organization. In fact, retaining quality employees begins with how well they are first received by the organization. Companies that demonstrate intentional caring about their employees are more likely to be effective at keeping those employees motivated and engaged.

The HR team provides the orientation to the company in the form of policy guides, initial personnel data uploads for the enterprise digital information systems, history of the company and shared values, supervisory and staff introductions, and other helpful insight into the company operations that help employees acclimate during the first few days to the first week.

Onboarding lasts longer than the first few days of employment and does not include just HR-related activities, although often the responsibility to ensure that all onboarding tasks are completed falls to the HR professional. Such activities may include observing downstream or upstream tasks related to the job duties of the new hire to see how their work fits into the overall organizational structure, attending specified internal training based on the position or responsibilities, and attending organizational meetings or other key events in the company.

Assessing the Effectiveness of Talent Planning and Acquisition

HR professionals should seek continuous improvement in the talent planning and acquisition processes. It requires ongoing assessment of the internal workforce to ensure that the available talent meets the demands of the company to accomplish its goals. Metrics are developed and implemented to provide data for analysis to make strong hiring decisions. When the data shows that talent is no longer meeting the needs of the organization, transition techniques are applied to move the company to restructure or realign the talent as part of a necessary change.

Internal Workforce Assessments

Techniques are available to conduct internal assessments of the current workforce in an organization and the available labor pool from which to draw talent. Some of the techniques are as follows:

- Skills testing
- Skills inventory
- Workforce demographic analysis

The skills testing and inventory are the parts of career development modeling that look at job positions and requirements in an organization and then systematically look at where the gaps are. In this gap analysis, the HR team may conduct assessments to quantify the skill level and knowledge and abilities of the talent. The goal is to determine the proficiency of the individuals with the skills and if the skill is readily available. Beyond testing, the HR team must take an inventory of the required and available skills to perform the tasks needed to accomplish the organizational mission. Sometimes these are technical skills; at other times they are soft skills.

In some highly technical jobs in the United States, the skills inventory exists within an aging population. A *workforce demographic analysis* looks at the region and the available talent pool from which to draw the needed skills. This could include the number of people with college or technical education, years of experience, age of the workforce, and other statistics that can enable HR professionals to plan and understand how a talent pipeline is influenced by the available population. The Bureau of Labor Statistics has a website at www.bls.gov that consolidates and presents workforce data that can be used in this kind of analysis. Figure 2.1 shows information from the website.

Establishing Metrics

HR professionals must collect data, analyze and report findings, and evaluate trends to make decisions regarding successful recruiting practices. Table 2.1 provides some categories of human capital metrics to follow.

FIGURE 2.1   Bureau of Labor Statistics website

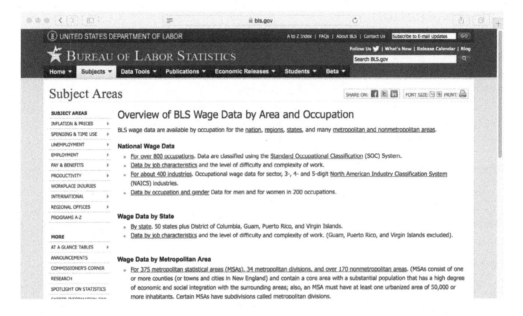

TABLE 2.1   Human capital metrics

Data Category	Metric
Organizational data	Revenue
	Positions included in succession plan
Compensation data	Annual salary increase
	Target bonuses for employees
	Area income levels and cost of living increases
Employment data	Number of positions to fill
	Time to fill
	Cost per hire
	Employee tenure
	Annual overall turnover rate
	Annual voluntary turnover rate
	Annual involuntary turnover rate

Methods to Assess Staffing Effectiveness

Figure 2.2 shows how to calculate a basic cost per hire. By determining how much a company commits in resources to hiring each employee and examining the turnover ratios, HR professionals can determine how effective their recruiting efforts are. The goal should be to bring on board the best talent in the shortest time possible for the lowest cost, while keeping new hires in the company productive beyond the time to recoup the initial investment.

FIGURE 2.2   Cost-per-hire calculations

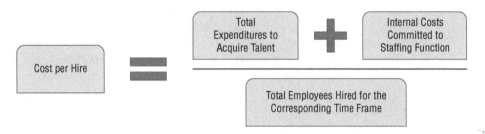

Another important metric is selection ratios. A quality hire comes from having a good pool of qualified candidates and finding the best fit from among those best qualified. HR should know how to track, using either a manual process or an automated applicant tracking system, the number of applicants, the number of minimum qualified applicants, and how many are interviewed to obtain a candidate to present an offer to. This process should also determine the numbers of minority applicants and women to ensure equal opportunity hiring practices and correlation to an affirmative action plan. Companies must be aware to prevent adverse impact in hiring because of internal practices that may have biases.

Transition Techniques

Knowledge of corporate restructuring, mergers and acquisitions (M&A), due diligence processes, offshoring, and divestitures is required for HR professionals. As a company expands or changes, the HR team must be aware of these transition techniques and how to employ them to achieve certain objectives.

Corporate Restructuring and Mergers and Acquisitions

Companies change through the process of restructuring and by joining or acquiring a separate business to form one organization. As part of corporate restructuring, some positions may be added or eliminated based on new job requirements. HR professionals must know how a restructured company might need new training for its employees or need to hire new talent that possesses skills and knowledge that is not available internally. When a company merges with or acquires another company, HR must examine each company and the workforce to see where duties and jobs overlap that can be consolidated. They also find gaps to hire individuals that fill new roles needed for the new structure.

Real World Scenario

Acquiring Automotive Body Repair Shops

A collision repair company that was expanding its operations into new markets had as part of the strategy the ability to acquire smaller shops that did not have the financial ability or business relationships to compete in the market in the long term. When a suitable prospective company was examined, the HR team needed to assess the behavioral and technical capabilities of the current employees and make recommendations on whether they had the prerequisite knowledge, skills, and abilities to keep pace with the larger company or could be trained to meet the standards in a relatively short time. While the goal of a company should be to retain as much personnel as possible from a merger and acquisition, HR must understand the business needs and focus on keeping talent that meets those needs.

Due Diligence Processes

An important part of a transition is the process of due diligence. HR determines any liabilities, including compensation and benefits, that may impact payroll. These processes seek to identify and reduce the risks associated with changing the talent structure of the company. Items to consider may include reviewing employee files, documentation, and employment contracts or union agreements. Transparency and communication during a due diligence review will identify any issues early in the process and mitigate any negative consequences to items that are discovered to be of concern.

Offshoring and Divestitures

In some instances, the company may decide it is necessary to offshore certain job functions, relocating the function to elements of the company located outside the parent company's host nation. Different laws and regulations in each country can provide a competitive business advantage to the company. In a similar manner, the company may decide to remove part of its structure through divestiture of a portion of the organization that may no longer be profitable or is not a core business competency. As these two transition techniques often result in a reduction of force and loss of jobs internal to the organization, HR professionals must be prepared with all necessary compliance and actions taken with the transition of talent from the company.

Exam Essentials

Know the various recruiting strategies available to HR. An organization can use several methods to find and hire the right people to achieve the company's mission. You should understand the different means and the pros and cons they present. Especially important is to review the costs associated with each recruiting option because that may have a direct impact on business decisions as to what methods are available to a particular organization.

Also important is to know the timelines associated with each choice because some recruiting options can take time to mature and develop.

Understand how to perform retention analysis.   Human capital is expensive and should never be wasted. You should understand the direct correlation between employee turnover and lost opportunity or productivity costs. By performing analysis on the effectiveness of retention strategies of the company, you will be able to reduce turnover costs and keep a company performing at optimal levels.

Responsibilities

The PHR® exam reviews an HR professional's understanding of the basic practices surrounding talent planning and employment. The key responsibilities cover the entire employment life cycle including recruiting, selection, retention, and separation of employees. The major tasks that an HR professional must accomplish are the planning and execution of the talent acquisition processes.

Federal Laws and Organizational Policies

A significant responsibility for HR professionals is the development and implementation of organizational HR policies and ensuring that they comply with laws and regulations governing talent acquisition. Through adherence to these rules, HR professionals can meet legal and ethical standards in hiring employees. They have influence with the decision-makers to help the company avoid practices that, though technically legal, may have a negative long-term impact on the corporate brand.

Legal and Ethical Practices

HR professionals should create practices in the hiring process to comply with Title VII, avoiding discrimination of protected classes. Developing standard interview questions, avoiding biases in screening questions or application forms, and reporting hiring results through annual submissions to the EEOC are examples of responsibilities that should be accomplished. It is not enough to avoid disparate treatment, but practices must be evaluated to determine if there is disparate impact, as such impact would be illegal.

Additionally, to comply with the FLSA, each position in the company should be properly classified, have wages established, and not create unfair labor practices. Chapter 5 discusses more requirements with respect to labor relations.

Compliance

It is essential that recruiting practices comply with all applicable laws and regulations. Earlier I discussed the laws that an HR practitioner must be familiar with. However, knowing the law is only the first step. The proper procedures and tasks will help ensure that the organization remains compliant. Table 2.2 outlines some practices that ensure compliance with existing rules.

TABLE 2.2   Recruiting practices

Recruiting Phase	Compliant Practices
Job analysis, duty description, competencies	Determine essential job functions.
	Determine whether any qualifications may have disparate impact.
	Determine whether duties classify positions as exempt from overtime provisions of FLSA.
Posting and advertising	Avoid preselection of candidates.
	Do not solicit any prohibited information (related to protected classes, physical limitation, or pregnancy).
Review candidates and conduct interviews	Ensure the same review process and questions for each candidate.
	Use panels to avoid bias and encourage diversity.
	Ensure that all qualified candidates meet the established minimum qualification based on the duty description and required skills.
Maintain records	Retain information used in the selection process for top candidates based on retention schedule as justification to any challenges or inquiries to the process.

Nepotism

The practice of hiring family members or close personal relations can create ethical issues within the company. It also has the potential to create morale problems with the current employees. It is extremely difficult to maintain accountability and independent judgment in situations where there is a perception of favoritism or undue influence. HR professionals should develop policies that eliminate nepotism practices in the organization.

Independent Contractors

A critical issue in today's business environment is the classification of the business relationship between the company and the worker. Independent contractors perform duties for the company, but the control of day-to-day activities of the worker is outside the scope of the company, and the permanency of the work relationship is temporary. Employees, on the other hand, have an expectation of ongoing work, and the company dictates their day-to-day activities with much more oversight and control. Misrepresenting employees as independent contractors could have serious legal and financial consequences, and a skilled HR professional should review the work relationships of all employees and classify them appropriately.

Recent legal cases have looked at the differentiation between independent contractors and employees as it relates to workers who may be full-time temporary staff provided by an agency. In those situations, if the company has a great deal of control over the employee, such as hours, duties, and other direct working conditions, the company and the temp agency have joint employer responsibilities, and both are required to follow the wage and hour laws with respect to employee classification. Generally, the company pays the temp agency an administrative cost for each worker, and the agency is responsible for paying the employee and handling all employer and payroll taxes. The W-2 generated for taxes would come from the temp agency and not the company.

Sourcing Methods and Techniques

Finding talent is a primary responsibility of HR professionals. Ensuring that the company has the right person, with the right skills, at the right time is an essential duty. There are a variety of methods to source this talent, and each has advantages and disadvantages. The end state should be a diverse talent pool that meets the goals and objectives of the company.

Employee Referrals

Employee referral is the process of using current employees to solicit qualified individuals to apply for open positions; a company may offer a financial incentive or other reward if the applicant is hired and performs the desired duties as required. HR professionals will set up procedures for employees to nominate candidates and facilitate processing their applications. To be effective with employee referrals, a company must have a strong, positive company climate. Employees must have a desire to share their work experiences and invite friends and acquaintances to join them in the workforce. The strongest motivation for recruiting is engaged employees. These engagement techniques are discussed further in Chapter 5.

 Real World Scenario

Increasing Social Media Use in Recruiting

A company was attempting to increase the talent pool from which applicants for jobs were coming. The HR team began to redesign job postings and place them on social media websites. This approach reached a different audience that may not have accessed the more traditional venues previously used for posting jobs and might not otherwise have known of hiring opportunities. It also included more applicants from out of the region willing to relocate for jobs with the company. As a result, a more diverse, skilled workforce could be recruited and hired. The company increased the total number of applicants and improved the overall quality of the applicants.

Talent Acquisition Life Cycle

The talent acquisition life cycle covers the period of time from initial contact with a prospect through their interview and assessment and concludes with a negotiated offer. The HR professional may not be part of the recruiting aspect of the process because this can also be done by third-party vendors that specialize in finding talent. Usually, the initial contact beyond the recruitment is the selection process beginning with interviews. Here are some considerations for choosing an interview process:

- Initial screenings for qualifications can be done by HR, but more in-depth assessments should include the hiring manager or supervisor of this position.

- There may be multiple interviews including telephonic, in-person, and practical or technical interviews that evaluate skills such as in a trade.

- Internet-based televideo interviews can be used but should not be given any less or more weight than other forms to avoid bias.

When the interviews are being conducted, the HR professional should maintain records of all interview notes and evaluations in the process to comply with equal opportunity guidelines.

When a candidate is identified for hire, the HR professional should ensure that the company has a process to conduct a background check and perform due diligence to verify the bona fides of the candidate's application and/or résumé. As a best practice, this process must be conducted before the company extends an offer for employment.

Finally, the HR professional prepares an offer and works with the hiring manager, supervisor, or other decision-maker to handle any counteroffers or negotiations in the process to get an acceptance and agreement of employment terms and conditions. Usually, an HR professional who has excellent communication skills will facilitate this process in a timely and professional manner. Figure 2.3 shows a graphic representation of this life-cycle process.

FIGURE 2.3   The talent acquisition life cycle

Interviews and Assessments → Extending Offer → Background Checks → Negotiation → Onboarding

Exam Essentials

Understand the talent acquisition life cycle.   Know how the entire process a company undergoes to convert individuals from an eligible talent pool into employees. This includes the recruiting process, the interviews of qualified candidates, job offers, due diligence through background checks, and finally the negotiation processes that end with an acceptance of an offer of employment.

Know tools and techniques for recruiting and hiring software.

Applicant tracking systems   HR should know how applicants access an ATS, the information usually provided, certain features such as résumé scanning or autofill that an ATS may feature, the methods of qualifying and referring candidates to the hiring manager, and any notification features.

Background screening   HR should know the types of background checks available, which include credit history; driver records; names and aliases; address verification; federal, state, and local criminal records checks; and sex offender registry. They should also know how to obtain and record consent for checks and maintain the results to include any rebuttals from the applicants if there is negative information revealed in a background screening.

Summary

Finding the right people at the right time and with the right knowledge, skills, and attributes is an ongoing challenge for any organization looking to maximize its human capital potential. Proper talent planning is an essential skill that HR professionals must possess. The added complexity of understanding the legal parameters to hire a diverse workgroup free from bias and prejudice is equally challenging. Companies may have the intent not to discriminate, but in practice, historical patterns and practices can get in the way. HR professionals must be sensitive to a company's culture while still helping them overcome outdated practices. By using effective tools and resources, along with external partners, HR teams can become very effective in delivering the necessary workforce that meets the needs of the company to perform its mission.

Test-Taking Tip

Look at a company's website and their careers or employment page. Review the job application process and recall the steps to hire that you went through to get your current position. Review any checklists or onboarding packets that new employees are required to complete during the hiring process. Pay close attention to the mandatory disclosure statements about equal opportunity or other antidiscrimination hiring practices and policies.

Review Questions

1. In some states applicants are no longer required to disclose a criminal record history in the preselection process because too many otherwise qualified applicants that were disproportionately minorities were being screened out. This is an example of _____ .

   A. ADA violation

   B. Disparate impact

   C. Disparate treatment

   D. Unfair labor practice

2. Which of the following is a protected class of people under the Civil Rights Act of 1964?

   A. Veteran

   B. Gender

   C. Disabled

   D. Sexual orientation

3. The federal government requires an employer to verify a worker's eligibility for employment using _____ .

   A. The I-9 form

   B. A state-issued driver's license and social security card

   C. E-Verify

   D. A background check

4. When determining whether a test is reliable in selecting an applicant for hire, it is important that the test _____ .

   A. Consistently measures what the employer intends to measure during the test

   B. Predicts how the employee will perform in their new duties

   C. Is effective in measuring an applicant's qualities

   D. All of the above

5. When interviewing an applicant, choosing to have several technical experts conduct the interview is an example of what?

   A. Situational interview

   B. Behavioral interview

   C. Panel interview

   D. Working interview

6. Onboarding a new employee is the responsibility of _____ .

   A. The HR department

   B. First-line supervisors

   C. Senior management

   D. All of the above

7. When terminating an employee for cause, it is essential that the HR professional _____ .

   A. Clearly explain the reason (or reasons) for the termination

   B. Send security or others to escort the employee to ensure that they do not remove company property

   C. Offer the employee the opportunity to resign

   D. First determine whether the employee is classified as an exempt employee

8. To assess the skills of the available workforce, an HR department could _____ .

   A. Use a timed, written exam not tied to the essential elements of the job

   B. Hire a third party or outside vendor

   C. Create a skills team to determine what job duties are needed in each position

   D. None of the above

9. Essential job functions _____ .

   A. Are performed only by top executives and experienced staff

   B. Can be generic tasks that must be completed by all employees

   C. Are defined by their critical or highly specialized nature

   D. Change each time a new employee is hired into a position

10. An offer of employment should have all of the following *except* which one?

    A. Be provided in writing

    B. Provide the working conditions, start date, and other essential information about the job

    C. Discuss salary including terms for payment and any benefits

    D. Include any noncompete clauses for competitors if an employee is terminated

11. A company located in Seattle, Washington, as part of the post-employment activities for a new employee residing in Boston, Massachusetts, may engage in which of the following?

    A. Contact references to verify employment history

    B. Assist the employee with relocation

    C. Use online teleconferencing technology to facilitate the interviews

    D. Offer a signing bonus

12. An organization's employment records are _____ .

    A. Essential to demonstrate consistent hiring practices that are compliant with regulations and the law

    B. Required to be maintained in accordance with prescribed retention schedules

    C. Allowed to be completely digital without paper copies

    D. All of the above

Chapter 3

Learning and Development (PHR® Only)

THIS CHAPTER COVERS THE PHR® EXAM CONTENT FROM THE LEARNING AND DEVELOPMENT FUNCTIONAL AREA AND CONSISTS OF THE FOLLOWING RESPONSIBILITIES AND REQUIRED KNOWLEDGE. FOR SPHR® PHR® EXAM CONTENT, REVIEW CHAPTER 8. RESPONSIBILITIES:

✓ 01   Provide consultation to managers and employees on professional growth and development opportunities

✓ 02   Implement and evaluate career development and training programs (for example: careerpathing, management training, mentorship)

✓ 03   Contribute to succession planning discussions with management by providing relevant data

IN ADDITION TO THE PRECEDING RESPONSIBILITIES, AN INDIVIDUAL TAKING THE PHR® EXAM SHOULD HAVE WORKING KNOWLEDGE OF THE FOLLOWING AREAS, USUALLY DERIVED THROUGH PRACTICAL EXPERIENCE:

✓ 25   Applicable federal laws and regulations related to learning and development activities

✓ 26   Learning and development theories and applications

✓ 27   Training program facilitation, techniques, and delivery

✓ 28   **Adult learning processes**

✓ 29   **Instructional design principles and processes (for example: needs analysis, process flow mapping)**

✓ 30   **Techniques to assess training program effectiveness, including use of applicable metrics**

✓ 31   **Organizational development (OD) methods, motivation methods, and problem-solving techniques**

✓ 32   **Task/process analysis**

✓ 33   **Coaching and mentoring techniques**

✓ 34   **Employee retention concepts and applications**

✓ 35   **Techniques to encourage creativity and innovation**

Chapter 3 covers the area of learning and development. This important topic composes 10 percent of the PHR® exam. HR professionals will be responsible for the growth and development of the talent in their organization. Additionally, HR most often coordinates and develops training for companies and must understand how employees learn and retain new concepts and ideas to create training that is impactful.

The key concepts to master in this chapter are how to provide consultation to managers and employees on professional growth and development opportunities; learning and development theory and practices; and techniques that are employed by HR professionals in this area. The goals of learning and development include aligning employee behaviors with desired outcomes and ensuring that the organization has the proper talent with the necessary knowledge, skills, and abilities to meet the needs of the company and the employees, now and in the future.

Required Knowledge

The desire of all HR professionals is to help their company transform into a learning organization, helping its employees to reach their maximum potential to grow and support the organization as it continues to improve its business and achieve its goals. To do this, HR professionals must be proficient in assessing learning and development needs, developing and implementing training, and determining the effectiveness of the training delivered. HR practitioners must have knowledge of learning theory, and they must master techniques of facilitation and delivery of instruction, as well as methods of teaching and coaching to encourage learners in the learning process.

Laws and Regulations

Even in learning and development there are legal compliance requirements to ensure that training is unbiased and delivered in a manner that provides equal opportunity to all employees who require access to training. In some cases, it is also important to know the legal restrictions governing the use of training materials such as copyright law. With the increase of materials freely accessible on the Web, it is still the responsibility of the training developer and those offering training to guard against infringement of other people's work without proper compensation or acknowledgment.

Title VII and ADA Compliance

Chapter 2 discussed the impact of civil rights legislation on hiring and promoting talent within the organization. These laws also have requirements that mandate equal opportunity in training employees. For example, to determine who needs training and when they can attend, companies should use processes similar to those used in selecting new employees. In cases where an employee might have a disability that is covered under the ADA, employers must again provide reasonable accommodation to such an individual. This might mean modification to support visual or hearing impairment, for example.

> Most e-learning training developed today is designed to comply with the ADA regulations. For example, in an online test review, correct answers will be identified in multiple ways to ensure comprehension. These may include a visual cue (such as the word *Correct* in a green box) or audio cue (a bell "ding"). An individual who may have difficulty determining red or green shades, commonly referred to as *red/green colorblindness*, is not solely dependent on the green box, as there are two other cues to show the correct answer (the word and sound). Recording narration and narration text appearing are other common techniques to ensure compliance.

Title 17 (Copyright Act of 1976)

This law is important to HR professionals responsible for the creation and implementation of training for an organization. With the extensive amount of material available on the Internet, it may seem reasonable to use whatever can be found in presentations, training products, handouts, and other developmental material. However, it is essential to understand that some of that work is the intellectual property of others and that using it may have restrictions or be prohibited.

There are five points to copyright law that HR professionals should know with respect to the copyright owner and the material.

- The owner has the right to authorize others to copy it.
- The owner has the right to authorize others to distribute it.
- The owner has the right to authorize others to alter it to create a new product or version (known as a *derivative*).
- The owner has the right to authorize others to display it.
- The owner has the right to authorize others to perform it.

In summary, it is not permitted to use, copy, distribute, alter, display, or perform any work created by someone without assigning proper credit and when required properly compensating the owner for the permissions discussed. The reasoning is that it wouldn't be right for someone to go through the hard work to create something and have it used by someone else without any consideration given.

Of course, there are always exceptions. One is material that is in the public domain. There are certain provisions that dictate how and when material enters the public domain and may be used freely by all. The other significant exception is the "fair use" doctrine. While fair use doesn't have a clearly defined standard, in general it looks to how much of the material is being used, for what purpose, and the impact financially for its use that would deprive the owner of benefiting from the work.

Learning and Development Theory

Much of developmental learning and training applies knowledge of how the human brain thinks, learns, retains, and uses information. The body of knowledge of the multiple theories on these subjects is well beyond the scope of this book. However, there are some basic principles common throughout them that impact how an HR professional designs and implements training for the organization. The Association of Talent Development (ATD) is an organization for talent developers, instructional design professionals, and professional coaches. It can be a great resource for HR professionals working in this field. Among these professionals are some who hold the Certified Professional in Learning and Performance (CPLP) credential. For more information, you can visit www.td.org.

Instructional Design Principles and Processes

When designing instructional material, it is important to understand the basic design principles and processes. The general intent is to know how the adult human brain learns and design a presentation in such a way as to maximize the retention and comprehension of the information. Through the use of developed instructional design techniques, content material can be learned faster and more efficiently with greater simplicity.

The first step is a needs analysis. As discussed in other chapters about total rewards or talent management or anything that requires HR input into business operations, a needs analysis clearly shows what the organization requires to meet its goals and objectives. A proper needs analysis in instructional design will reveal what needs to be learned and the best methods to achieve learning.

HR professionals should be familiar with such design models as Analysis-Design-Development-Implementation-Evaluation (ADDIE). This five-step process begins with analysis of the problem or objective, followed by intentional design and development of the training and its implementation. It then concludes with an evaluation of the results. This dynamic and flexible process provides necessary structure for learning development.

Another example is Robert Gagne's nine events of instruction, a model that attempts to capture the process of learning in concrete events as they occur in the instructional process. Figure 3.1 shows the events that were first defined by the American educational psychologist. The process begins with capturing the attention of the learner and flows through to practical use of the information gained, where the knowledge is transferred to long-term memory and can be recalled and used over and over.

FIGURE 3.1   Gagne's nine events of instruction

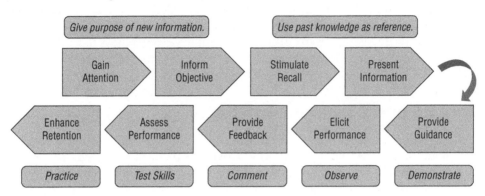

Process Flow Mapping

When a process is created in the organization, process flow mapping allows for the steps in the process to be visually displayed so that the learner can review the process and have greater understanding and comprehension. It allows for the learner to identify non-value-added steps, facilitates teamwork and communications, and keeps everyone on the same page. There are standard graphics used in modern process flow mapping. Figure 3.2 provides an example of a basic process shown in a flow map. Creating the map is often part of the instructional design process to facilitate the employee learning visually how the process is to be followed.

FIGURE 3.2   Process flow map

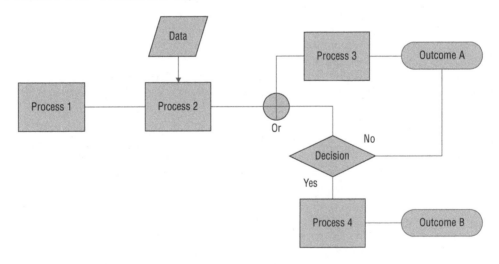

Adult Learning Processes

The classic adult learning theory was popularized by Malcolm Shepard Knowles (1913–1997), who developed these four concepts related to adult learning:

- Adult learners want to have a voice in deciding the content and method of delivery.
- Adult learners are most interested in learning about something that has immediate impact and relevance in their world.
- Adult learning is experiential, meaning that adults draw upon their own experience to learn new concepts.
- Adult learners use problem solving as the primary method of learning and retention of ideas and concepts.

In addition to Knowles's learning theory, Benjamin Bloom (1913–1990) defined what has become a standard taxonomy of learning; it has three levels of learning based on senses, emotions, or knowledge. The cognitive level, based on knowledge, has six levels: Remember, Understand, Apply, Analyze, Evaluate, and Create (or Synthesize). This is important to understand for adult learning because it shows the levels of retention and ability to integrate new concepts from the lowest level (just understanding) to the highest (creation of new thoughts based on what has been learned).

A full dive into the adult learning process is beyond the scope of this guide, but a general understanding will help with concepts outlined in the rest of this chapter. For more information on this subject, I recommend the Department of Education information paper at https://lincs.ed.gov/sites/default/files/11_%20TEAL_Adult_Learning_Theory.pdf.

Task and Process Analysis

HR professionals must know how to deconstruct a task or process and understand where employees may struggle in understanding how to perform it. This is a critical step in the needs analysis process to fit the right training or remedial steps to improve performance.

1. Review the job requirements and identify the tasks or actions that are essential to successfully do the work.
2. Determine the required knowledge, skills, attributes, or other behaviors that are needed to most effectively perform the task or process.
3. Compare the requirements against the current performance of the employee and identify any deficient areas.
4. Determine which of the deficiencies can be corrected through training.
5. Design or acquire training that supports the needed changes.
6. Implement the training and monitor progress of the employee.
7. Evaluate any changes in performance to measure the effective of the training.

Techniques

HR professionals responsible for the development of the human capital of their organization must be familiar with the various training techniques available. Training is designed to align knowledge, skills, and behaviors of employees with the needs of the organization to achieve goals and objectives. There are also a variety of techniques to evaluate the performance of employees and assist them to continually improve.

Career Development and Leadership

Great organizations have intentional paths for how an entry-level employee grows and progresses throughout their tenure with the company. For example, in the United States Army, how does a new private who enlists today grow up to be a senior noncommissioned officer, an officer, or potentially a four-star general? Every career field has a career development model that is designed to plan the steps needed to advance, and that includes experience, education (both formal and informal), and professional development. Not only the *what* but the *when* in the timeline of a career are essential.

This is equally true in civilian companies. It is important when employees join the company that they understand what they need to do to continue to grow and advance. Sometimes they may not seek increased responsibility or supervisory roles, so there should be consideration paid to how to enrich their current role to maintain engagement and keep the employee motivated to achieve the goals and objectives that support their role and the company's mission, vision, and values. A career development map can show which positions have similar skills or duties that facilitate an employee switching jobs or career paths. From this, an individual can create a personal career development plan that takes into account their goals and desires and the needs of the company.

It is not always possible for the employee's ideal work and the reality of the job requirement demands for the company to align perfectly. In these cases, it is necessary for the leadership of the organization to motivate, coach, and develop the employee to maximize their contributions. Leaders select leaders and must be involved in succession planning to identify future leaders. They intentionally plan for their development to assume roles of greater significance, determining how to close or minimize any skills gaps in these prospects.

Organizational Development

Organizational development (OD) theory looks at both processes within an organization and the implementation strategy. A learning organization is one that continually assesses its situation, determines what it needs to improve, and develops a plan to make those improvements. It then evaluates the results at the end and starts the process again. As part of this theory, HR professionals should know change management and the variety of quality and control improvement methods that exist. Table 3.1 lists some common methods and their key points.

TABLE 3.1 Quality improvement methods

Method	Key Aspects
Total Quality Management	▪ Find issues that affect quality ▪ Identify stakeholders in the process ▪ Eliminate wasteful steps ▪ Establish conditions that support continuous improvement

Method	Key Aspects
ISO 9000	▪ Benchmark standards that define quality processes in a company
	▪ Implement continuous improvement
	▪ Focus on reducing defects
Cause and effect	▪ Establish major factors in defects to process and what elements cause them
	▪ Create a visual map to improvement
Lean process	▪ Establish principles on which to do work, such as the 5S methodology (Sort, Set in Order, Shine, Standardize, Systems)

In addition to quality improvement methods, HR professionals determine how to implement desired changes in an organization. There are three basic areas: people, technology, and structure. Figure 3.3 shows their relationship and how they may interact within an organization. It is important to know and understand how each type of change affects the other areas and how to adapt these changes over time.

FIGURE 3.3 Organizational development change theories

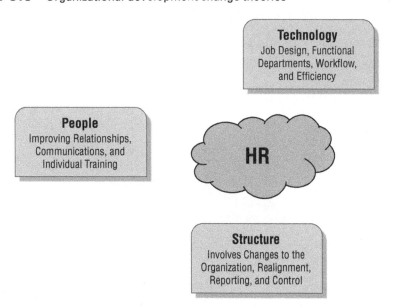

In all cases, an HR professional must know how to act as the change champion, embracing the continued growth and development of the company and reassuring its human capital that to be successful companies must continually change to meet the current demands that are informed by the current operational environment. HR professionals must communicate with leaders and employees about how people are accepting and adjusting to the reality of change within the company.

Motivation Concepts and Applications

A key point of knowledge for HR professionals is an understanding of motivation for employees and its relationship with organizational behavior. There are many different models and academic studies on this topic, each with a different variation on what compels people to behave in certain ways and how to use that knowledge to lead and inspire others to perform in a manner consistent with the desired values and behaviors of the company. It is not necessary to study every single motivational method in detail, but HR professionals should be familiar with the concepts and how they are applied in decisions related to the business.

Maslow's Hierarchy of Needs

Probably the most popular motivational structure is Maslow's hierarchy of needs, first developed by Abraham Maslow in his research published in 1943. This model lists six levels from the basic physiological to self-actualization and explains that individuals move along the hierarchy only after each lower level is satisfied. Figure 3.4 shows the hierarchy model. It is important for HR professionals to understand these basic needs to help the organization provide for its employees and allow them to develop. For example, according to the hierarchy, physiological needs (such as food, shelter, and clothing) are well below esteem (accolades, rewards, and recognition). Therefore, it is logical that an employee's basic compensation so that they can buy those items to meet physiological needs is of greater importance than a certificate of appreciation for their quality of work. However, for an employee to progress to self-actualization, those points of recognition are also needed.

FIGURE 3.4   Maslow's hierarchy of needs

Theory X and Theory Y

Motivation of employees is important to their development and continued effective performance in an organization. Developed by Douglas McGregor at MIT in the late 1950s and 1960s, the two competing philosophies known as Theory X and Theory Y reflect on the nature of the generic worker and the corresponding management techniques that should be applied. Theory X views workers in a generally negative light, holding that they are not motivated to work and when given a choice will choose not to work and be generally lazy. The management technique that is required under this theory is one of punishment and reward to constantly motivate employees to meet demands of the organization and segregate those workers unable to perform from those that can. Managers focus on tasks to be performed more often than the workers that perform such tasks in this scenario.

The converse to this is Theory Y, where the employee is assumed to be motivated internally to succeed and do the necessary work, but obstacles or restrictions limit the performance of most employees. Therefore, the manager's role is to eliminate barriers to performance by communicating with the employee and help find ways to help the employee. These managers are more proactive and people-oriented than task-oriented. In the first theory, the relationship is more transactional, while in the second case, it is more transformational. In Theory X management, the results last only as long as the desire for reward or punishment is greater than the consequences of not completing the task in the mind of the employee. However, Theory Y will have a longer effect if the known barriers are removed and the employee is free to develop.

Problem-Solving Techniques

An eight-step problem-solving method is an example of a practical series of actions to take when solving complex problems. There are many versions of this method, but not all problems require a formalized step method. Many small issues get solved without the need to address each step. However, for difficult issues, HR professionals should be aware of the following steps:

1. Define the problem.
2. Gather facts and assumptions.
3. Define the goals and objectives and establish success criteria.
4. Determine root causes and develop possible solutions.
5. Analyze and compare the solutions and choose the best option.
6. Implement the proposed solution.
7. Evaluate the results.
8. Continue to monitor progress of results and recommend any changes or future action.

Coaching and Mentoring Techniques

HR professionals must know proper coaching and mentoring techniques to reach employees and to work with managers and executives who are in the role of mentor or coach to help them be more effective. Many times asking questions that drive critical thinking is a key task for a coach. For example, "What happened?" or "What did you intend?" and "What did you learn?" or "How can you improve next time?" are the types of questions that will help the employee learn from a given situation and process the knowledge gained. Coaches and mentors must gain the respect of the subject of their coaching to be effective, and trust is important in this regard. They have strong influence to help employees create and achieve goals. They must know how to help identify strengths and weaknesses of a learner or employee so that they can cooperatively develop strategies to overcome challenges.

Encourage Creativity and Innovation

HR professionals should encourage creativity and innovation within the culture of the organization. In a similar manner to those techniques employed by coaches and mentors, encouraging creativity allows for the free flow of information and newly generated solutions to problems that can negatively impact the organization. To truly be innovative requires the removal of fear of failure. That does not mean removing consequences for poor performance or bad actions, but rather that when mistakes are made in the learning process, the focus is on correction and growth, not shame and blame. An organization that inspires dialogue and continuous improvement in the learning process will see resulting innovation.

Training Program Delivery

Training programs can be for specialized technical needs or more generalized. When developing a program, a needs assessment begins the process to determine exactly what training is required, who will sponsor the project, the available resources, the method of delivery, and the time allotted for the development of training. HR professionals should know how to research and determine the needs of employees, coordinate with subject-matter experts for specialized training, and prepare or coordinate for the delivery of more generalized training.

In many cases, there is already training available for common business topics such as conflict management or leadership fundamentals, and it's not necessary to create this training from scratch. However, a company may choose to present these topics in the context of its individual business by personalization. The bulk of internal resources dedicated to training program development is usually for more specialized training, since it isn't commercially available off the shelf to purchase. Training specific to a company's operation or proprietary processes or systems can be tailored as needed.

HR professionals must know how to prioritize training resources and understand the effect that training will have to determine return on investment. This includes metrics to determine how employees retain the knowledge learned over time. Instruction that is not implemented or used quickly will not have as strong a retention, lessening the likelihood that it will be used by employees.

Training Program Facilitation

HR professionals will know how to facilitate training events. As part of the adult learning model, the lead trainer is not an instructor providing all the knowledge and information but instead takes on the role of group advisor to help the collective team discover and learn using their own experience and understanding. The material is available for the group to draw upon, discuss, and collaborate, and the facilitator keeps the team motivated and sets milestones and general guidelines to ensure that learning objectives are met.

Training can now be delivered in a traditional classroom presentation or through online content or blended using both methods. HR professionals must know how materials and subjects are best presented to ensure maximum retention. Some complex tasks require hands-on experience to learn. Training on equipment, on complex machines, or in specific locations cannot be easily replicated in a classroom.

In a classroom, there can be interaction with the instructor. With e-learning, an instructor must anticipate questions that will flow naturally and prepare the response within the script. It is beyond the scope of the exam to know instruction design software for building online learning; however, it is the responsibility of HR to be able to review, evaluate, and select the platforms available to deliver the training.

Training Techniques

HR professionals are often responsible for training managers, employees, and colleagues in a variety of subjects. It is required that they understand different training techniques. With the availability of modern technology, there are now more options available including simulations and virtual environments, along with more traditional classroom methods or on-the-job (OJT) training. OJT offers a unique opportunity for hands-on learning in the actual environment where the work is performed under real conditions but doesn't allow for many mistakes or errors. The classroom works for learning theory or basic concepts related to the job, but it does not lend itself to realistic training because the environment doesn't account for real working conditions. A virtual environment is helpful when communicating and learning across distances or with multiple learners, but again may not be the optimal learning environment for real conditions. In those situations, it also limits the amount of direct interaction between the learners and the instructor. HR professionals must contemplate the training that will be conducted and determine the best technique to use to achieve learning. These techniques are used in combination with other core elements discussed, including the adult learning process and motivational concepts.

Employee Retention Concepts and Applications

HR professionals must be knowledgeable about concepts that improve employee retention and know how to apply those concepts in the organization. Providing growth and learning opportunities for employees will improve retention. Companies that strive to improve organizational effectiveness will align employee behaviors that the company desires. These individuals are naturally disposed to perform at high levels for the company, and this makes them more desirous to remain with an organization where they are successful.

Improving Organizational Effectiveness

Training should be tied to the overall goals and mission of the organization, and each individual position in the company should have required training to sustain and improve the team. As part of the training needs assessment, HR should look at the critical tasks performed by each employee and the necessary skills or behaviors that an employee should possess to perform the tasks properly. Using performance appraisal methods discussed later in the chapter, supervisors and management can determine where an individual employee needs to improve, and training can be matched to meet the needs. Surveys and assessments are conducted post-training to see whether there are changes in performance, improved efficiency, or other tangible results because of the training. Training the individual must align with the needs of the company to improve organizational effectiveness. The training must be balanced so that the employees' improvements are related to the areas the company needs to remain successful.

Evaluating Program Effectiveness

HR professionals are responsible for evaluating the effectiveness of employee training programs. There are several methods for establishing the metrics and collecting data to compare the program results with the desired results. Surveys are a comprehensive method for quickly collecting results and depending on the type of survey can measure various levels of responsiveness. Table 3.2 shows examples of surveys, the type of information they solicit, and how that information is used by an organization.

TABLE 3.2   Surveys

Survey Type	Information Gathered	Allows Measurement Of
Immediate reaction	Responsiveness/quality of instruction or instructor	Initial response to training format and delivery
Short-term follow-up	Check on learning/implementation of instruction	Utilization of knowledge obtained in training
Long-term follow-up	Determination of incorporated practices	How much the information from training has improved the process output or results

Using Metrics to Evaluate Training Effectiveness

Cost for training and the retention of information in post-learning surveys or tests are commonly used metrics that a company can use to measure training effectiveness. It is important that HR professionals know how to capture all costs associated with learning and development, not just paid courses external to the company but the internal committed resources to build in-house learning. They can develop tests that are administered after a short period of time following training to reinforce and measure retention of information of the class provided.

Exam Essentials

Understand organizational development theory.   While it is not required to know every theory in detail, exam participants should know the basics and be able to identify more commonly used theories.

Know techniques related to instructional design and adult learning models.   All organizations must understand how to design training around adults and know how their learning and retention are impacted by effective design. The components, the various measuring methods, and how those training techniques are used to improve the technical knowledge or capabilities of employees in the company are important knowledge points for HR professionals.

Responsibilities

The responsibilities associated with the functional area of human resources development are critical to a successful organization, but often in smaller organizations some or all of the key tasks are outsourced. The tasks of other functional areas tend to have immediate impact on employees or support the immediate needs of employers, such as payroll, or have compliance requirements that mandate work for HR, such as record keeping. Because these short-term needs can overwhelm even the most efficient small HR teams, human resources development is often viewed as a nice-to-have and not a need-to-have function by companies. Unfortunately, this is common, so HR professionals must strongly advocate for the continued development and training of the organization's talent or risk stagnation and complacency throughout the company.

Provide Consultation

HR professionals are responsible for providing consultation to managers and employees on professional growth and development opportunities both internal and external to the organization to maximize the human capital potential of the entire company. HR professionals must work with supervisors and managers throughout the learning and development process. Managers often are highly skilled and knowledgeable about technical processes, but that doesn't necessarily mean they are able to teach and groom others or can identify untapped potential performers in the group. HR must use interpersonal skills to build relationships with managers to help them develop all their employees to constantly and consistently achieve the goals set by the company. HR professionals use their role as advisors to coach managers to have deliberate discussions about employees' desire for progression, career goals, and development plans. Both HR and management develop training to provide the needed skills for employees to advance and improve. HR must also ensure that managers understand their internal biases and ensure equal opportunity for all high-potential performers. HR professionals should routinely meet with managers to discuss their teams and the best course of action to develop them that meets the goals and objectives of the company.

Developing the Organization

HR professionals must help the organization to grow and meet the ever-changing needs of its employees, stakeholders, and customers. As companies transform, there must be systematic processes that ensure that no part of the team gets left behind or that change does not happen haphazardly. As a skill, HR professionals must know how change disrupts and are responsible for minimizing the impact of those disruptions or mitigating the potential negative consequences that often follow change.

Implement and Evaluate Career Development and Training Programs

HR professionals assist the organization by implementing and evaluating career development and training programs in the company by providing relevant data. This could be statistics about numbers of trained employees, the percentage of retirement-eligible employees that requires a career development model to grow internal replacement candidates over time, or active management of high-potential employees.

Talent Management

HR professionals must manage the talent of the organization and continually invest in the employees to ultimately benefit the company. They must build career development models and identify high-potential employees to ensure that those employees are managed more closely, to groom them for positions of increased responsibility or complexity, and to provide training at the right time in a career timeline to possess the right skills needed to do the work. Finally, HR professionals ensure that dedicated workers whose performance is aligned with the behaviors desired by the company are provided job enrichment opportunities to keep them engaged and performing at a high level.

Building a Career Development Model

HR professionals must know how to chart the career progression of the various positions in the organization to stabilize the workforce and develop talent internally. It requires an understanding of the knowledge, skills, and abilities required of each position and how those positions might be developmental to other more senior positions such as supervisors or executives. Career development models also show HR planners where skills of positions overlap to enable cross-training or suggest lateral transfers across the company.

Ideal models can clearly demonstrate to new employees the career progression of a job within the organization and provide guidance as to how an employee can grow and develop their skills over time to advance in the company over an entire career. A career development model will show a combination of experience, education, and professional development that someone must possess to advance. It is important to note that while this process may show what is required, it doesn't evaluate the potential or performance of an individual. So, it is possible that an individual's career is limited by how well they are able to reach some of the milestones determined by a career development model. Figure 3.5 depicts a career development model for an administrative position within a human resources department in a company.

FIGURE 3.5   Career development model

CDM for HR Generalist
- Promotion potential to HR Lead or Supervisor
- Specialization as Benefits Administrator; Labor Relations Specialist; Organizational Trainer; Recruiter

Educational requirements: High school diploma, preferred two- or four-year degree from accredited institution

Technical progression: HR training; certification (PHR)

Experience: Exposure and relevant work in HR subject areas of workforce planning, HR development, employee relations, and compensation and benefits. Firsthand knowledge of company procedures and practices governing HR delivery.

Managing High-Potential Employees

As the term suggests, high-potential employees are those who have shown the ability to perform high-level tasks and are capable of management or supervisory responsibilities. HR professionals have a duty to help current managers identify, select, train, and advance these individuals to help the company sustain its corporate leadership over time. HR professionals use a variety of techniques and tools designed to measure the potential of certain employees and then assist supervisors to cultivate skills. HR professionals might use an individual development plan (IDP) to coach talented individuals and assist their leadership in determining the areas that may need attention. Figure 3.6 shows a potential versus performance matrix, commonly referred to as a *nine-box*.

FIGURE 3.6   The nine-box model

High Potential Low Motivation	High Potential Moderate Motivation	High Potential High Motivation
Moderate Potential Low Motivation	Moderate Potential Moderate Motivation	Moderate Potential High Motivation
Low Potential Low Motivation	Low Potential Moderate Motivation	Low Potential High Motivation

Potential (vertical axis) — Motivation (horizontal axis)

For high-potential employees, you are looking at those employees who would be categorized in the far-right column but not necessarily in the top-right corner. It is the job of management along with the assistance of HR to determine what limitations are preventing those employees in the spectrum to the right of the matrix from being placed in the upper right and how to overcome them.

Creating Job Enrichment Opportunities

In some cases, employees have reached their potential for advancement through either desire or capability but are still competent in their role and have a strong desire to perform their job functions well. HR professionals must ensure that these strong employees remain engaged to prevent a decline in their performance. They must creatively find opportunities to enrich the jobs these skilled individuals already have. In some cases, training on new technology or processes will better equip employees to do their job. Adding depth to their understanding of the role, which may include increased knowledge or control over certain aspects, can be considered enrichment. For example, an employee who is highly competent may be given a lead role for their job but not supervisory responsibility. They may instead be responsible for training new team members initially or perform quality control checks because of the quality of their work and knowledge of the right processes.

Training for Evaluators

HR professionals are responsible for providing training to supervisors on how the evaluation process works for the organization. Technical training, including the specifics of how any instruments are completed and submitted and the time frame to do so, is one form of training. The other, often more beneficial training requires HR professionals to help supervisors develop clearly defined performance success criteria. Evaluations cannot be arbitrary, but often tasks are hard to measure from a quality standpoint. In manufacturing jobs, production numbers compared to goals are straightforward, and comparisons can be done from rating period to rating period. However, it is harder to measure qualitative results for manner of performance.

Supervisors must measure both technical and behavioral competencies in the evaluation to provide a comprehensive look at an employee's performance. Technical competencies are connected to what tasks are being completed and to what degree. Behavioral competencies seek to show how an employee is performing. Too often employers will overlook one side in favor of the other. Someone who produces great results but has a negative attitude can still be a performance problem, as is someone who struggles to meet goals but is positive and gets along with co-workers. HR professionals can help supervisors navigate difficult conversations.

Contribute to Succession Planning

While succession planning is often done at higher levels in the HR structure, all HR professionals are responsible for contributing to succession planning. Front-line HR managers or generalists may have more personal knowledge of employees and can comment on potential or their training needs with more detail than may be available in information systems. Providing relevant data on vacancies and potential losses as discussed previously is a critical role for HR. In many cases, HR professionals evaluate the required knowledge, skills, and abilities at the position in question and then identify any skills gaps among potential successors. They must determine the time and cost to close the gap and evaluate where resources should be committed to this process.

It is critical to understand that succession planning does not mean identifying one person as an heir apparent to take a senior-level position. This creates potential for a single point of failure and could also be a violation of equal opportunity laws. Instead, the HR team will look at the skills needed and several potential replacements in a cohort to train and evaluate together. Sometimes this planning may even require going externally from the company to find the right individual if it is deemed that no suitable internal candidates exist with the right skills. Succession planning is an ongoing process, so as solutions are developed, they must be reevaluated and updated especially as people leave the organization.

Exam Essentials

Know how to provide consultation to managers and employees.   An organization can use several methods to find and hire the right people to achieve the company's mission. You should understand the different means and the pros and cons each presents. Especially important is to review the costs associated with each recruiting option, as that may have a direct impact on business decisions as to what methods are available to a particular organization. Also important is to know the timelines associated with each choice, as some recruiting options can take time to mature and develop.

Understand how to evaluate career development training programs.   Human capital is expensive and should never be wasted. You should understand the direct correlation between employee turnover and lost opportunity or productivity costs. By performing analysis on the effectiveness of career development and training programs, you can develop retention strategies for the company. As a result, you will be able to reduce turnover costs and keep a company performing at optimal levels.

Summary

Learning and development is the effective management of talent within an organization. It is a critical function for HR professionals to master and understand. They must be able to assess needs and remain compliant with existing laws, rules, and regulations governing the opportunities for employees to participate, the design and creation of the training, and the performance assessment of employees.

Training development is the responsibility of the HR team by either creating the necessary training to improve performance or determining what available training may be outsourced to reduce cost and time to deliver. Understanding generally how the training cycle runs from need to design to implementation to evaluation is part of HR professionals' knowledge base. HR professionals have the added responsibility for program development and providing coaching and mentoring directly to managers and employees.

Test-Taking Tip

Talk with the individuals responsible for training in your organization and ask them about their important functions and daily job duties. Get a sense of what priorities they have to create and deliver effective training and how those priorities relate to the overall company mission and strategic goals and objectives.

Review Questions

1. When developing training for use in a company, it is important that HR professionals remember _____ .

   A. To add multimedia to enhance a presentation, regardless of the source

   B. To use any third-party material properly in accordance with copyright law

   C. To provide training in only one format to reduce complexity

   D. To alter any original work from another author so that it can be used in a presentation as a new creation

2. The fair use doctrine states _____ .

   A. If material is available on a public platform like the Internet, it can be used.

   B. Any government or public institution's material needs approval before using it.

   C. Small portions of the work can be used, if it would not create a negative financial impact to its author by its use.

   D. Material enters the public domain 50 years after its original creation.

3. A company is looking to correct errors in its manufacturing process. There appears to be inconsistency in how employees perform certain tasks. The HR team should do which of the following first?

   A. Conduct a needs assessment by interviewing supervisors and employees involved in the process

   B. Develop training for managers to better lead their employees for more consistent results

   C. Purchase commercial off-the-shelf training for employees on time management

   D. Rewrite the employee manuals on how to perform the task correctly so that it is better understood

4. When selecting training programs for an organization, an HR professional should consider the following *except* which one?

   A. Number of employees to train

   B. Time to implement

   C. Method of delivery

   D. ROI

5. When conducting surveys to assess the effectiveness of training, the best results are with surveys that _____ .

   A. Measure the learners' immediate feedback on the class

   B. Collect data on learners' performance changes over time

   C. Test short-term retention of the material covered

   D. None of the above

6. High-potential employees are
    A. The primary focus of training within companies
    B. Easy to identify within the organization without any additional resources
    C. Critical to identify within the organization for succession planning
    D. Immediately capable of management or supervisory positions and should be promoted

7. Succession planning is best described by which of the following?
    A. A systematic approach to identify, assess, and develop talent for leadership roles in an organization
    B. Predetermining employees within the company to fill management roles
    C. Planning the career path of entry-level employees to fill different roles in the company
    D. None of the above

8. Organizational development (OD) theory has which two general categories?
    A. Change process and implementation
    B. Technology and personnel
    C. Design and implementation
    D. Quality control and execution

9. The following are examples of instructional methods *except* which one?
    A. Blended
    B. Facilitated
    C. Classroom
    D. eLearning

10. An employee in the company is having difficulty with their job performance. The job requires certain skills that the employee does not do well. Providing the appropriate training to improve the employee's performance requires which of the following?
    A. External support
    B. An e-learning course
    C. A task analysis
    D. A supervisor to monitor progress

11. An HR professional should understand executive coaching as part of their role in human resources development. Which choice shows how this is best demonstrated in a company?
    A. An HR professional helps the chief operating officer develop a strategy to improve time management for all supervisors and managers.
    B. An HR professional delivers training on performance management to all supervisors in the company.
    C. An HR professional counsels an employee who is having difficulty performing tasks that a senior manager requires them to perform.
    D. An HR professional meets with the chief financial officer to understand the company growth plan for the next five years.

Chapter 4

Total Rewards (PHR® Only)

THIS CHAPTER COVERS THE PHR® EXAM CONTENT FROM THE TOTAL REWARDS FUNCTIONAL AREA AND CONSISTS OF THE FOLLOWING RESPONSIBILITIES AND REQUIRED KNOWLEDGE. FOR SPHR® EXAM CONTENT, REVIEW CHAPTER 9. RESPONSIBILITIES:

- ✓ 01 Manage compensation-related information and support payroll issue resolution

- ✓ 02 Implement and promote awareness of noncash rewards (for example: paid volunteer time, tuition assistance, workplace amenities, and employee recognition programs)

- ✓ 03 Implement benefit programs (for example: health plan, retirement plan, employee assistance plan, other insurance)

- ✓ 04 Administer federally compliant compensation and benefit programs

IN ADDITION TO THE PRECEDING RESPONSIBILITIES, AN INDIVIDUAL TAKING THE PHR® EXAM SHOULD HAVE WORKING KNOWLEDGE OF THE FOLLOWING AREAS, USUALLY DERIVED THROUGH PRACTICAL EXPERIENCE:

- ✓ 36 Applicable federal laws and regulations related to total rewards

- ✓ 37 Compensation policies, processes, and analysis

This chapter covers the important topics of total rewards. *Total rewards* is the term referring to all policies, programs, compensation and benefits, recognition, and rewards designed to attract and retain the necessary talent to meet the organization's goals and objectives. For the PHR® exam, it represents 15 percent of the total exam content. The day-to-day administration of a total rewards program is the implementation, promotion, and management of the compensation and benefits programs in compliance with federal laws. HR professionals who understand the full details of such programs are much better equipped to analyze and develop strong programs that benefit all the employees of the company. Fairly providing compensation and benefits to company employees is critical to all successful organizations.

This chapter focuses on total rewards for all employees that support the company's mission, vision, and values and help achieve its underlying goals and objectives. In smaller companies that do not have specialists in particular HR disciplines, the priority is the correct administration of the company's payroll. In fact, many HR departments grow out of necessity from the payroll clerk as the number of employees grows and the company begins to reach thresholds that have legal and regulatory implications. Emerging companies that grow to this point do well to invest in a strong HR professional with knowledge of total rewards to administer the programs involved and ensure compliance with the rules.

Required Knowledge

This chapter has the most complex knowledge requirements of all the topics in this book. Because this is a review guide, the assumption here and throughout is that individuals preparing to sit for the PHR® exam already have a base knowledge and are reviewing the exam content in this book as a refresher. However, I highly recommend that even if you have experience and in-depth knowledge that you spend a little more time with this chapter.

The knowledge areas of compensation and benefits can be viewed in different ways: compliance, policies, and methods or means to deliver.

Compliance

The primary transactional function of the HR department and therefore the primary role of HR professionals is the administration of the total rewards programs of the company. Simply put, if the employees don't get paid, you don't have a company! This may be obvious, but once the company size grows beyond a handful of workers, rules and regulations take over. It is the complex regulatory landscape that is time-consuming and burdensome for a chief executive, operations, or finance officer to handle and takes away focus from the mission of the company. It isn't a core competency of the company, and it is delegated to the professional with the expertise and knowledge to handle the daily work and ensure compliance with the law.

Laws and Regulations

As stated previously, HR professionals are not attorneys and are not legal advisors. However, a great deal of their work has legal implications and liability to the company, so it is important that HR professionals understand how their work intersects the law. In compensation and benefits, there are numerous federal, state, and local laws that apply to the proper conduct and execution of this HR function. While an in-depth discussion of all the laws would be its own review guide, this section will discuss the most significant laws that HR professionals should be most familiar with. The following sections discuss the most important of these; Table 4.1 lists several other major laws and their significance regarding compensation and benefits. For more information on these and other Department of Labor laws, visit https://www.dol.gov/general/aboutdol/majorlaws.

TABLE 4.1   Additional major compensation and benefit laws

Law	Covers	HR Significance
Davis-Bacon Act	Requires contractors using federal funds to pay wages and fringe equal to or greater than the local market wage	Applies if receiving federal funds for work or projects
Walsh-Healey Act	Establishes the time-and-a-half overtime rule for hours in excess of 40 in a week for nonexempt employees	Must properly classify employees and track hours worked for nonexempt employees
Portal-to-Portal Act	Created general rules for compensatory time	Understanding when employees are on "company time" for pay purposes and when developing policy
Dodd-Frank Wall Street Reform and Consumer Protection Act	Creates rules for executive compensation to include reporting and provisions for recapturing certain compensation in cases of misconduct or highly substandard performance	Important when establishing executive compensation packages and employment contracts

Law	Covers	HR Significance
Sarbanes-Oxley Act (SOX)	Places restrictions on executives and administrators of benefits plans within public companies to prevent certain transactions that would create unfair or illegal business earnings for benefits programs such as company stock	Necessitates the monitoring of plans and ensuring compliance by all company leaders that are involved with benefits plans
Lilly Ledbetter Act	Affirms equal pay for equal work regardless of gender and provides recourse and legal avenues in cases of discrimination	Requires policies and procedures to ensure that men and women in the company are not paid at different wage rates in the same jobs with similar experience and qualifications
Uniformed Services Employment and Reemployment Rights Act (USERRA)	Provides provisions for members of the Armed Services called to military service to allow returning to civilian work upon completion of their duty	Has special tracking and monitoring consideration of any individual that is serving in the Armed Forces and was required to give up their civilian employment
Consolidated Omnibus Budget Reconciliation Act (COBRA)	Provides employees and dependents the ability to maintain continuous healthcare coverage in the group plan by covering the employer cost and additional admin fee	Requires notification of rights under this law to all employees accepting healthcare benefits and notice upon a qualifying event of eligibility
Health Insurance Portability and Accountability Act (HIPAA)	Allows for someone to obtain healthcare coverage even after the loss of a job if the individual or eligible family member has a serious illness	Restricts the release of personal medical information to third parties without consent and places provisions on maintaining the integrity and security of the information held
Genetic Information Nondiscrimination Act (GINA)	Prevents discrimination on the basis of genetic information in obtaining employment or access to healthcare	Mandates the protection and unauthorized disclosure of genetic-related information of employees or applicants

Fair Labor Standards Act

The Fair Labor Standards Act (FLSA) of 1938 is the prevailing law that governs wages and hours worked by the workforce. It is the most significant legislation with respect to compensation, as it has the broadest application and reach concerning labor practices.

It applies to any organization that engages in interstate commerce, produces goods for interstate commerce, or otherwise uses materials or goods that were transported as a result of interstate commerce. While there are some exceptions and limitations, such as those based on total volume of business, it is safe to say that the provisions of this important act apply to virtually every business. The Wage and Hour Division of the Department of Labor is chiefly responsible for the enforcement of many of the provisions of this law and is a primary source for clarification on rules, interpretations, and requirements of employers.

After determining applicability, it is then necessary for the HR professional to understand to which workers this law pertains. There is a difference between independent contractors and employees. The determining factors as to whether a worker is an independent contractor or an employee has mostly to do with autonomy over the work being done, the relationship between the worker and the company, and the work itself being a central part of the company's core mission.

At the time of publication of this book, the Department of Labor was reviewing its guidance on the interpretation of contractors versus employees and the concept of "dual responsibility." However, in general, HR professionals must be careful in classifying workers properly within the organization. When comparing two workers side by side and determining which is a contractor and which is an employee based on duties and general working conditions, the IRS will use 20 different factors to determine a worker's status as an employee or an independent contractor.

Workers who are employees of the company work hours during working days that are totaled each week. Under the law if an employee works more than 40 hours in the established workweek, they are entitled to overtime pay. There are rules and caveats that determine the workweek and the calculation of working time. HR professionals should know some of the nuances that affect pay and can have implications for the employees. One example would be employees who temporarily work in a different location than their normal place of duty and must travel to and from this location. The travel time potentially has different calculations based on the circumstances. To understand more, see the U.S. Department of Labor website at www.dol.gov for a frequently asked questions section worth reviewing.

Of course, with any rule there is an exception. This overtime rule applies to a certain group of employees. Those in the other group, based on certain qualifiers, are exempt from this portion of the law. Hence, the terms *exempt* and *nonexempt employees* refer to their status with respect to the overtime rule. To be exempt, an employee must work in certain fields such as executive, administrative, professional, technical, or sales *and* perform certain duties in those fields *and* be paid in a salary (as opposed to hourly) making more than a threshold salary of $455 per week or $23,660 annually. Table 4.2 describes some exempted employees and the criteria.

In 2016 the Department of Labor issued a ruling changing the annual salary threshold to more than $47,000. At the time of writing this book, the State of Texas and several other states filed a federal lawsuit to block implementation of that rule. An injunction was ordered, and the case is still pending. For an HR professional, this is an example of how compliance is impacted by outside influence that requires your attention.

TABLE 4.2 Exempted employees from the wage and hour law (FLSA)

Employee Type	Criteria
Administrative	▪ Office type work ▪ Has independent judgment and discretion on matters of significance ▪ Salaried above the established threshold
Professional ▪ Learned ▪ Creative	▪ Learned—requires specialized education and experience ▪ Creative—requires talent and work in the arts professions or creates intellectual work
Executive	▪ High salary ▪ Management of an organization or subcomponent and regularly directs two or more full-time employees ▪ Authority to hire and fire
Computer professional	▪ Systems application or analysis ▪ Design, creation, or modification of programs ▪ Documentation design, creation, or modification related to operating systems
Outside sales	▪ Primarily works making sales beyond the confines of the company (traveling)

Employee Retirement Income Security Act

The Employee Retirement Income Security Act (ERISA) is the key legislation that governs actions concerning a company's benefits, establishing minimum controls and ensuring that benefit plans are administered in a financially responsible way. The key point is that it does not require a company to provide certain benefits, but if the company elects to do so, it must comply with the law and regulations. The general provision of the law states that the plans are operated for the benefit of the employees who participate and their beneficiaries, not the company. Therefore, the company must act in the way a prudent person would when managing the assets of the company. This is called the *fiduciary responsibility* of the plan.

ERISA sets the vesting requirements of a plan, defining when the employee is entitled to all or a portion of the benefits without penalty. An employee has the right to all of his or her money invested, but the vested portion pertains to the amounts that an employer matches or contributes over time. The vesting may be all at once or over a period of time depending on the plan. The vesting period is also determined by the type of retirement plan such as a defined benefit plan or a defined contribution plan.

ERISA requires that the employer, the benefit plan sponsor, provide a summary plan description (SPD) to the participants at least once every five years. Also, an annual report is submitted to the IRS and must be available to the participants upon request. Since these requirements are very particular and have significant fines attached for noncompliance, it follows that HR professionals should coordinate with benefits administrators and legal advisors with experience in this area to have a full understanding of the law.

Family and Medical Leave Act

Created in 1993, the Family and Medical Leave Act (FMLA) applies to organizations with 50 or more employees for at least 20 weeks of the current or preceding calendar year. This law applies equally in the public and private sectors, including nonprofit companies. The law allows leave to an employee who has worked in the organization for at least 12 months and at least 1,250 hours in that period at a location within 75 miles of where 50 or more employees also work. The law allows for up to 12 workweeks of unpaid leave in which their job is protected based on certain medical cases involving pregnancy, childcare after birth or adoption, or the serious medical issue of a spouse, child or parent, or the employee. Serious medical issues as defined by the law requires incapacity for more than three consecutive calendar days plus two visits to a healthcare provider or one visit and continuing treatment (such as physical therapy).

This law may also be applied with intermittent conditions such as a chronic care situation that requires periodic medical treatments or doctor's care or convalescence. There are different means by which the 12 months can be calculated, but they must be consistent once determined by the company:

- A calendar year
- A fixed 12-month period (fiscal year)
- The 12-month period based on the employee's first use of FMLA leave
- A rolling 12-month period

HR professionals must understand the calculation of the time and the required documentation needed to be maintained to provide advice and work with employees who need to exercise this leave right. Upon return from this leave, the employer is required to restore the employment at the same job or one with equivalent benefits and compensation.

The Uniformed Services Employment and Reemployment Rights Act

This important legislation protects our uniformed service members' employment when they are called upon to serve the country, whether that service is voluntary or involuntary. The Uniformed Services Employment and Reemployment Rights Act (USERRA) was originally signed in 1994 and amended by the Veterans Benefits Improvement Act signed in 2004. This law also applies to applicants to a position if a company uses pending military leave as the reason for denying employment or rescinding a bona fide offer of employment.

There are some provisions that the employee must meet to be covered under USERRA. It requires that they or their command provide written notice of the reason for leave with sufficient notice being 30 days when possible. This is often a challenge to the employee and employer because sometimes orders take time to be processed in times of national military call-up. In all cases, it's beneficial to everyone for an employee to provide a "heads-up" advance warning to the HR professional or the employer directly to allow sufficient time to plan and prepare for the absence. An employee can take military leave for up to five years (and even more under certain rules), and the right of the employee to return to their job or an equivalent position within the company must be maintained.

While the employee is on military leave, they retain the same benefits as individuals in other, nonmilitary leave statuses. They also must maintain the same level of benefits based on seniority as if they had not left the company, which means general increases in salary for longevity and promotion opportunity upon return. Retirement must remain unaffected without a break in service including any vesting and accruals. There are specific time frames that must be adhered to for the employee to return and restrictions on the position to return to, including additional requirements for disabled veterans. Finally, employees under the provisions of USERRA are not entitled to compensation from the employer except that exempt salaried employees must be paid the difference between their salary and their military pay for their time on military orders if applicable.

The Patient Protection and Affordable Care Act

The Patient Protection and Affordable Care Act (PPACA or ACA), more commonly referred to as Obamacare, mandates certain healthcare provisions for certain classifications of employers (called *applicable large employers*) and their employees. They must provide health coverage that is deemed to be affordable and provides a minimum value to their employees and the employees' dependents. This provision applies generally to companies with more than 50 full-time equivalent employees. There are reporting requirements to the IRS for employers to demonstrate compliance with the law. While there are numerous restrictions and provisions with this legislation, there is a frequently asked questions section on the IRS web page located at www.irs.gov. HR professionals must be familiar with how to determine coverage compliance and which employees are covered under this law, as well as all the reporting requirements.

There has been a great deal of controversy and political discussion about the Affordable Care Act and its viability as a matter of law. While the outcome of legislation is still being determined in the courts and through the political process, it is still important as a subject for HR professionals to study and understand. It is likely that this law or a similar provision will govern healthcare coverage for employees, and therefore, HR professionals will be responsible for the compliance with the law.

Budgeting and Accounting Practices

In today's complex business environment with tax laws and other external forces impacting budgetary decisions, companies must use generally accepted accounting principles (GAAPs). While HR professionals are not required to be certified public accountants or know the details of these principles, they should have a working knowledge of what the accounting practices are and how to review portions of accounting and financial statements of the company where HR is impacted, such as payroll.

The Financial Accounting Standards Board (FASB) is a nongovernmental organization that decides how company financial statements are to be organized and reported in public companies by their chief financial officer. All these rules impact financial reporting, but a few also have consequences for HR-related topics such as retirement benefits and healthcare costs to the company. An HR professional should be able to review financial disclosure statements prepared by the finance and accounting department and understand where the numbers come from, especially if they are related to the topics discussed. HR should ensure that all budget items that are reportable related to personnel functions are as accurate as possible.

Plans and Policies

In conjunction with the overall corporate strategy and aligned with the HR strategy, HR professionals must help the executive leadership establish a compensation and benefits plan that meets the needs of the organization and its valued employees. They are required to know and understand the factors that impact compensation and benefits within a market. HR professionals should be familiar with the company's mission, vision, and values to know how to design a compensation and benefits plan that matches them. Organizational culture will impact the strategy as well.

Compensation and Benefits Strategies

HR professionals must know how to establish a comprehensive compensation and benefits strategy to attract and retain the right employees capable of performing the duties required to accomplish the goals of the organization. It begins with the company's pay philosophy, which determines how it will structure its compensation plan and the types of benefits that can be offered. The strategy must take into account the available resources and consider when and under what circumstances increases will be given.

The strategy first looks at external factors, which include the industry in which the company exists. Industries that have a shortage of qualified talent, like emerging technology or information age companies, will have higher wage demands. Higher technical and skilled craftspeople will elicit a higher compensation scale as well. As a result, even the support functions and roles may have some pay affected by the other core occupations of the organization. Finally, where the company is located will also impact the compensation plan. Geographic distribution may have variations in labor costs, and this is magnified in international markets.

HR professionals must know the market and the company's competition and with this knowledge make a decision on where to place the company's pay. If the organization matches the market, they will strive to be in balance with what others will pay for talent. They will use metrics to establish the median salary point and try to target employees' salaries in a band on either side of this target. Companies with more available resources or seeking to be an industry leader will seek to lead the market by paying the highest salaries and providing the best benefits to the employees. Their objective is to pull the best talent from the market to the company. However, it is important to be careful with this methodology as the highest paid is not always the best qualified; employees can be under- or overvalued. However, bringing in higher-paid employees should result in a more productive workforce, increasing profitability. Finally, a company may choose to lag the market wages because of costs or an availability of talent that allows the company to pay less and not fear loss of employees. It is also possible that any or all of these strategies may be employed at one point in the company's history or even at the same time with different occupations within the organization. Figure 4.1 shows the relative position of the wages in the market and their pros and cons.

FIGURE 4.1   Comparative wages

Methods

Having an overall strategy for how a company will provide compensation and benefits for its employees is only the first step in the process. There are several methods of executing the plan, once developed, that HR professionals must have knowledge of to be successful. These methods cover examining the jobs themselves and the pay structures that result. The pay and benefit programs that include executive compensation are the direct results of the methods discussed here.

Job Evaluation Methods

A job evaluation determines the relative worth to the company of any particular position. An HR professional can rank the positions in degrees of importance to the company or can compare each job to another using a predetermined value scoring. When comparing jobs in an organization, it can sometimes be difficult to determine the more important job when the jobs vary significantly. For example, it is challenging to compare the value of the controller with that of an area HR manager or the IT supervisor. All are critical, but how they are paid compared to each other could be different in different companies.

A technique that can be used simply is to compare each job, one by one, with another in the organization in a matrix. That will result in a one-to-*n* list, where *n* is the total number of different jobs in the company in order of value. This process looks at the whole job, not individual skills or competencies required. Determining skills and competencies was discussed previously in Chapter 2, "Talent Planning and Acquisition." This is the fastest method, but it isn't useful in knowing why one job is favored over another.

Another method is the classification of jobs into a set number of grades, as in the federal or state government systems. These job classes group common knowledge, skills, or attributes (known as *essential job functions*) needed for the successful execution of the jobs in that category and may have common work done by all. In many cases, the HR function may list example jobs, or benchmarks, that fit in the category. This is a highly effective method for grouping large numbers of jobs, as would be required by the federal government. The downside of such a system is that by its nature it is general and broad. A company may have two unrelated job functions in the same classification. As you will see later in this chapter, when those jobs in the same classification are banded together for pay purposes, it highly restricts certain positions from being paid at a higher wage.

A quantitative approach as shown in Figure 4.2 uses established compensable factors to score each job in a point comparison. Compensable factors are value added to the organization. To ensure compliance with the Equal Pay Act and Title VII, the following factors should be considered:

- Skill
- Responsibility
- Effort
- Working conditions
- Supervision

FIGURE 4.2   Quantitative approach

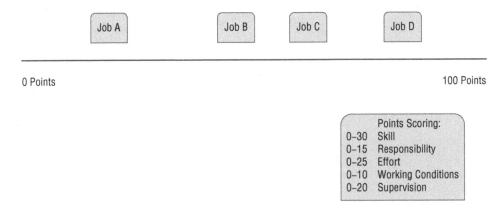

These factors take into account the actual work performed, documented in a job description, and supporting the organization's mission, vision, values, and goals. They should be reviewed periodically and be valued by the stakeholders of the company.

HR professionals may choose to examine the jobs in their organization compared to the current market value. This takes external factors into account such as the availability of qualified individuals and what competitor organizations are willing to pay for the same knowledge, skills, and abilities. This can be scaled on a local area, state level, or nationally. There are several companies that specialize in doing pay studies that can help by analyzing large quantities of data to refine market-based pay. It is important to know the pros and cons of using external market values. For example, a company may value a particular position or job skill as more important than other companies and therefore have a higher pay value. Or it may be part of an emerging industry that does not have a lot of useful data yet, meaning that its market is not mature enough to price-compare.

Job Pricing and Pay Structures

HR professionals must know how to price a job, that is, find a competitive wage to pay for the right skills and talent that will further the company's mission without losing profitability. To do this, HR professionals rely heavily on data that includes information obtained from surveys, regularly published information from the government, and historical trends recorded over time. While no single survey can capture all the information, the combination of various data points helps to create a picture of the target pay area that can help when making decisions. The data when collected should capture a range of salaries and a time frame to determine how current this information is. For instance, if salary information in the company is reviewed once every four years, there could be significant economic changes that have impacted the organization during that time. As a result, it will be harder to compare the data and determine the right range. Likewise, if the information is new, it may be the result of a spike with no other data trend for comparison.

When the information is collected, HR professionals must know how to look at the data and find averages in a particular pay band or by occupation. The goal should be to find the midpoint of the range of comparable salaries to have a target from which to base offers and set salary ranges. The pay structure is created by analyzing the data and creating either graduated steps or tiers from the lowest salary point to the highest. There is no specific rule on how to create structures for companies, and it is largely determined by the characteristics of the company itself. However, within the structure there will be pay grades and pay ranges that are established, and this will be the foundation for determining the salaries of the employees.

Pay grades band together jobs that have a similar value to the overall company. They may not be closely related in terms of duties or job function, but they have the same worth to the bottom line of the company. Pay grades will differ between larger or smaller organizations where the total numbers of employees being grouped are different. There may be different levels in the company from line employees to leads, supervisors, department managers, senior staff, or executives. The more complex a hierarchy in a company, the broader or more numerous pay bands needed. How people advance and grow in the company also will impact pay grades. If certain promotions carry increases in salary, it is possible that someone would need to move to a different band with promotion or risk reaching the upper ceiling of a pay range.

Pay ranges are the limits of pay for any employee who may have their pay determined by being in a pay grade. As shown in Figure 4.3, these upper and lower limits bracket the salaries within a pay grade, but that does not necessarily mean there is no overlap between grades. The determination should consider how often a company moves individuals across pay bands and how an employee whose salary is at the maximum level of one band would be shifted to another band based on an increase in salary.

FIGURE 4.3   Pay ranges in a company

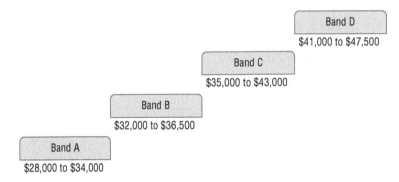

HR professionals should calculate the range spread by subtracting the minimum pay in a band from the maximum and then dividing the results by the minimum. In larger organizations, the midpoints of the pay grades may become compressed, and the result is an unmanageable system. In those cases, a company may choose to broadband the pay bands, putting multiple grades inside one band for the purpose of simplification.

Noncash Compensation

A large portion of the compensation at the executive level is the noncash part, which can consist of a variety of offerings depending on the organization. While there may be a cash value, there is often a conversion that is required to realize the full monetary potential of the compensation provided. Perks are those select items that are provided for executives and have some intrinsic value. A company car, for example, has some value, as does a company expense account in the form of a company credit card. Other items might be event tickets, passes to amusement parks, exclusive fitness club memberships, or any other item that is not available to the general employees but reserved only for executives to recruit and retain their commitment to the organization.

Another portion of the noncash compensation is the written consideration to provide an amount of money if a top executive were to lose their job as a result of the company being sold or acquired by an outside entity and they would otherwise have difficulty finding a similar job and compensation elsewhere. Designed to lessen the burden to the individual from the fall from the executive level, this is more commonly known as a *golden parachute*. Such items might include early access to benefits or the company contributions of a retirement account.

Stock in the company is the most common component of the noncash compensation. There are many tax implications that must be considered for each of the choices, but they are beyond the scope of this book. Some companies may choose to offer stock options; that is, they provide the executive with the opportunity to obtain stock in the company when the value of such stock is higher than would be the purchase price. Because this leverages certain invested amounts, there are restrictions and tax implications that should be considered for both the company and the executive.

Another stock program would be the purchase of stock itself. The stocks could be a diversified package that is managed to provide returns as dictated by the market but also could be portions of the company stock itself. In the second choice, federal law and regulations place restrictions on company executives, especially those who have responsibility over the financial performance of the organization where they might be in a position to manipulate the financial decisions in such a way as to increase the profitability and therefore the value, which would inflate stock prices. Legal limitations created under Sarbanes-Oxley in 2002 and Dodd Frank in 2010 have greatly restricted the practices of stock purchase plans in publically traded companies. There are other stock choices that closely resemble the ones previously mentioned but take a different form to meet different situations that can be advantageous to both the company and the executive. Figure 4.4 shows some comparisons of two common miscellaneous stock plans that an executive might receive.

FIGURE 4.4   Miscellaneous stock plans for executives

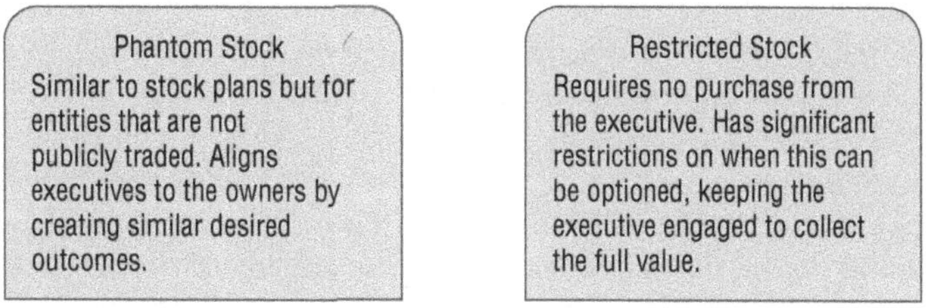

Phantom Stock
Similar to stock plans but for entities that are not publicly traded. Aligns executives to the owners by creating similar desired outcomes.

Restricted Stock
Requires no purchase from the executive. Has significant restrictions on when this can be optioned, keeping the executive engaged to collect the full value.

Align and Benchmark Compensation and Benefits

It is important for HR professionals to know methods to align and benchmark compensation and benefits. Today, the most common practice in benchmarking compensation is to use an external source and purchase or craft compensation studies to compare an organization's pay scales with the market. Often these studies include factors such as locality, availability of talent, and job specifications to ensure a consistent comparison. Companies may look at what industry trends are to compare their pay. A company must also look at the total rewards to include perks, bonuses, vacation, and other tangible elements of value.

A large portion of total rewards consists of the benefits a company provides its employees. In some cases, employees may opt for a lower base salary if there is an increase in available benefits such as healthcare, retirement savings, continued education, or a general sense of work/life balance. To align benefits to employees, HR professionals must know how to conduct periodic needs assessments and evaluate the benefits program to determine what is most desired by employees that can be provided.

Mandatory Benefits Programs

In addition to paying a fair wage, employers provide benefits to their employees. While the choice of benefits varies from company to company, HR professionals must know what the typical benefits are and the process to deliver them. Certain benefits are mandated by laws and regulations at the federal and state levels. There are only a few that fall in this category, but they are important.

- Social security and Medicare
- Unemployment insurance
- Workers' compensation
- Benefits provided under other legislation

These benefits require the employer to pay the government for each employee based on an employee's salary, the amount and number of claims filed, or a fixed structure set by rule. However, these amounts are consistent and can be budgeted by the company as part of the payroll budget.

Social Security and Medicare

The social security program has been in existence since 1935 and has been part of the U.S. employment landscape ever since. HR professionals should be intimately familiar with all the components of this program because it plays an important role in many employees' decision of when to retire. This program is for workers who have contributed into the program over a cumulative period of at least 10 years, determining the benefit based on their highest-paid 40 quarters in which they paid into social security. Additionally, there are amounts paid in case of disability or death and separately to the survivor of an eligible employee.

Based on the age of the employee, they may receive full benefits between age 65 and 67 but could draw a reduced benefit as early as age 62. There are some caveats based on means testing from other income sources that would result in a reduction in the benefit provided. The employee and employer are jointly responsible for contributing an amount based as a percentage of the employee's yearly salary and deducted each pay period. The disability benefit is provided when an employee who has not yet attained the eligible retirement age has a qualified disability that limits their ability to work and is expected to prevent their ability to return to work for at least 12 months. Survivors may also receive benefits based on age, as children, or as dependent parents where the employee is responsible for a majority of their financial support.

Medicare is part of the social security program that provides medical insurance coverage and includes hospitalization coverage. Again, the employer and employee pay an amount based on a percentage of salary with eligibility beginning at age 65. If a company has more than 20 employees and provides health insurance, under the law the employee cannot use Medicare as their primary medical coverage. This prevents employers from encouraging their employees older than 65 to decline coverage in favor of a government program. This program also has a prescription drug benefit provided the employee is eligible for and paying into the hospitalization and medical coverage portions of the entitlement program.

Unemployment Insurance and Workers' Compensation

Unemployment insurance is another product of the social security program; it benefits workers who are involuntarily terminated from employment with some exceptions that include misconduct. This program is employer-funded and managed in a trust at the federal level. However, each state administers the program for the workers who file claims in that state. One particular feature of this program is that in most states employers who have fewer claims from employees enjoy a lower rate. This is a direct result of employers less frequently terminating employees from their jobs without cause.

Workers' compensation is handled at the state level and aids employees (or survivors in the case of death) who suffer work-related injuries or illness. It's a benefit to the employer to cover the expenses that are the direct result of a work-related accident (such as acute or extended medical care) and is independent of who is faulted for the accident. This ensures that it is reported and the employee receives timely medical attention without the need for legal action against the company. All parties benefit by reducing the cost and actually working to mitigate the risks that tend to cause accidents in the first place.

Additional Benefits Provided by Legislation

While there are several pieces of federal and state legislation that provide benefits to workers, two that are critical are FMLA and COBRA. FMLA was discussed earlier in this chapter and provides a benefit to employees where there is a qualified medical event with either the employee or their immediate family. The Consolidated Omnibus Budget Reconciliation Act (COBRA) ensures that employees and their dependents who would have their benefits terminated as a result of separation from employment can pay both the employer and employee portion of any coverage for which they are eligible for a period of 18 to 36 months depending on the qualifying event, that is, the reason they are now eligible for this coverage.

HR professionals are required to ensure that employees are notified with specific information about coverage when the qualifying event occurs and a more general notice within 90 days after initial eligibility for coverage in the group benefit plan. HR professionals must know the reporting requirements and the documentation needed and must have an understanding of the general eligibility rules to counsel and advise employees and the employer on this important benefit.

Employer-Provided Benefits

As discussed previously, there are as many types of benefits as there are employers, and all have distinct features. It is impossible to detail each single type of program within the scope of this review, but HR professionals should be familiar with the general types and examples from each. In general, there are deferred compensation plans (often viewed as retirement or savings plans), health plans (such as medical, dental, and vision), and supplemental plans (including short- and long-term disability, life insurance, leave, employee assistance, and wellness). Table 4.3 shows these various examples and important knowledge points for HR.

TABLE 4.3 Employer-provided benefits

Benefit	Examples	HR Professionals Must Know
Retirement plans	▪ Defined benefit plan (pension) ▪ Defined contribution plan (401k, 457, Roth, 403b)	Plans in these categories allow the employee to save money either pre- or post-taxes and make scheduled regular contributions with a cap amount and withdrawal restrictions or limitations. All have significant tax implications.
Education plan	▪ 529 plan	
Healthcare	▪ Managed care ▪ Dental ▪ Vision ▪ Prescription drug ▪ Health savings accounts	These plans usually have employer and employee portions and offer many choices based on the needs and population of the employees; insurers may provide incentives to lower costs with wellness exams and fitness opportunities.
Supplemental	▪ Disability ▪ Other insurance ▪ Employee assistance programs ▪ Leave programs ▪ Tuition assistance	Employers choose from a variety of options based on the needs of the employees; many employees may elect to not have some of these options or may choose the minimum benefit provided.

Exam Essentials

Understand the major laws that govern compensation and benefits.   It is not necessary to know historical events around the laws themselves, but understand the impact to organizations from an HR perspective. The most significant of the laws is the Fair Labor Standards Act (FLSA), which covers wage, overtime, and exemptions. For other legislation, review Table 4.1 for some solid examples and familiarize yourself with the areas covered.

Know the FLSA exemptions and rules for overtime.   It is important to understand all the laws governing compensation and benefits. However, by far, this particular element is the most confusing and challenging to HR professionals. You should clearly understand the provisions that classify an employee as exempt versus nonexempt from overtime pay. Additionally, review how worked time is defined and determined when calculating overtime. Remember that these rules are interpreted by the Department of Labor's Wage and Hour Division and that you must understand the context of these decisions and how they apply to your company.

Understand how job evaluations inform compensation structures.   As an organization defines the roles in the company, each job must be evaluated to understand its relative worth and importance to the performance of the company's mission. Once these roles are established, you should be able to evaluate the compensation structure to ensure that individuals are paid properly based on the role and duties associated with their job. You should look at objective measures that are used in determining a pay scale and compare them to the difficulties of the tasks a certain job performs. Review job descriptions and essential job functions for some key roles in your organization, and if you have the ability, examine the relative pay.

Responsibilities

Ensuring that employees are paid and receive the benefits to which they are entitled is one of the most critical responsibilities of HR professionals. The timely compensation for the hard work rendered by workers shows they are valued and respected and demonstrates the ongoing commitment of the organization to see that their employees' basic needs are met. HR professionals will determine the needs of employees and develop and implement the procedures and policies that are legally compliant to deliver pay and benefits to all eligible employees.

Ensuring Compliance

As discussed in the "Knowledge" section of this chapter, several laws at the federal and state levels govern compensation and benefits. It is not expected for the exam that you are an expert on all of them and every nuance they contain. However, HR professionals must know how to research the rules, determine which ones are applicable, and lay out a course of action to ensure that the company remains compliant. In the big picture, often this requires record keeping and documentation to provide auditability of pay actions. In other words, if an external party examined the policies, practices, processes, and procedures of the company, they should be able to ascertain how a pay decision was reached, why it was done (justification), who conducted the action, and how it was recorded. The documentation should match the amount in the general ledger that finance has recorded.

Real World Scenario

Showing Auditors How a Bonus Was Paid

A company has external auditors review its financial records annually as a public company. In one year, the auditor examines pay records in a given time period and for a particular pay date requests the documentation for all the associated pay transactions. For one employee, they found a $1,000 onetime bonus. Cross-referencing this ledger entry, the employee file should have documentation stating that the employee received the bonus (such as an official letter or notification) signed by someone with the authority to authorize payment and additional documentation justifying why the bonus was paid (such as an award for a special circumstance like employee of the quarter). The auditor may also request to review the policy on bonuses, which would likely indicate the amount a bonus can be for such items and who the approval authority is in the company. This would then demonstrate that the policies are effective and being followed in practice.

HR professionals must establish clear practices and policies and follow them to ensure that the company complies with the laws and regulations. They are responsible for communicating with managers, employees, and executives on the importance of documenting and being consistent when it comes to compensation and benefits. This also includes documentation for benefits such as leave taken under the Family and Medical Leave Act (FMLA) and notifications associated with the Employee Retirement Income Security Act (ERISA).

Developing and Implementing Benefits Programs

As most companies grow and become more profitable, they will have the ability to offer benefits to remain competitive and retain top talent. What benefits are offered depends on the needs assessment discussed earlier and what the company can afford to provide. Companies will provide certain benefits such as health and dental early in the company's growth life cycle, and then other benefits follow depending on the company demographics and needs. HR professionals are responsible for helping corporate executives decide which programs meet the needs of the company at an affordable cost. Over time, they evaluate the effects and benefits that the program produces and make recommendations to change and then implement those changes.

HR professionals will often meet with third-party providers that offer consolidated services to broker benefit plans from a variety of providers. In many circumstances, these plans are highly subject to compliance laws and regulations discussed in the first part of this chapter. Because HR professionals are not legal advisors, it is recommended that these sources be used as they have the legal foundation and support to ensure that all regulatory requirements are met in providing these programs. This is especially important for organizations with a small HR department that may not have the breadth and depth of experience in benefits administration.

HR professionals are responsible for periodically assessing the programs and work with the executives to determine when changes are needed. They may solicit new proposals for services to be provided, such as employee assistance programs or other nonmandated benefits like supplemental insurances. They develop the evaluation criteria and review proposals from vendors. When a suitable program is found, they become the primary point of contact for the company and keep the company informed of the pending changes. If the program is new, then HR professionals develop an implementation plan with start dates, communication plans, and other necessary actions to ensure a smooth start. If, however, this is a change in providers or a new benefits program replacing an existing one, then they are responsible for the transition plan, which may include facilitating new registrations, updating any employee information, and monitoring the changeover.

HR professionals will develop policies and documentation for the benefits programs for new employees as part of the onboarding process and to inform current employees. They may schedule and conduct information briefings on the new plans and their costs to employees and be available to answer any questions. They must work with employees to validate data so that benefits providers have the most accurate employee information when beginning the delivery of the services and benefits program.

Communication and Workforce Training

The key role in all HR actions surrounding compensation and benefits is maintaining the continued communication between the company and the employees. While this seems intuitive, when companies grow and there is constant turnover of employees, or geographical separation between divisions, it is a continual battle. HR professionals must develop policies and procedures to keep the employees informed of changes to their benefit plan and pay structure and ensure that application of those policies is fair and consistent across the organization.

Training the Workforce on Compensation and Benefits

HR maintains the responsibility of training employees on the company's benefits and compensation plans. This starts from the beginning of the employee work life cycle with recruiting and continues through separation or transition with the company. When HR recruits prospective candidates, they will educate and inform applicants of the benefits the company has to offer. They will market benefits to attract talent seeking better opportunities with better plans. Applicants selected for employment will go through an orientation and onboarding process. During this process, it is the HR professional that will answer questions from new employees and collect the necessary information for these plans as part of their function. This includes verifying eligibility of the employee and dependents. They often provide critical information so that an employee can select the right plan that meets their needs.

Each year during open enrollment, the HR team will prepare information presentations to train the workforce, including management, on any specific changes to current benefit plans. This is a great time to discuss and answer questions about premium changes,

changes in coverage, or new providers that the company has partnered with. In growing companies, sometimes a new benefit will be rolled out with the details on how to obtain coverage and the cost.

In addition to health benefits, HR is responsible for monitoring any retirement programs and ensuring that the information about such programs is delivered to the employees. This is a more difficult task because HR professionals do not have the credentials required to discuss financial investments from an advisory capacity and must be careful not to dispense advice, but rather information, about programs and facilitate discussion between the employees and qualified individuals to discuss such programs.

Retirement Briefings

In many companies, HR will facilitate presentations by retirement-benefits subject-matter experts to come in to the company and meet with a group of employees to discuss retirement options and investments. These meetings are important, and HR must work diligently to encourage maximum participation. Some topics that will be discussed are as follows:

- Eligibility to retire and the various plans with a company
- Typical concerns in retirement plans grouped by age demographic
- Historical data on the performance of the retirement plans and other relevant statistics

The subject-matter expert may also have one-on-one meetings with retirement-eligible employees to discuss individual plans and concerns. Companies have many options and may have more than one retirement plan, so these subject-matter experts can provide insight to help employees decide which plan meets their needs most effectively.

HR is also responsible for training when there are changes to pay structures. While this may happen from time to time based on the company's financial position or growth, it can also occur sometimes with regulatory changes. When minimum wage rules are changed in states or at the federal level, for example, the HR team must train both management and employees on the impact to the organization. It is the responsibility of the HR professional to consult with employment attorneys, the finance department, and other key stakeholders to develop a communication plan to present the changes, execute any necessary actions that bring about the change, and then, finally, conduct a review of the changes and preserve any lessons learned for future analysis and follow-on decisions.

Promote Awareness of Noncash Rewards

HR professionals have the responsibility to implement and promote awareness of noncash rewards. Among some of these types of company benefits are paid volunteer time, tuition assistance, workplace amenities, and employee recognition programs. While each type of program is generally tailored to the organization according to its needs, HR professionals play a vital role in the execution of these programs and ensuring that employees understand what is available to them.

Paid Volunteer Time

As companies continue to enhance and develop their corporate responsibility plans, they promote social responsibility as a value of the organization. Often companies will develop policies to allow employees time away from the organization to volunteer in the community and, in some cases, ensure that time is paid. HR professionals work with managers and executives to develop policies and identify the types of volunteer organizations that meet these requirements. They also develop and implement procedures to track hours and properly compensate the employees. Some examples include reading programs in schools, nonprofit organizations such as United Way, and in cases where a company has a particular service or product, donating a portion of those assets as part of the volunteer effort.

Tuition Assistance

Tuition assistance may be offered by some companies to help with the continued professional development of employees. Companies establish policies to reimburse employees that enroll in higher learning to help defray the costs to obtain degrees that could be of additional benefit to the company or increase an individual employee's knowledge, skills, or abilities related to their job. HR professionals must track the enrollment and ensure that the employee successfully completes the course to provide payment. As with other benefits, HR professionals must also ensure that employees have fair and equal opportunity to these benefits to be in compliance with existing regulations.

Workplace Amenities

Workplace amenities may create visions of the proverbial "executive washroom," but in fact companies today strive to create a comfortable workplace environment that has elements designed to inspire creativity and motivation of employees. Coffee bars, free snacks, resting areas, and workplace wellness such as massages or fitness rooms are just a few of the creative ideas companies now offer on their campus. Smaller companies need not be extravagant to entice workers to join the organization, requiring only such items that demonstrate genuine care and concern for the well-being of the workers.

Employee Recognition Programs

The retention of employees is affected by the perception of the employees related to their value to the company. Companies that highly value their employees recognize and reward their contributions to the overall success of the organization. HR professionals assist the company in establishing and maintaining an effective employee recognition program. They must have criteria for awards and a method for identifying eligible employees. They must maintain a fair system that truly rewards contributions in a consistent manner that promotes the best efforts of the group and highlights achievements worthy of recognition. The program might have a financial component or may be honorary such as public recognition.

In all cases, such programs must align with the company values and reward behaviors of employees that support those values.

Managing Payroll Information

The old adage "If it's not recorded, it didn't happen" is accurate when it comes to the maintenance of payroll documentation and information. HR professionals are responsible for maintaining the human resources information systems or the paper files that contain the critical information discussed throughout this chapter and to support any payroll issue resolution. To do this effectively, HR professionals must devise a standardized system to capture, index, retain, recall, and purge payroll information. Policies and procedures will define how new hires, transfers, and other typical HR actions are handled that impact payroll. Some companies choose to make effective dates correspond to certain calendar dates to coincide with payroll events for simplicity.

Whether it uses advanced technology or old-fashioned paper copies in a filing cabinet, the system must be easy to follow and consistent. Documentation should be easy to recall during audits or when needed to confirm or justify why payroll actions were conducted. This information must be secured, and safeguards must be in place to prevent its unauthorized disclosure. When necessary, HR professionals will coordinate with in-house or external counsel, information technology, or the finance department for the proper sharing and use of payroll information in the execution of other important tasks by a company.

When an employee separates from the company, HR professionals must ensure the retention of payroll information for the appropriate period of time based on a retention schedule that is determined by the company and in accordance with relevant regulations. The HR professional will either correspond directly with the employee concerning the continuation of benefits or receipt of retirement or severance pay or use a third-party administrator in this role. These workflows are standard in most companies in the private and public sector and independent of size. What changes with size and growth are the governing regulatory requirements. However, the HR professional who strives to input a strong system from the outset of the organization can layer added protocols on a solid foundation easily instead of dismantling an ad hoc system once the company has outgrown patchwork structures.

Resolving Payroll Issues

HR professionals are responsible for quickly and accurately resolving payroll-related issues. In some cases, it may be that additional information is needed to resolve an issue related to payroll. HR professionals must communicate directly with the employee to notify them of the discrepancy, what may be required to reach resolution, and an expected time frame to solve any outstanding issues.

HR must work with the finance department or external provider to solve payroll issues quickly. For example, cases such as direct deposit errors resulting from errant bank routing information can be detrimental to an employee's financial well-being. Failing to correct mistakes quickly can impact morale and performance of the employee.

Exam Essentials

Understand how to develop and implement total rewards programs.   These areas are important from an ethical and corporate responsibility standpoint, but most often HR generalists have limited interaction with these topics unless they work in this area specifically. Reviewing health plans, retirement plans, other insurance, noncash rewards, and base compensation will familiarize generalists with these specific topics.

Understand the responsibilities associated with managing outsourced compensation and benefits components with third-party vendors.   In addition to managing these programs, the knowledge of the roles and responsibilities when the function is distributed to third parties is critical. The key points include the ongoing communications, notifications to employees, coverage, and compliance. The intent of any outsourced function is to reduce burden of the HR team, so it's important that these vendors deliver, or the HR department may see an increase in workload.

Summary

Total rewards will continue to be a core competency of HR professionals, but the landscape of the delivery of these important functions continually changes, impacted by legislation, the market, and the changing workforce population. The needs of workers should be assessed and reviewed periodically to ensure the alignment of compensation and benefits and to meet the burden of taking care of the lifeblood of any organization—its people.

For additional information on this topic, candidates for the exam should visit the Department of Labor website at www.dol.gov, the Social Security Administration at www.ssa.gov, and the Internal Revenue Service at www.irs.gov. At these websites a keyword search of the topics discussed in this chapter will provide regulations, guidance, and rulings to review for a more in-depth understanding of the role these federal agencies play in compensation and benefits for employees.

Test-Taking Tip

The PHR® exam is now available year-round at testing centers. In the past, this exam was offered only two times per year, which meant having to adjust preparation and study time to those windows, which may not work with an HR professional's busy schedule. Take your time in the preparation of this comprehensive exam. Review the material in this book, including the references, to ensure that you have a good practical base of knowledge prior to test day.

Review Questions

1. When reviewing what constitutes compensable time, what should an HR professional review?

   A. Policies previously established by the company

   B. Guidance from the Wage and Hour Division (WHD) of the Department of Labor

   C. The Fair Labor Standards Act

   D. Regulations from the Department of Commerce

2. An office employee is earning a salary of $49,500 annually with no supervisory responsibility but oversees and makes decisions on a major project that generates significant income for a company. This employee should be classified as what?

   A. Nonexempt

   B. Exempt

   C. Full-time

   D. A contractor

3. A lawyer working for a company serves as a reserve officer in the United States Army and receives orders to mobilize. The company must do which of the following?

   A. Maintain the employee's right to return to their company job for up to five years or in some cases longer

   B. Continue to pay the employee's salary because they make more than their military pay

   C. Leave the position vacant during the military absence

   D. Both A and B

4. A company that is looking to conserve resources and reduce costs when there is an abundance of available talent may choose to _____ the local market with comparative wages.

   A. Lag

   B. Lead

   C. Match

   D. Lower

5. A company's systemic evaluation of jobs in the organization may result in the establishment of which of the following?

   A. A comprehensive benefits program

   B. A performance improvement plan

   C. A general increase in pay

   D. A grade system

6. When taking a type of quantitative approach to a job evaluation, which of the following compensable factors are included in the Equal Pay Act or Title VII?

    A. Skill

    B. Effort

    C. Working conditions

    D. All of the above

7. A manufacturing company is paying employees who make widgets a base salary and additional compensation based on the average daily output each employee is able to build that meets the specifications. This is an example of what kind of pay program?

    A. Time based

    B. Performance based

    C. Person based

    D. Productivity based

8. Workers' compensation is paid for by _____ and is _____ .

    A. The employee, optional

    B. The employee, mandatory

    C. The employer, optional

    D. The employer, mandatory

9. As a company grows and expands, the desires of employees may change, affecting the types of benefits the company provides. To determine what to do, HR may take what action?

    A. Recommend changes to pay scales

    B. Provide a cafeteria plan

    C. Conduct a needs assessment

    D. Consult an outside provider

10. An employee has requested to take leave under the Family and Medical Leave Act to support a family member and has submitted the proper documentation to the HR department. Later it is discovered that their manager requested the employee to take only part of the time and work from home because a project is due in a few weeks.

    A. No action is required by HR as the documentation was submitted and the employee can choose to help if they desire.

    B. The HR professional should tell the employee that they should do what they can to support the organization if the company is willing to provide resources such as a laptop.

    C. Leave under FMLA is like other leave in that it must be approved by management and can be limited if it affects the mission of the company.

    D. The HR professional has an obligation to ensure compliance with the law and should speak to the manager and supervisory chain to eliminate any interference.

11. It is important that the payroll administrator communicate changes to pay to the employee in advance for any of the following *except* which one?

   A.   General increases in the amount

   B.   Changes resulting in structure such as exempt to nonexempt or salaried to hourly.

   C.   Employee self-directed changes to withholdings or allotments done through a pay portal

   D.   Bonuses received as part of a Performance Incentive Plan

12. In general, when an employee chooses health coverage under the company's group plan, they cannot make changes unless which of the following occurs?

   A.   A period of open enrollment

   B.   A qualifying event occurs

   C.   The employee waits a period of 60 days

   D.   Both A and B

Chapter

5

Employee and Labor Relations

THE PHR® EXAM CONTENT FROM THE EMPLOYEE AND LABOR RELATIONS FUNCTIONAL AREA COVERED IN THIS CHAPTER CONSISTS OF THE FOLLOWING RESPONSIBILITIES AND KNOWLEDGE AREAS. RESPONSIBILITIES:

✓ 01 Analyze functional effectiveness at each stage of the employee life cycle (for example: hiring, onboarding, development, retention, exit process, alumni program) and identify alternate approaches as needed

✓ 02 Collect, analyze, summarize, and communicate employee engagement data

✓ 03 Understand organizational culture, theories, and practices; identify opportunities and make recommendations

✓ 04 Understand and apply knowledge of programs, federal laws, and regulations to promote outreach, diversity and inclusion (for example: affirmative action, employee resource groups, community outreach, corporate responsibility)

✓ 05 Implement and support workplace programs relative to health, safety, security, and privacy following federal laws and regulations (for example: OSHA, workers' compensation, emergency response, workplace violence, substance abuse, legal postings)

✓ 06 Promote organizational policies and procedures (for example: employee handbook, SOPs, time and attendance, expenses)

✓ 07 Manage complaints or concerns involving employment practices, behavior, or working conditions, and escalate by providing information to appropriate stakeholders

✓ 08 Promote techniques and tools for facilitating positive employee and labor relations with knowledge of applicable federal laws affecting union and nonunion workplaces (for example: dispute/conflict resolution, antidiscrimination policies, sexual harassment)

✓ 09 Support and consult with management in performance management process (for example: employee reviews, promotions, recognition programs)

✓ 10 Support performance activities and employment activities by managing corresponding legal risks

IN ADDITION TO THE PRECEDING RESPONSIBILITIES, AN INDIVIDUAL TAKING THE PHR® EXAM SHOULD HAVE WORKING KNOWLEDGE OF THE FOLLOWING AREAS, USUALLY DERIVED THROUGH PRACTICAL EXPERIENCE:

✓ 44 General employee relations activities and analysis (for example, conducting investigations, researching grievances, working conditions, reports, etc.)

✓ 45 Applicable federal laws and procedures affecting employment, labor relations, safety, and security

✓ 46 Human relations, culture and values concepts, and applications to employees and organizations

✓ 47 Review and analysis process for assessing employee attitudes, opinions, and satisfaction

✓ 48 Diversity and inclusion

✓ 49 Recordkeeping requirements

✓ 50 Occupational injury and illness prevention techniques

✓ 51 Workplace safety and security risks

✓ 52 Emergency response, business continuity, and disaster recovery process

This chapter focuses on the important tasks of human capital management: managing, monitoring, and promoting legally compliant programs and policies that impact the employee experience throughout the employee life cycle. Key points of knowledge for this chapter include developing, implementing, administering, and evaluating the workplace to maintain relationships. Additionally, HR professionals have the responsibility to ensure safe and secure working conditions that balance employer and employee needs and rights in support of the organization's goals and objectives. This functional area is 39 percent of the PHR® exam. The percentage for the exam demonstrates the overall importance and significance to HR professionals of this functional area. While employee and labor relations may not take up all the daily duties, HR professionals still execute some significant responsibilities in this functional area that are vital to a company.

While the other chapters focus on knowledge and responsibilities that impact the talent of the company, the topic of this chapter is more the organizational climate and its relationship to the ways employees behave. Specifically, these behaviors are the actions that must be aligned to the company values to achieve its goals and objectives. Employee and labor relations are, as the phrase implies, about fostering strong, positive relations with the workforce.

This chapter also reviews risk management. It covers a wide array of threats to the organization, from internal and external sources, and the necessary actions to mitigate potential outcomes. This should not imply that every accident is preventable or that plans to prevent them are 100 percent effective. In fact, it is more likely that one of these significant events will occur within an organization than not, and therefore risk management is often about the response and actions taken after an incident has occurred to review what occurred, why, and what steps should be taken going forward. This section reviews the knowledge and responsibility required to provide a safe, secure working environment and to protect the organization from potential liability.

Required Knowledge

The general practice of employee and labor relations is a vast subset of an HR professional's responsibilities, and there is a great deal of information to know and understand. As in other chapters of this book, important aspects of the law that govern these areas are critical points of knowledge. However, it is also important to understand negotiation and working with groups with both competing and aligning interests. In much of business today, companies often seek out specialists who are entirely focused and experienced on this topic. Knowledge of labor practices, employee and employer rights, and how to foster a strong organizational climate are all required to be a successful HR professional.

As with other functional areas covered in the PHR® exam, HR professionals must know the applicable laws and regulations at the federal level that will govern procedures and practices in an organization to ensure compliance. Beyond the laws, HR professionals should be familiar with the types of programs that are typically found in a company in its field and how they should be administered and developed. HR professionals will often execute the procedures across several different areas that impact risk management, including emergency response, business continuity, and investigations. Finally, HR professionals must know the categories of risks to be found in a company and the general practices that are undertaken to mitigate those risks and the damage that can be done to a company.

General Practices, Laws, and Procedures

Just like the functional areas covered by other chapters of this Review Guide, employee and labor relations requires HR professionals to have a working knowledge of key legislation related to this functional area. In this case, labor laws are a critical part. As in other chapters, there are overlapping provisions of Title VII to ensure equal opportunity and consistency in how employee relations are handled, but there are also other provisions, addressed in the following sections. HR professionals must know general employee relations activities and be able to analyze the effectiveness of efforts by the company to engage their employees.

Many of the laws covered in this chapter define compliance and the minimum required standards a company must have in place related to the health, safety, security, and privacy of employees. However, just because a company is compliant with the letter of the law doesn't mean that it's "safe." The minimum standards are just that—the absolute minimum but not necessarily all that can be done. Once again, there is a balance the company must achieve and maintain: it must remain viable as a company but also do what it can to provide the best possible protection to its employees. As previous chapters have discussed, the behaviors of the company must align with its values and ethics. The conduct of the employees, managers, and executives when it comes to practices are no exception, and care should be taken that the company consistently places the value of its human capital above a product or sale.

Union and Nonunion Environments

There is a lot of discussion in the modern business world over the relevance and purpose of unions. Collective bargaining among workers has been part of the fabric of the United States for well over a century but continues to have both advocates and detractors. This book does not take a position on the subject of unionization, nor should any HR professional in a generalist role establish a practice of being "pro" or "anti" union, as they must be reliable professional advisors on what the regulations require and should not be biased in their approach.

As of the publication of this book, 28 states have some form of "right to work" provision that impact how unions operate within those states and require them to allow non-union workers to be covered by the same provisions agreed to in collective bargaining without paying union dues or being a member. Essentially, these employees benefit from the work of the union without requiring union participation or financial support. Additionally, several states have provisions about union activity that add to federal statutes and must be followed. HR professionals must be knowledgeable about the specific legal requirements within their state to be effective in this functional area.

As mentioned in previous chapters, companies have a responsibility to create a workspace that is free from discrimination and respects all employees. Harassment and equal opportunity legislation applies equally to union and nonunion companies. However, there may be requirements or provisions that are established in collective bargaining agreements that provide for procedures or policies to adjudicate these issues. HR professionals must possess the requisite knowledge of how these agreements have been implemented and practiced and work with legal counsel to ensure that they do not run counter to the law or subject the company to an unfair labor practice complaint, as discussed later in the chapter.

National Labor Relations Act

The National Labor Relations Act (NLRA), also known as the Wagner Act, was created in 1935. Prior to this act, dating back to before the turn of the century, there were a series of legislative acts that tended to favor businesses over the employees. As industries grew and the need for skilled labor changed, especially during the times of World War I and II, organization of labor experienced changes. Table 5.1 lists some of the legislation and its effect on labor relations over the years.

TABLE 5.1   Historical labor laws

Law	Impact
Sherman Anti-Trust Act, 1890	Outlawed contracts that were considered to limit trade and commerce, effectively outlawing unions.
Norris-LaGuardia Act, 1932	Prohibited federal injunctions resulting from labor disputes.
Taft-Hartley Act (Labor Management Relations Act or LMRA), 1947	Balanced the interest of unions and companies; regulated the interaction between the parties.
Executive Order #13496	Required federal contractors to notify employees of rights under federal labor laws

The NLRA took into consideration the needs of the employer and the rights of employees in the workplace. The act also established the National Labor Relations Board (NLRB) to be the oversight agency designated to enforce the provisions of the law. Over the years, it has issued regulations and interpretations to the law, some that have been challenged in court and others upheld. HR professionals must know the role the NLRB plays in the establishment of a union and during the collective bargaining process.

One of the arguments about provisions in the NLRA, or about how the NLRB interprets them, is whether they have been superseded by later legislation such as the Fair Labor Standards Act (which sets rules for wages and compensation) and are no longer necessary. All of these laws intersect and overlap, but each serves a legitimate purpose in protecting the integrity of the labor system in the United States. As we have seen in other chapters and examples, the HR professional's knowledge of these various rules often directly contributes to a company's ability to quickly address concerns, establish effective policies, and implement proper procedures.

Title VII of the Civil Rights Act of 1964

As discussed in previous chapters, this act is the centerpiece of antidiscrimination legislation in the United States. Along with the other laws discussed in Chapters 2 and 4, this act provides for the equal protection and opportunity of employees in the workplace. In this respect, these federal employment laws have made mandatory rights that formerly needed to be established by agreement between the employer and employee. What is now commonly accepted practice in companies once required the intervention of the NLRB and a collective bargaining agreement. Therefore, today's function and purpose of unionization doesn't need to cover the areas that are basic with respect to compensation and benefits or hiring and training practices under other laws. Instead, the focus is more often on training, equipment, standards, safety, and grievance procedures.

The Workers Adjustment and Retraining Notification Act of 1988

The Workers Adjustment and Retraining Notification (WARN) Act creates provisions requiring an employer to notify employees 60 days prior to an action that results in the closing of a business unit or layoff that impacts more than 50 employees. The basic provisions are set in the law that generally applies to companies with more than 100 employees. The law establishes triggering events such as a plant closure or mass layoff, notification requirements, definitions of terms like "employment loss," and exemptions to the rule. The intent of the legislation is to provide warning and notice to employees when a business decision is reached that will have a significant impact on the future employment of employees in the company to give them some time to prepare for transition, prepare for unemployment, or seek training for a change in profession. Closings covered include one company selling to another, in which case the provisions also address the responsibilities for both parties. HR professionals must know the timeline provisions and reporting requirements to remain in compliance.

There are exceptions for the 60-day requirement, such as unforeseeable business circumstances and natural disasters, but the notices must still be made as soon as practical. The notices must be in writing and specific to the circumstances. Besides going to the employees, the notices in many cases must also go to the local subdivisions of government.

Failure to make proper notification subjects the company to penalties that could include the back pay and wages of the employees up to the 60 days. A part of the act allows for the notification to go through the designated representative of workers supported by a union. Often, collective bargaining agreements will have provisions for such notice and the actions required.

Occupational Safety and Health Act

This law, passed in 1970, was the first of its kind to address safety standards and practices concerning safety in the workplace. It established the Occupational Safety and Health Administration (OSHA) as part of the U.S. Department of Labor as the regulatory oversight agency of the federal government. The goal of the law is to reduce hazards in the workplace and improve programs in organizations that are related to safety or health. The Secretary of Labor is tasked with developing or implementing required occupational safety and health practices.

OSHA conducts studies and records data that shows trends in health and safety within companies, and it looks holistically at the information gathered to improve the overall physical well-being of the workforce in the workplace. When necessary, it has the power of enforcement to ensure that companies comply with necessary health or safety practices. It also places an important focus on training to improve the overall safety posture of companies. Employees have a fundamental right under the law to work in a place that is not hazardous or could cause injury or death to an employee as a direct or indirect result of the workplace conditions. These rights are summarized as follows:

- Safety and health are protected while working.

- An employee can request an inspection that may be attended by a designated representative.

- An employee may file a complaint and must be informed when hazards are discovered at the workplace free of reprisal or similar action.

- An employer must correct or mitigate hazards when discovered.

- Employees are entitled to be properly trained to identify and reduce hazards and risks related to safety or health.

OSHA Standards

The standard practices established by OSHA have four categories (general industry, maritime, construction, and agriculture) and can be reviewed further on its website (www.osha.gov). In general, these standards are the conditions that an employee should expect to have as part of the working environment. In fact, they are so common as to be expected in the modern business world, and today we often forget that not long ago these practices were not in place, resulting in serious injuries or deaths to workers. For example, companies must identify emergency exits and procedures on how to evacuate a building. It is common to see the red-lighted exit signs above doors in public buildings and commercial spaces.

Other types of standards include noise and hearing protection, which covers annual hearing tests for employees exposed to loud noise; hazardous communication, which provides material safety data sheets (MSDSs) to tell employees about the hazards and necessary precautions needed around chemicals and other substances that they are exposed to in the workplace; and blood-borne pathogens, which present potential risk to health by entering the bloodstream of exposed workers, causing illness. There are also a variety of precautionary measures to reduce exposure to injury in confined spaces, around heavy machinery, and for jobs needing specialized protective equipment that must be worn by workers.

Documenting Illness and Injuries

HR professionals must be familiar with the record-keeping requirements of OSHA, specifically, the standardized government forms that are to be completed and used to log work-related illness or injury. It is necessary to know when circumstances warrant the completion of these forms. In general, if the incident results in the death of an employee, loss or restriction of work, or a recordable illness or injury (often defined by a doctor with an employee having a chronic illness such as a terminal disease or acute injury such as broken limbs), it must be recorded. Further, these reports must be available for inspection by OSHA representatives and posted for employees to be advised about incidents.

Inspections

The law provides for representatives to conduct inspections of the workplace without notice to ensure compliance with the standards. Employers do have a right to protect their proprietary work from release, but in most cases, confirming that working conditions are safe and reasonable should not create a risk of company trade secrets being disclosed. Therefore, companies must allow unfettered access by inspectors to verify the working conditions and report on any findings where standards are not being followed. The inspection process uses a series of tiers that are driven by the immediacy of the dangers posed to employees, with the most critical first and a programmed or routine inspection last. Upon arrival, it is expected that inspectors should communicate to management the purpose and intent of a visit and the inspection process; they should conclude the visit with a preliminary report, especially if critical findings exist.

Metrics

HR professionals should know that evaluating the number of cases against the total time that labor is on the job provides an incident rate that can be compared against the industry to help gauge how effectively risk prevention, training, and communication are working in the company. When these rates lag the industry, it means that safety practices are not meeting requirements and could trigger inspections or create a need for an improvement plan. The intent is not to punish but to correct practices to improve the conditions of work for all concerned. Ultimately, safe practices established under OSHA will drive down costs that result from lost productivity and damage to equipment or from injury/illness to employees.

Violations

As of January 2017, violations of OSHA can result in fines that are more than $12,000 per occurrence for serious violations or failure to abate a violation after the abatement date. For cases where the violation is determined to be willful, the amount is 10 times the fine at more than $126,000 per occurrence. Such fines and potential criminal repercussions indicate the importance of complying with the law. As a result of such strong enforcement and attention, today's modern workforce has exponentially safer working conditions and environments and, just as importantly, organizational leadership that focuses on the well-being and safe practices of its employees factored into its business model.

Drug-Free Workplace Act

Companies that have federal contracts valued in excess of $100,000 or those that are given grants must certify that their organization is drug free and that programs and policies are maintained to keep the company drug free as well. It is permissible for the company to conduct random drug screening for its employees as part of the hiring process. This is usually done after there is an offer and acceptance by the applicant as part of the prehire process. As federal contractors, a company has an added incentive to maintain a drug-free workplace. This also requires the organization to maintain the appropriate documentation of inspections and results along with any training that is conducted to benefit the employees.

Several states in recent years have changed their laws to allow the use of marijuana for medical or recreational purposes in their state. While these laws vary, the federal law prohibition is still in force, and therefore companies must abide by the federal standard to remain compliant as a federal contractor. As a matter of practice, it is a good idea to have a clear drug use policy and set the expectation across the organization.

Of course, there are cases where employees will fail random drug screening or have incidents resulting from drug use. The law requires that employers notify the federal contracting agency within 10 days of discovery of the violation. There must also be consequences to the employee for violation. This does not necessarily mean termination but may require treatment or rehabilitation as part of the mitigation and response by the company. It is also essential to understand that drug abuse is not limited to illegal substances but could be the abuse of prescription drugs. For example, a worker who has a physical injury, is prescribed narcotics as pain management, and then abuses them beyond the prescription can be considered or "in violation" of this act.

Americans with Disabilities Act (and Amendments)

This legislation also pertains to risk management. As discussed in previous chapters, the Americans with Disabilities Act (ADA), including its amendments, imposes restrictions on employers and mandates reasonable accommodations to qualifying employees. These accommodations also must be considered in evaluating risk to the employee in the performance of their duties or with equipment or other accommodation to a disabled employee required to maintain safety standards. One area that is also considered under the ADA would be infectious diseases. In many medical facilities, universal safety protocols are in place to prevent transmission of disease between an employee and a patient. Individuals must be protected, and the organization is responsible for the enforcement of the practices and standards.

Health Insurance Portability and Accountability Act

The Health Insurance Portability and Accountability Act (HIPAA) is important to protect the medical information of employees and, for organizations in the medical industry, the patients and customers. Because of the sensitive nature of personal medical information, there is a compliance requirement that this information is safeguarded and disclosed only as required and authorized by the patient while properly informing the individual of the need and nature for disclosure. As part of risk management, HR professionals must know how to collect and safeguard this information to prevent unauthorized use. HIPAA information must be separate and distinct from employee personnel files. When dealing with a workers' compensation incident, for example, the HR team must not disclose private medical information that is not needed to make a management decision or release information to parties without a legitimate need to know.

Another limitation on risk management is on the implementation of fitness and wellness programs. Companies may choose these programs to reduce healthcare costs or improve physical abilities and therefore reduce illness and injuries that may occur on the job. However, they cannot mandate or force employees based on knowledge of previous illness or other medical conditions that is illegally obtained in violation of HIPAA.

There are two specific rules associated with the law that pertain to risk management. For more information, visit the Department of Health and Human Services website on this topic located at www.hhs.gov/hipaa/for-professionals/index.html. The Privacy Rule sets the standards for protecting personally identifiable health information by certain entities. One such entity is any health plan that would impact businesses; the goal is to prevent unauthorized disclosure from health plan managers to other elements in the company. The second is the Security Rule, which protects the confidentiality of electronic health information. This is why it is imperative that in establishing electronic files, the HR team must keep employment and health information with separate access and restrictions. Health files should not be included among files normally accessible by managers and supervisors.

Sarbanes-Oxley Act

As discussed in previous chapters, Sarbanes-Oxley (SOX) is legislation passed to prevent fraud and establish financial requirements and ethical conduct standards for public companies. Shareholders have an expectation that the company is being run properly with financial integrity and in compliance with governing laws and regulations. HR professionals must have knowledge of the principles and requirements of this law. Even for companies that are not publicly traded on the stock market, the foundation of this law shows the necessity for a company to develop and implement a variety of financial controls to protect the organization.

Section 404 of the law outlines the required controls that an organization must have in place to mitigate fraud, waste, and abuse of the financial structure of the organization. The United States Securities and Exchange Commission has developed a guide for small businesses to help establish internal control practices that is available at www.sec.gov/info/smallbus/404guide/intro.shtml. While these companies are not necessarily subject to the full provisions of the law, following those provisions helps create good practices that would facilitate conversion to a publicly traded company in the future as the organization grows.

Procedures for using corporate credit cards, purchasing, and other means of committing funds should be enacted and individuals in the company held accountable. Disclosing conflicts of interest and other financial obligations such as large debt can be part of policy, and the HR team must know how to properly develop and use such policies to include any regulatory limitations that could be protected by privacy restrictions (discussed later in the chapter).

In reducing financial risk, the company demonstrates good stewardship of the resources that are available and provides confidence to shareholders and other external stakeholders affected by its financial practices. The intent of the law is to ensure that a company is not solely focused on profit or share price to the detriment of its long-term financial stability and that any actions that are taken to obscure the potential misconduct or financial mismanagement have penalties by force of law.

Researching Grievances, Working Conditions, and Reporting

HR professionals must know how to thoroughly research grievances of employees and assess the working conditions that may need to be adjusted. They must have working knowledge of the various means that employees can use to report problems in the workplace that require resolution by or involvement of management. For example, there may be an anonymous reporting line that allows employees to report a problem without identifying themselves. This encourages reporting without fear of retribution or reprisal. Employees must believe that issues concerning working conditions that are reported will be addressed in a timely and fair manner. When researching a grievance, HR professionals should be familiar with company practices and policies that are directly related to the complaint. They should be able to discuss concerns and listen to the employees who are aggrieved. They should know what the working conditions should be and determine whether there are any discrepancies. The goal in this process is to demonstrate a commitment to the employee's well-being and to take all concerns that are raised seriously.

Conducting Unbiased Investigations

A key point of knowledge for all HR professionals is how to conduct an investigation. Most important is knowing when an investigation should or should not be handled by HR. The company should develop clear policies and guidance to determine which circumstances should be handled in an administrative capacity and which others require legal counsel, internal audit, or external oversight. Criminal matters should be handled by the appropriate law enforcement authority, and if during the course of any internal review or investigation HR believes that criminal conduct has occurred, HR should refer the matter to the authorities immediately.

When the investigation is within the purview of HR, HR professionals must be deliberate, thorough, and complete in their investigation. They must collect and review the facts of the matter, keeping in mind that they hold no compelling powers for employees to provide information, nor is their communication privileged should there be any subpoena. Therefore, HR professionals should, to the best of their abilities, try to maintain discretion and confidentiality but understand that there are limits. When conducting an investigation, HR should keep in mind the following:

- Interview all parties involved in the incident under investigation as quickly as possible to limit possible collaboration of statements.
- When possible, obtain statements in writing.
- Maintain discretion and do not discuss findings until after the investigation has been completed and the findings submitted to the appropriate decision-makers.
- Limit the scope and purpose of the investigation and where practical establish a time limit to avoid endless investigation that covers areas beyond what is germane to the incident.
- Stick to the facts; do not let individuals speculate or add commentary to their statements.
- Confer with legal counsel, internal auditors, or similar positions to interpret rules or regulations that may govern the investigation and provide guidance or expertise.
- Ensure that you have the appropriate authority to conduct the investigation.

Corporate Culture

In an age when there is a shortage of available qualified talent, often corporate culture is what attracts and retains good employees. These workers seek a strong culture that is values-based and helps align their goals and promote growth within the organization. HR professionals should know the close correlation with culture and values and the impact on human relations in general. Additionally, the ways the company views diversity and inclusion and manages performance are all indicators of the corporate culture.

Human Relations, Culture, and Values

HR professionals are experts at relating to people and understanding their needs at a personal level. They must leverage this knowledge and capability to ensure the optimal performance of each employee. They must be astute at recognizing elements of emotional intelligence in themselves and others. Emotional intelligence measures how well an individual perceives their own emotional state and that of others and also how the emotions of others affect them and the impact of their emotions on others.

Being self-aware of one's emotions is an important skill for anyone, but especially for HR professionals. They must understand how emotions impact judgment and decisions and then be able to manage these emotional states. Being aware that you are angry and being able to manage that anger are two different skills to consider. Simultaneously, the individual must learn to sense the emotions of others and understand why those emotions are present. People with a strong emotional intelligence can predictably understand why certain emotions that they exhibit affect others in certain ways. Once someone can master these emotional intelligence concepts, they can improve and be more impactful to the organization.

Another aspect of human relations is organizational culture, or how a company collectively acts based on certain parameters. This concept is important because the organizational dynamic is largely based on how the group behaves and responds to leaders and conditions that exist in the company. HR professionals who can accurately predict how the organization will respond to decisions, policy changes, accomplishments, and setbacks is valuable to modern business models. They can maximize the human capital potential in the organization through their understanding of human relations and the response to corporate culture. This culture is based on the values of the company and how the individuals and collective group prioritize values when they conflict.

Diversity and Inclusion

HR professionals should strive for a diverse organization to draw from different thoughts and experience within an organization. They should know concepts about diversity and how those apply in their company. Diversity is not just about the protected classes discussed throughout the book related to Title VII of the Civil Rights Act. It goes beyond those limits to look at differences among generations, cultures, and even learning styles.

We are at a unique point in today's business world with as many as five generations in the workforce. This unusual dynamic plays a crucial role in the introduction of technology to a company, the values the company espouses, and the general work ethos of each generation. The younger generations are more globally connected and have access to much more information in a shorter period of time. They will be challenged by synthesizing such vast data and being able to discern the reliability of the information available. At the other end of the timeline, older generations are more traditional and will have a harder time embracing new concepts or ways of doing business. While this doesn't seem new as there is always generational overlap, the fact that people are working longer and life spans have increased, combined with the exponential advancements in technology, has greatly affected organizations.

HR professionals must also be attuned to cultural competencies and understand the impact of globalization in the marketplace. Being aware of the role that culture can play in a company will help HR professionals develop diversity and inclusion programs that reach out to all cultures and respect their contributions to the company. These programs enhance an organization's capabilities with respect to employee relations. These slight differences among all employees will impact how they each assimilate information that is learned by the organization. HR must know how to manage this process and ensure that no group is marginalized or not allowed to contribute to the growth and development of the organizational culture.

Collective Bargaining

One of the key processes in labor relations is collective bargaining. HR professionals must have extensive knowledge of the process, concepts, and strategies. At its core is the successful negotiation of an employment agreement between the management of a company and the union representatives that are authorized to negotiate on behalf of the company's employees. This collective bargaining agreement is a contract that governs the working conditions and employment settings for the employees along with the responsibilities of both management and the workers. These agreements take into account many factors, including the labor skills, overall economy, prevailing wages and benefits, and accepted practices of employers.

The agreement covers both mandatory and voluntary subjects. The voluntary subjects include areas such as retiree benefits for members of the union or processes for handling unfair labor practices. These may or may not be subject to negotiation. The National Labor Relations Act sets out which category a subject falls under, including those items that cannot be discussed under any agreement (illegal items such as requests that would violate other laws or regulations). The mandatory subjects include the following:

- Pay and Overtime
- Terminations
- Disciplinary and Grievance Procedures
- Reductions in Force
- Promotions and Seniority
- Holidays, Vacations, Time Off
- Promotions, Demotions, Transfers
- Safety Procedures

Collective bargaining can be done by first negotiating with one company in an industry, such as an industry leader or one a union feels will create the best deal for workers, and then attempting to promulgate the agreement with other competing companies in the industry. While this was a prevalent method in the past, it is less common today because industries now have standard practices that cover most of what would be negotiated by a union and offer no competitive advantages to either side. A second option would be for a group of employers to negotiate with the union seeking to represent employees at the companies. In industries where there are multiple unions represented (such as the airline industry), the unions can coordinate their bargaining processes with the employer to maximize their negotiation power. Finally, the process can be broken up to discuss complex details in a variety of committees to reach a consensus.

A collective bargaining agreement will have several articles that discuss each mandatory area and any voluntary area that is agreed to by the union and management. Within the agreement there will be provisions for who will be members and the dues and the rights of the union to exclusively represent the interests of the employees. If they work in a right-to-work state, HR professionals must understand that there are additional restrictions and provisions that limit a union's ability to collect dues or fees for representation. The biggest difference is that in the right-to-work states, union shops are illegal, which means a union cannot require new employees to pay dues and become union members. While the employee's employment is protected, they cannot attend union meetings or have a vote concerning the approval of an agreement without being union members.

HR professionals must understand how contracts are administered and how various provisions are handled such as grievance procedures and arbitration. They must understand what actions should be taken in cases of litigation or allegations of unfair labor practices, as well as how to handle inquiries by the National Labor Relations Board if management is not negotiating in good faith as part of the collective bargaining process. They must also understand the protected activities that sometimes are the by-product of negotiations or failure to reach an agreement. Table 5.2 discusses some of these items and the role of the HR professional.

TABLE 5.2   Activities related to collective bargaining

Activity	Example	HR Considerations
Lockout	Management shuts down a plant to prevent workers from entering the facilities.	Works with management to control access to the facility; informs secondary managers of policies and procedures
Strike	Workers refuse to work as required to include slowing down processes or throughput.	Works with management to find temporary workers to maintain production; some strikes may not be authorized by a union or may not be allowed by contract making them a ULP
Picket	Employees exercise free speech usually at locations in proximity to work sites to protest management actions.	Ensures that management responses are compliant with regulations and continues efforts to reach negotiated settlement on contract; may arrange for additional company security

Performance Management

To align behaviors of employees with the organizational goals, HR professionals should know how to provide evaluations, corrective actions, and coaching to identify an employee's strengths and weakness. They should provide suggestions to managers on how to improve employee performance over time. Performance management is the entire process and includes the tools, such as formal reviews, and the procedures, such as one-on-one coaching sessions to discuss expectations and outcomes related to an individual's performance.

HR professionals must help employees understand the uses and limitations of a performance management system. There are a multitude of options available in the modern business environment, but there is no one-size-fits-all solution. However, if you view the ultimate goal of performance management as alignment of employee and organizational goals, then the required performance management is the system that most effectively accomplishes this task.

Terminations

When it is determined that an employee must be involuntarily separated from employment with the organization, HR must know the proper procedures and work with management to ensure that these steps are followed. Failure to do so may result in litigation over unlawful termination. Managers should refrain from firing an employee outright without first following the due process described earlier. It is better to put the employee on an administrative leave with or without pay until a determination can be reached. It is important to remember in the cases where an employee is suspended without pay that should a determination be made in favor of the employee, the back pay will be due to the employee.

The determination should be made in the same manner as outlined previously after a thorough, complete, and timely investigation, with relevant facts and information that have been collected. The employer must lay out clearly the reasons for separation and promptly notify the employee. HR must be aware to document the incident and all related information on the case and maintain the file for record. HR professionals must recognize potential misuse of disciplinary procedures that may violate protected classes and jeopardize equal opportunity for employment. Disciplinary actions to include separations cannot be used as an alternative means to terminate someone who would otherwise be protected in their employment.

Safe and Secure Workplace

HR must have extensive knowledge of the variety of programs that protect employees from occupational illness and injury. Other programs also protect the company's and employees' rights on matters of substance abuse and the impact on operational risk. While the structure and execution of these kinds of programs are very different, both types are means of reducing risk to the organization with the goal of maintaining a strong and capable workforce.

Record-Keeping Requirements

The retention schedule of documents refers to how long documents must be stored by the organization and how they are disposed of at the end of the required storage period. HR professionals must know how documents are to be stored. They can be in hard copy form or electronic, although federal or state regulations may have specific requirements as to how documents must be physically maintained. In all cases, the documents must be readily available if required for validation or inspection during a review. Some documents may be required to be maintained until no longer needed for current operations. Other documents could be required to be kept for more than 20 years. HR professionals should be aware of the retention schedule of critical records because often a company keeps records beyond the required time. This can create additional risk or subject the company to additional scrutiny when documents are requested by outside agents. Finally, HR professionals should be aware of how to properly destroy records that are to be purged. While it may seem simple to shred physical files, with modern technology there are challenges to ensuring that data files that are kept electronically are in fact purged. Too often copies and backups exist that are beyond tracking for compliance purposes, which exposes a company to risk should it be determined that those files should have been destroyed.

Injury and Illness Prevention

General safety programs seek the reduction and elimination of hazards that cause injury or illness. Table 5.3 provides some examples of creating the conditions to prevent incidents. HR professionals must know how to drive these programs and evaluate their effectiveness. In some cases, HR professionals in conjunction with managers will assign additional duties to an employee to be the responsible agent for safety in a particular department or division.

TABLE 5.3   Prevention methods

Example	Result
Safety suggestion program	Allows employees to present ideas on how to improve safety practices
Proper equipment training and fitting	Ensures that employees exposed to hazards know how to use proper personal protective equipment (PPE)
Universal precautions	Industry standards in the medical, health, and food services industries that prevent transmission of bacteria or viruses
Safety equipment	Eye wash stations, first aid kits, fire extinguishers, safety showers to reduce or minimize injuries

In addition to individual appointments, HR professionals should understand how to implement committees to promote safety practices and general awareness of risks that employees are exposed to within the organization. They can help with incentives that are awarded to individuals and teams that are safety focused and have solid practices that result in a reduction of preventable illnesses and injuries in a company. Inspections and reviews are an important part of any safety program, and HR professionals should know how to conduct and record the results of these inspections. When incidents occur, part of the program must focus on understanding the proximate cause of an incident that resulted in illness or injury and quickly identify any failures in protocols or procedures that may have contributed.

🌐 **Real World Scenario**

Explosion on Set

A licensed pyrotechnician on a movie set was working to rig explosives on cars for a scene to be filmed outside a warehouse. As the individual was carrying the charge to the place where it would be attached, it detonated, causing injury to the individual. Fortunately, the individual was following all of the established protocols for handling the explosive cord, including proper distance from the body and location. While the injury sustained was severe, it was not fatal. An investigation was conducted to examine whether the individual missed a procedure or created an unsafe condition. This included other witness statements and a review of the area. It was ultimately discovered that this particular remote location was a former factory with iron filings scattered in the soil surrounding the building. These filings happened to create sufficient static charge when walking across the lot that the explosives ignited. This was unforeseen by the production crew or the experienced technical expert. It shows that even with procedures and trained personnel, incidents can still occur. However, it also is worth noting that the severity of the occurrence was mitigated precisely because proper practices were being followed.

Workers' Compensation

This benefit is an insurance product designed to cover employee compensation as a result of a work-related incident. HR professionals must know how this program works and how premiums are determined. It is based on results and claims, so companies and industries with higher likelihood of incidents will pay more as would be expected. These claims usually have a medical component for any treatment, along with any rehabilitation and a portion of wages lost. These packages can be several thousand dollars, so each claim will have a significant impact on the resulting premium increases.

Workplace Safety

Safety protocols are intended to reduce accidents and the extremely high costs associated with workers' compensation and other financial liability. However, these safety points work only if they are implemented and followed by the employees. Generally, safety risks are those specific risks that come from hazards that result in physical illness or injury and subsequent losses in work time, productivity, efficiency, or resources (such as money). Hazards such as those that cause slips, trips, or falls can be reduced. Table 5.4 gives some examples of hazards, the possible losses that they cause, and the prevention or risk mitigation method.

TABLE 5.4   Hazards and risk

Hazard	Potential Loss	Mitigation
Wet floor	Fall causing injury with loss of work days	Wet floor signs or other barriers to alert employees
Dust particulates	Inhaled by employee causing respiratory distress and lost days	Breathing respirator or other similar PPE
Blood-borne pathogen	Illness or sickness resulting in lost days	Universal precautions like latex gloves, gown, and face shield or mask

Certain safety risks, as shown in Table 5.4, require different means to reduce the threat. The measures needed to protect employees against tripping are quite different from the measures to protect against blood-borne pathogens, but the steps to identify these hazards and implement controls are the same.

Workplace Security

HR professionals should be familiar with a variety of security risks, from both physical and virtual aspects. Theft is a large risk that can create loss for an organization if access controls are not present; it's also a risk if there are situations where employees or outsiders perceive an opportunity to steal, if the consequences are low, or if there is a low chance of being caught. Without proper standards, some employees may feel entitled to take company property or feel that it's acceptable behavior. HR professionals must ensure that the company clearly defines the disciplinary outcome if a theft occurs.

In addition to general theft, corporate espionage is a specific kind of theft that involves trade secrets and insider information about a company and its activities. This is an intentional act by someone who intends harm or damage to a company by stealing proprietary information that can be used to damage an organization's reputation, market share, or products. This person seeks for an outside entity to gain a competitive advantage over the company by using deceptive means to gain access and use the information. In a similar fashion, sabotage doesn't seek to take information out of the organization but to take action that harms the company from within. Sabotage is a deliberate act to disable, destroy, or break equipment that is needed for operations to delay or stop production or delivery of service.

HR professionals should know how to reduce physical risk, by controlling access and establishing procedures for who may perform certain tasks in the company. For example, suppose a company that uses a direct deposit system for payroll transposes an account number, causing an employee to go unpaid. To correct the situation, the finance department generates a handwritten check to be issued to the employee. Without proper controls, the check could be approved for any amount. The accounting department, without knowledge of the transaction, could improperly report the payment as an error resulting in a stop to payment on behalf of the bank. These controls ensure that the right individual is approving money movement, and if there are any changes to procedure, that they are communicated throughout the organization to individuals who need to know this information to properly fulfill their duties.

Business Continuity and Disaster Recovery Plans

Like general emergency preparedness plans, business continuity and disaster recovery plans have components that HR professionals must know. Specifically, they must know the ways that their organization chooses to back up and protect sensitive data. This may include using a cloud service or third-party vendor to store data off-site. By having a backup of information stored at a separate location, the company reduces the risk that may be caused if an incident happens whereby the primary storage location is destroyed (fire, tornado, flood, and so on). HR professionals must take care to develop and know the parts of a disaster recovery plan, which includes items such as alternate work locations. In some situations, especially with companies that have multiple locations, it may be possible to re-establish work in another place while waiting for recovery operations to restore primary locations.

 Real World Scenario

Hurricane Katrina

In 2005, Hurricane Katrina devastated the Deep South of the United States and specifically was responsible for causing a catastrophic flood of New Orleans. The United States Military Entrance Processing Command (MEPCOM) is responsible for the accession and qualification of individuals joining the U.S. Armed Forces. It has 64 military entrance processing stations (MEPSs) around the United States, including New Orleans. At the time of the disaster, the personnel needed to evacuate themselves, along with files including hard copies and vital records such as birth certificates for those candidates who were in processing to the military and headed to basic training from that region. They successfully stored and secured thousands of files and moved them to alternative locations, including Atlanta and two other MEPSs to continue operations. These alternate work sites were able to take the increased workload and displaced workers until operations in New Orleans could resume. This is a great example of preparedness and planning in a short time to respond to a disaster.

Internal Investigation, Monitoring, and Surveillance

HR professionals must know the limitations and capabilities of monitoring employees in the workplace and surveillance techniques. This includes internal investigations of employees suspected of violating policies or those who may pose a risk to the organization. In the modern workplace, the most readily identifiable example of this type of activity is email monitoring and website visits. The IT department has the capability to track and store data elements that are transmitted across company equipment. HR must understand how to notify employees that they may be subject to this kind of surveillance as a condition of having access to and using company computer systems. HR professionals should know that communications transmitted in the conduct of work should not be considered private or personal and therefore may be accessed as part of routine work operations. It should be clearly communicated with active acknowledgment by the individual employee that they may be monitored while working. While a company should respect the privacy of its employees, it has an affirmative responsibility to protect its IT infrastructure, and any risk imposed by employees disregarding policies is too high.

Data Integrity

Data integrity means ensuring that the digital information a company collects and stores is authenticated and secure from intrusion. Modern organizations store much of their information digitally on servers located within the company or externally maintained by third-party vendors. In all cases, HR professionals should know common practices to reduce the risk associated with data breaches and how to report incidents if they occur. The greatest risk to a company's data is the very personnel who work for it. In most cases, it's not malicious actors from within but complacent employees who do not follow proper procedures and are unaware of threats to data integrity.

Data transmitted across email or the Internet can be stolen. It is important that HR professionals know which critical data should be encrypted. Personally identifiable information (PII) such as social security numbers, bank information, and credit card data should be protected. Files that are stored on servers should be restricted for access to those individuals with a legitimate business interest. Shared folders, therefore, should be routinely checked to determine whether people have appropriate credentials for accessing the data contained in the files. Most files and computer systems are protected by passwords. It is an important practice in HR that passwords should not be shared to prevent unauthorized access or disclosure.

Because employee complacency or negligence poses the greatest risk to data integrity, data hackers will exploit this vulnerability. One successful technique is social engineering. This is a construct where someone attempting to gain access uses a variety of practices that take advantage of the human nature to help or assist others. For example, someone may pose as a customer and ask questions in an attempt to get an employee to reveal sensitive information. This approach relies on good customer service standards and the employee's desire to answer the client's questions. Employees can be tricked into giving away passwords that can be used to gain unauthorized access to the data being protected. HR professionals must be aware that training and vigilance are the best risk mitigation strategies for any organization.

Exam Essentials

Understand the process of unionization.   The terminology related to unions and the unionization process including card checks, petitions, elections, voter eligibility, and determination of bargaining units should be reviewed. More information can be reviewed at the National Labor Relations Board website (www.nlrb.gov). HR professionals should review what conduct is allowed and the restrictions on actions that could be considered as unfair labor practices to avoid unintentional violations.

Understand how OSHA impacts an organization.   Whether it is just the rules for general workplace safety or those for a specific industry such as manufacturing, a company is responsible for complying with OSHA regulations. You should review investigation procedures in your organization and especially any recent findings or notices where there may have been compliance violations. Talk with the individuals responsible for filing reports and maintaining documentation when accidents occur and understand their process. If possible, compare the practices of different organizations.

Responsibilities

The responsibilities of HR professionals for employee and labor relations can greatly impact the overall climate of the company and therefore organizational effectiveness. HR professionals must diligently execute these duties as part of the job. Often these responsibilities are neglected because the negative impact of neglect is not readily apparent. However, the consequences can be severe and long-lasting for inattention to this important role.

While safe practices must be part of a company's everyday operations, HR professionals must understand the importance of the responsibilities they have in this area. A personal investment in the well-being of all employees is often the hallmark of a good HR professional. This means the proper administration of the safety program is paramount. However, it's not just about documentation and compliance; it is about developing and encouraging a culture of safety throughout the company. Effectively managing risk to prevent illness and injury will help the organization reduce loss and liability. HR professionals can demonstrate through their actions a continued commitment to the organization's employees and their health and safety.

Legal Requirements

HR professionals are responsible for ensuring that an organization conducts labor relations in accordance with the applicable laws and regulations. They are the primary advisors to executives and management on the conduct of the organization during labor negotiations and when responding to labor complaints. It is imperative that the organization establish clear policies and procedures and that HR manage the process to avoid charges of unfair labor practices.

Compliance

HR professionals are responsible for ensuring that the organization is compliant with the rules under the National Labor Relations Act and other companion laws. If a company is union-free, HR professionals should work with management to continually create a positive, strong culture that keeps employees engaged. HR professionals have the responsibility to review labor practices with management to remind them of unfair labor practices and how to avoid them. Generally, there is a need for proper training and awareness of what constitutes unfair labor practices and the restrictions and limitations that are imposed on management with respect to union activities.

If the company is currently going through a union-organizing process, the HR professionals have the responsibility for properly identifying the eligible employees to participate in the election process. They also work with management to help craft opinions and counterarguments to unions, which is permissible under the NLRA. If the union is successful in its organizing campaign, HR professionals will work with executives and management to liaison with union representatives for the purpose of collective bargaining. HR professionals are responsible for all records management for documents related to union activities.

Policies and Procedures

HR professionals are responsible for developing internal policies that govern the relations between employees and the company. Most often these take the form of an employee handbook that covers the expectations and standards for all employees. A handbook must be current and must be available to and understood by each employee to be enforceable in cases of disciplinary action or termination as a result of violating a policy contained in the handbook. Documenting changes and their distribution to employees should be maintained in the personnel files to alleviate questions about employees' awareness of a particular policy.

Policies should be routinely reviewed and updated to meet current practices. If a policy exists in a handbook but is not enforced, it could create challenges should an employee claim disparate treatment in being subjected to policy provisions. HR professionals can work with management to ensure that written policies are kept to the minimum required to successfully enforce standards so as not to limit the company's available courses of action. They should encourage managers to review policies and standards before taking any actions on employee behavior to maintain consistency in their approach. It is also prudent to discuss changes or implementation of new policies with all affected parties before implementation to have all sides be heard. This will often prevent policies from being enacted in a knee-jerk fashion, usually following an employee incident. Providing employees with a chance to comment on new policies and get feedback demonstrates that they are valued by the company and builds positive relationships.

Fostering and Cultivating Strong Employee Relations

In fostering and cultivating strong employee relations, HR professionals must analyze functional effectiveness at each stage of the employee life cycle (hiring, onboarding, development, retention, exit process, and alumni). They will identify alternate processes and implement them to improve functionality. Figure 5.1 shows the employee life-cycle stages and the HR role during each phase.

FIGURE 5.1   The employee life cycle

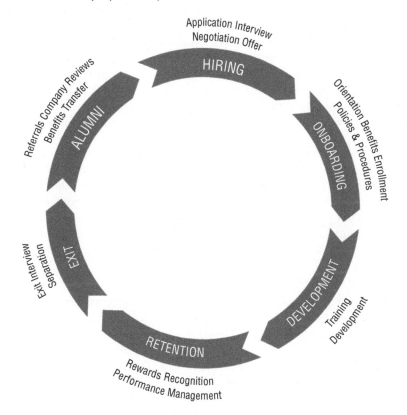

HR professionals have a responsibility to help management create and maintain an organizational culture that fosters positive employee relations. They must assess the culture and climate, implement programs that build on the foundation of the company, and measure the effectiveness of the programs once created to ensure that the company stays on the right track. To do this effectively, HR professionals are responsible for responding to emerging issues in a timely and fair-handed manner, investigating the circumstances using an unbiased approach, and then addressing any employee grievances. When cases warrant such, HR professionals are responsible for carrying out legal termination procedures that can withstand legal scrutiny to mitigate or prevent litigation.

Employee Engagement Data

HR professionals will collect, analyze, summarize, and communicate employee engagement data with managers, employees, and key leaders throughout the organization. Through a variety of metrics such as turnover ratios, survey results, and customer feedback, HR professionals should be able to gauge the level of employee engagement. Employee engagement is directly correlated to a positive organizational climate.

Organizational climate can be considered the pulse of the company. If the pulse is weak, it indicates something is not healthy within the body, whereas a strong pulse indicates strength internally. In the same way, HR professionals can establish practices to assess the pulse of the organization and determine its relative strength. Many tools can be used to assess the climate. We have discussed the wide use of surveys to get a general sense of concerns or perceptions. This last point is important. Surveys measure perceptions as the employees see things, which may or may not reflect the truth. However, it doesn't matter with respect to facts, as perceptions can often dictate actions that will impact the outcome. Strong employee relations mean that the HR professionals, management, and executives are managing the perceptions to better reflect the situation.

Other options for the HR professional include having sensing groups or internal meetings. This can take the form of skip-level interviews where HR bypasses management to go directly to line employees and get direct feedback. Doing so can result in an unfiltered assessment as the employees may see it. However, HR professionals must still be aware of perception bias. They must organize and conduct the sessions with employees and systematically solicit, organize, and present information and concerns shared by employees to develop an action plan to address them.

Using Metrics to Evaluate Employee Relations

As we have discussed in other chapters, developing and using metrics and analytics are important responsibilities in the HR function. Since employee relations are tied to the corporate culture and have a significant impact on the recruiting and retention of a strong, positive workforce, it is imperative that HR professionals understand how to use these tools and metrics to advance the organizational climate in a positive direction. HR professionals may, for example, conduct exit interviews with employees, especially focusing on those voluntarily separating from the company. Individual reasons may not offer much insight, but collectively trends will be useful to see key reasons employees are choosing to leave. If those reasons are within the span of control of management, it is their responsibility to make adjustments.

In looking at trends, HR professionals can gather and present the turnover data on the overall cost to recruit or rehire replacements, the loss of productivity, and the average life span of an employee in the company. If a company is constantly rehiring and replacing key positions, it will be virtually impossible to grow or improve because the company will be using its limited resources on covering the same ground each time with new employees.

Developing Strong Employee Relations Programs

Maintaining or building a strong culture requires input and effort on the part of management. HR professionals are ultimately responsible for developing and implementing employee relations programs to inspire and encourage the workforce. These programs celebrate diversity in the workplace, recognize the accomplishments of employees, and highlight special events. HR professionals work with leaders to determine the focus for these programs and use a planning process to establish the parameters, goals, and objectives. Table 5.5 gives some examples of these types of programs and their purpose.

TABLE 5.5   Employee relations programs

Program	Purpose
Diversity and inclusion	Promotes minority opportunities and recognizes contributions to the organization and community
Community involvement	Enables employees to reach members of the community through volunteering or assisting with company resources
Mentorship/peer support	Provides coaching and developing to employees among each other
Tuition assistance	Helps with continuing education of employees for job-related course study
Flexible schedule/ telecommuting	Facilitates flexibility for employees that can complete work with less supervision required and the ability to work remotely

Although each employee relations program may have a slightly different purpose, HR professionals are responsible for their successful development and implementation, including the following steps:

1. Determine the overarching goal and theme for the program.
2. Establish a timeline with scheduled meetings, incorporating feedback on the program specifics.
3. Gather resources for the program as needed.
4. Establish metrics, benchmarks, or standards for determining the program success.
5. Conduct the program.
6. Assess the results and determine the way ahead.

Implementing and Supporting Workplace Risk Management Programs

Risk cannot be eliminated or prevented completely. Therefore, it is the responsibility of the organization to manage the risks that are identified; in many cases, it becomes a primary responsibility of HR professionals to establish procedures to identify the risks in operational processes that would result in loss to the company. They must determine the likelihood that a loss would result, along with the criticality of the loss should it occur. Once this risk matrix is created as discussed in Chapter 1 (see Figure 1.4), the next step is to identify ways to reduce either the likelihood of occurrence or the severity of the loss. In this way, an HR professional can manage the risk and assist decision-makers in the company with establishing strong procedures that still allow the organization to achieve its mission and goals but do so in a consistently safe manner.

Compliance

Like other areas of human resources, risk management has a compliance component. Other compliance legislation is centered on ensuring that employees have equal opportunity and access to employment and training free from discrimination so that as employees, they are treated the same and paid fairly for their work. HR must also ensure that the company creates a workplace that considers and protects the health, safety, security, and privacy of the employees. HR must follow regulatory guidelines to protect the general safety of employees from routine hazards that can occur in any workplace. There also may be additional requirements based on the specific industry. Generally, the more dangerous the line of work, the more likely there will be further restrictions and compliance requirements that must be met.

Protecting health and safety means ensuring the physical well-being of an employee and can pertain to short-term incidents such as slips, trips, and falls or to sustained health and safety hazards such as chemicals or toxic inhalation exposure. HR professionals must follow reporting requirements on accidents that result in losses, damages, or significant injuries. There are also requirements to investigate root causes thoroughly and establish prevention strategies when accidents do occur. When there are long-term, systemic risks, the organization is responsible for ensuring that proper training is conducted and documented as required to maintain certifications or operational compliance. In addition to training, there may be a need for proper protective equipment for employees. HR may be responsible for coordinating ordering or fitting employees for necessary safety equipment. An example might be breathing filter equipment for employees using aerosols.

Security is both physical and virtual. Examples of physical security compliance are laws that are intended to prevent domestic or workplace violence. HR must be proactive in helping the organization secure its employees and prevent harm. Companies may have liability if they do not have proper protocols that could protect employees from physical threat or danger while on the job. From a virtual standpoint, this includes the safeguarding of every employee's personally identifiable information from unauthorized release or disclosure. HR must also ensure that employee information is not used for any purpose that is unauthorized or inconsistent with regulations or law. For example, there are now laws that limit how a company can obtain information about credit history or criminal records of employees. Privacy cannot exist without security. A company may have security procedures (discussed earlier in the chapter), but privacy is how the company then chooses to share or release that information.

Investigating Employee Complaints

HR professionals must be capable of resolving conflicts and complaints by employees with respect to employment practices and working conditions. They are responsible for assisting and participating in investigations on actions filed with the National Labor Relations Board or other regulatory agencies with jurisdiction. In cases where there are validated complaints, HR professionals must work to comply with federal and state regulations. This may require working closely with outside resources that are specialists or experts on labor practices.

Many companies choose to retain legal counsel that specializes in labor disputes for legal terminations or if charges of unfair labor practices are submitted against the organization. Working with these professionals, the HR team must collect and preserve documentation and provide policies and standard operating procedures, along with any statements collected or other correspondence that can dispute the claims. In some instances, companies and employees with complaints may seek or be required to use mediation or arbitration. This practice allows both parties to avoid costly litigation by having an independent, disinterested party review both sides and make a binding determination. In other words, both sides agree that the decision of the arbitrator will be final.

Disciplinary Policy

HR professionals are responsible for developing a discipline policy for the company. In doing so, they must consider the organizational culture and establish a strong ethical climate that seeks to administer discipline in a fair and judicious manner. HR professionals are instrumental in assisting the company executives to develop and promulgate a code of conduct that defines how employees should conduct themselves. In cases where there is a violation of these policies and standards, HR professionals are responsible for working with supervisors to determine the appropriate actions.

Generally, a company will have a progressive disciplinary policy, which seeks to use the lowest form of discipline to resolve minor infractions but increases with each subsequent violation or for more severe violations. It is important to realize that a progressive policy is not intended to restrict or limit the company's ability to separate employees who do not exhibit the required behaviors or align to the company's values but to ensure that there is due process. It is also the responsibility of HR professionals to assess whether discipline practices create a disparate impact that would impact the equal employment opportunity of every employee. They should review actions to ensure that there are no potential exceptions to the "at-will" practices in employment, that they comply with laws and regulations, and that they are proportional to the circumstances to include actions in the past.

HR professionals gather all documentation, show clearly why there is a need for disciplinary action, and recommend the appropriate course of action to take in the matter, up to and including termination. In cases where there is a union or arbitration clause, they coordinate with the stakeholders to determine a time to meet and resolve the issues. Ultimately, they ensure a fair process that can withstand the scrutiny of review.

Grievance Procedures

When resolving employee relations issues, HR professionals must be aware of and follow proper procedures. In instances of an employee disputing actions taken by the company for disciplinary reasons, there should be a process to handle grievances. In union settings, an employee has a right to have another individual attend interviews during investigation processes that could result in disciplinary actions being taken. These rights are formally known as the Weingarten rights, named after a legal labor case ruling by the Supreme Court. Usually there are formal steps that are part of a grievance. Figure 5.2 shows a typical grievance process.

FIGURE 5.2 Formal grievance process

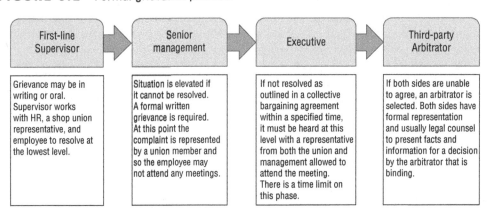

First-line Supervisor	Senior management	Executive	Third-party Arbitrator
Grievance may be in writing or oral. Supervisor works with HR, a shop union representative, and employee to resolve at the lowest level.	Situation is elevated if it cannot be resolved. A formal written grievance is required. At this point the complaint is represented by a union member and so the employee may not attend any meetings.	If not resolved as outlined in a collective bargaining agreement within a specified time, it must be heard at this level with a representative from both the union and management allowed to attend the meeting. There is a time limit on this phase.	If both sides are unable to agree, an arbitrator is selected. Both sides have formal representation and usually legal counsel to present facts and information for a decision by the arbitrator that is binding.

In the grievance process, HR professionals have the responsibility to do the following:

- Investigate thoroughly and be prepared for any litigation or mediation that may result from a complaint.
- Work with union officials that represent the employee and determine any company obligations as the result of union agreements.
- Document all findings and maintain all notes, records, or other correspondence related to the investigation.
- Avoid making individual concessions that set a precedent or conflict with existing policy or agreements with a union.
- Settle a grievance if the company is, in fact, wrong on the merits of the case.
- Continually communicate with the executives and decision-makers of the company on the progress of the dispute, grievance, and resolution.

The other circumstance in a grievance process is with performance. HR professionals must be responsible for ensuring that management has documented and truly performed the required steps in a performance improvement plan before dismissing an employee for failure to perform. This is certainly true in a union environment because it is likely that the collective bargaining agreement will have provisions that protect employees from being terminated for performance if these measures have not been done. HR professionals have the responsibility when developing performance policies to include the steps management must take to document employee performance deficiencies and corrective measures taken.

> In situations where a manager has a poorly performing employee, the manager will often seek HR's help in "getting rid of the bad employee." HR professionals must guard against this kind of action. This is because more often than not a manager has failed to document the deficiency properly and the failure has been going on for an extended period of time but there is now a catalyst that makes the manager want to take action. HR professionals must ensure that proper procedures are followed to avoid a grievance later.

Termination

HR professionals should develop and use a termination checklist when faced with separating an employee from employment with the company. This step-by-step procedure ensures that every termination is handled consistently and that nothing is left out that could result in litigation later. HR professionals are responsible for working with managers who have the authority to terminate an employee and cooperatively ensuring that the procedures are followed. This requires training for management in these practices, and HR should be present for any dismissal.

Terminations will always be an emotional event; however, it is imperative that HR professionals maintain a professional atmosphere even in the most hostile or tense situations where an employee may act out. If HR professionals ensure that the conduct of the termination is handled with dignity and respect for the employee, this may set the tone and result in a cordial separation.

A few years ago, I was required to terminate an employee with long ties to the organization. It was the practice of the company to offer the employee a chance to submit a letter of resignation instead of being terminated, which, in effect, removed their rights to formal grievance. It was felt that this individual would certainly file a grievance over the dismissal and that litigation was a likely outcome. However, in the course the termination meeting, the supervisor did a remarkable job of outlining the reasons for termination and still was respectful and professional with the employee. At the end of the meeting, the employee shook our hands and thanked us for being considerate and direct and offered the letter of resignation.

Another responsibility of HR professionals in developing a termination process is to examine other potential separation actions. For example, if a company downsizes, it may be necessary to terminate employees in a reduction in force or other structured action. By establishing proper guidelines and working with union representatives, HR professionals ensure that the company avoids claims of equal opportunity violations on any protected classes during separations. Things to consider as part of the termination process are who attends, the talking points, the collection and recovery of any company property, the removal of access to information systems or facilities, the retrieval of personal items or property from the work area, the arrangement for the continuation of benefits under COBRA and other mandatory disclosures, and any announcements to colleagues informing them of a change in status of employment (protocols).

Managing Labor Relations

While the organized labor movement changes over time and may not be as strong as in the past, it is a significant part of the U.S. workforce and therefore an important responsibility for HR professionals. Understanding the collective bargaining process and the associated requirements and being able to execute the task is something HR professionals must know how to do. It may be that the employees of a company never seek to organize; however, there is a responsibility to the organization that HR be prepared to participate in the election process, contract negotiations, and administration.

Senior HR professionals also have a responsibility to communicate with employees the benefits of remaining union free. However, they must ensure that they do not violate any rules that would result in an unfair labor practice charge, such as forming a select committee of employees to bring issues to management that would usurp a union's bargaining authority.

Exam Essentials

Review those programs and actions that improve organizational climate and promote strong, positive employee relations. It is an important function of the HR team to coach and develop managers and executives in improving their relationship with employees. The addition of programs and recognition of the contributions of all employees will continually motivate and encourage participation throughout the company. HR professionals should be aware that these programs rely on communications between the employees and the company to get feedback on the types of programs that best fit the culture.

Understand formal grievance and legal termination proceedings. Among the most difficult actions is the intentional removal from employment of an individual in the company. It is especially challenging if there are provisions within policies or contracts that require documentation or substantial justification to warrant termination. To avoid claims that could result in litigation or a successful grievance action, HR professionals must review each case and when necessary conduct an unbiased investigation and assessment for management to make a determination. It is important to consult with legal counsel to review procedures and case law.

Summary

The subject of employee and labor relations examines how to effectively manage the expectations and relationships between employees and management. It creates a framework to handle and resolve conflicts that arise between members of the team and, in some cases, provides guidance on disciplinary action. The labor laws of the United States are intricate and attempt to balance the needs of the company with the rights of the workers to have a fair wage with safe and reasonable working conditions. While union involvement and activity may not be as prevalent as in years past, they still play a vital role in labor within the United States and globally. It is vital that HR professionals understand the restrictions and limitations imposed by laws including the National Labor Relations Act.

The HR generalist taking the PHR® exam may be located in a right-to-work state or in a company without organized labor representation. However, this topic is still required knowledge and remains relevant even in these circumstances. It is still possible to violate provisions of the regulations and laws discussed in this chapter if one does not properly understand the context and requirements. Risk is a significant part of business, and great organizations take risks to ultimately succeed in their endeavors. However, unknown, unmitigated risks are unacceptable and will undoubtedly expose the organization to a great deal of potential litigation and liability. HR professionals must be able to effectively identify risks, understand how those risks can potentially disrupt the business, and offer solutions on how to reduce risk profile. They must champion safety practices and enforce standards that protect employees from illness and injury. At the same time, they must know proper procedures and practices to follow when an incident occurs and how to respond in the event of a disaster to recover the organization and maintain its viability. While there is technology available to use as tools to improve risk management, the most effective way is to have trained, knowledgeable workers and management that remain vigilant.

Test-Taking Tip

On the day of the exam, it is critical to remain focused. Testing centers are quiet and usually full of other testers. It is an atmosphere that most people are unaccustomed to. Since there are a lot of technical questions requiring analysis and understanding, you must prepare your mind to be ready for the environment. Read the questions carefully, but do not overthink the answer. Remember that the correct response is the best answer for the given scenario and may not necessarily be the same as how your particular company may choose to perform.

Review Questions

1. A company is located in a right-to-work state. In what way will this impact the organization?

    A. The company is permitted to establish committees that can represent employees on employment matters.

    B. The company is not required to hold elections to unionize if requested by the employees.

    C. Employees are not required to pay union dues within a required time frame to remain employed by the company.

    D. A company can terminate an employee for any reason with or without notice.

2. The NLRB was created as a result of _____ ?

    A. The WARN Act

    B. The Wagner Act

    C. Title VII

    D. None of the above

3. A company is facing possible unionization and has decided to counter the efforts by offering a $1,000 bonus to employees. This is an example of:

    A. A labor negotiation strategy

    B. A lock-out provision

    C. A rewards and recognition program

    D. An unfair labor practice

4. The at-will provision of employment means:

    A. An employee is not represented by a union.

    B. An employee must give and serve a notice if they voluntarily quit.

    C. A company can terminate an employee without any reason.

    D. Both A and C.

5. A company decides to conduct a climate assessment of the organization to gauge employee engagement. In conducting a survey, HR professionals should ensure which of the following?

    A. That employee responses are anonymous and free from retribution

    B. That the company discusses the results of the survey along with any plans to address the findings with employees

   C. That the survey is focused and asks specific questions to get answers to concerns by management

   D. All of the above

6. An employee who is involved in operations is offered an opportunity to be part of an internal quality assurance team because of their experience and in-depth knowledge of the process. What is this an example of?

   A. Job enlargement

   B. Job reward

   C. Job enrichment

   D. Performance improvement

7. Security risks can be categorized as:

   A. Physical and virtual

   B. Virtual and progressive

   C. Internal and external

   D. Progressive and advanced

8. All of the following are legal arguments that a senior HR professional can use in communicating to employees reasons for remaining union free, except which of the following?

   A. The company is in a better position to reward high performers if not restricted by a union agreement.

   B. The employees can provide input on committees formed by the company to represent their peers.

   C. Employees can have opportunities for cross training and new responsibility without union negotiation.

   D. The company already has policies and provisions in place that benefit employees without them being required to pay dues.

9. It is important that HR professionals conduct investigations in the workplace in an unbiased manner. Which of the following best describes actions they might take to ensure this?

   A. They interview only the supervisor in the course of the investigation.

   B. They investigate all past issues with an employee as part of the current problem or complaint.

   C. They do not require anyone to provide a written statement to allow them to speak freely.

   D. They attempt to resolve the issue in a timely manner and provide a written recommendation to the decision authority.

10. For minor infractions, a company may have a progressive discipline policy. Which of the following might be considered in deciding what would be best for a violation of an attendance policy?

A. Termination after two absences in the same month

B. A written reprimand for someone who has had no previous violations and has had only a recent series of tardiness incidents in which they informed their supervisor

C. A three-day suspension for an employee who previously was suspended for attendance issues last year

D. A verbal warning from the supervisor and a review of the attendance policy with the employee for failing to notify their supervisor in a timely manner

11. Employee relations programs are an important part of maintaining a positive, engaged workforce. Which of the following is *not* an example of these types of programs?

A. An employee-of-the-month award

B. A monthly history event that recognizes minority contributions to the company's history

C. A safety program established by the company

D. A suggestion box placed in the breakroom for the employees

12. A union employee is being disciplined for repeated policy violations and receives a three-day suspension. In a grievance action, the HR professional should ensure which of the following first?

A. That all incidents have been documented by the supervisory chain

B. That the decided action is covered under the union agreement

C. That the grievance is reviewed by the CEO before proceeding with a suspension

D. That the case is reviewed by legal counsel

13. The Occupational Safety and Health Administration provides support to organizations that seek to improve their operational safety program by doing what?

A. Providing standards and practices to establish proper procedures

B. Deciding who is at fault when an incident occurs

C. Allowing exemptions based on a successful track record without accidents in a company

D. None of the above

14. When employees believe that unsafe conditions exist in a company, one of their rights that they may exercise is to _____ .

A. File a formal complaint with the union.

B. Procure proper safety equipment or modify procedures as they see fit to address the conditions.

C. Notify their supervisor and demand that changes be made.

D. Request an independent inspection to determine compliance and provide recommendations.

15. Some examples of illness and injury prevention include all of the following except which one?

    A. Establishing protocols for preventing transmission of blood-borne pathogens

    B. Deciding to acquire an AED for the company

    C. Training new workers on the proper use of a forklift in a warehouse

    D. Completing accident reports and making them available to review by employees

16. The first action HR professionals should take upon notification of an incident that may result in a workers' compensation claim is which of the following?

    A. Secure the accident scene.

    B. Determine whether the incident was the result of negligence.

    C. File an accident report.

    D. Notify the insurance carrier.

17. In detecting potential warning signs of the threat of workplace violence, which of the following is most relevant?

    A. A disagreement between co-workers over the proper procedures to follow in a complex operation that gets a bit heated.

    B. A radical change in behavior, sudden loss of status in work, and multiple disciplinary actions in a short time of an employee.

    C. A repeat of minor mistakes that stems from a lack of training or job awareness.

    D. It is impossible to detect signs of workplace violence in advance, and employers should only focus resources in responding to crisis events.

SPHR®

PART

II

What This Part Covers

Chapters 6–10 of this book are dedicated to the SPHR®
exam and cover all the topics and information needed to successfully pass this exam for senior HR professionals. These
chapters stand alone as the only content portion of the book
needed. The first half of the book is not required reading if
you intend to take the SPHR® exam only. You may choose to
review some of the material and compare the difference, but it
is not necessary for the purpose of exam preparation.

Chapter 6

Leadership and Strategy

THE SPHR® EXAM CONTENT FROM THE LEADERSHIP AND STRATEGY FUNCTIONAL AREA COVERED IN THIS CHAPTER CONSISTS OF THE FOLLOWING RESPONSIBILITIES AND KNOWLEDGE AREAS. RESPONSIBILITIES:

✓ **01** Develop and execute HR plans that are aligned to the organization's strategic plan (for example: HR strategic plans, budgets, business plans, service delivery plans, HRIS, technology)

✓ **02** Evaluate the applicability of federal laws and regulations to organizational strategy (for example: policies, programs, practices, business expansion/reduction)

✓ **03** Analyze and assess organizational practices that impact operations and people management to decide on the best available risk management strategy (for example: avoidance, mitigation, acceptance)

✓ **04** Interpret and use business metrics to assess and drive achievement of strategic goals and objectives (for example: key performance indicators, financial statements, budgets)

✓ **05** Design and evaluate HR data indicators to inform strategic actions within the organization (for example: turnover rates, cost per hire, retention rates)

✓ **06** Evaluate credibility and relevance of external information to make decisions and recommendations (for example: salary data, management trends, published surveys and studies, legal/regulatory analysis)

✓ 07   Contribute to the development of the organizational strategy and planning (for example: vision, mission, values, ethical conduct)

✓ 08   Develop and manage workplace practices that are aligned with the organization's statements of vision, values, and ethics to shape and reinforce organizational culture

✓ 09   Design and manage effective change strategies to align organizational performance with the organization's strategic goals

✓ 10   Establish and manage effective relationships with key stakeholders to influence organizational behavior and outcomes

IN ADDITION TO THE PRECEDING RESPONSIBILITIES, AN INDIVIDUAL TAKING THE SPHR® EXAM SHOULD HAVE WORKING KNOWLEDGE OF THE FOLLOWING AREAS, USUALLY DERIVED THROUGH PRACTICAL EXPERIENCE:

✓ 01   Vision, mission, and values of an organization and applicable legal and regulatory requirements

✓ 02   Strategic planning process

✓ 03   Management functions, including planning, organizing, directing, and controlling

✓ 04   Corporate governance procedures and compliance

✓ 05   Business elements of an organization (for example: products, competition, customers, technology, demographics, culture, processes, safety and security)

✓ 06   Third-party or vendor selection, contract negotiation, and management, including development of requests for proposals (RFPs)

✓ 07   Project management (for example: goals, timetables, deliverables, and procedures)

✓ 08   Technology to support HR activities

✓ **09** Budgeting, accounting, and financial concepts (for example: evaluating financial statements, budgets, accounting terms, and cost management)

✓ **10** Techniques and methods for organizational design (for example: outsourcing, shared services, organizational structures)

✓ **11** Methods of gathering data for strategic planning purposes (for example: Strengths, Weaknesses, Opportunities, and Threats [SWOT], and Political, Economic, Social, and Technological [PEST])

✓ **12** Qualitative and quantitative methods and tools used for analysis, interpretation, and decision-making purposes

✓ **13** Change management processes and techniques

✓ **14** Techniques for forecasting, planning, and predicting the impact of HR activities and programs across functional areas

✓ **15** Risk management

✓ **16** How to deal with situations that are uncertain, unclear, or chaotic

This is the first chapter that examines content for the Senior Professional in Human Resources exam. In Functional Area 01, Leadership and Strategy, the senior HR professional learns the importance of leading the HR function by developing HR strategy, contributing to organizational strategy, influencing people management practices, and monitoring risk. This chapter covers material that represents 40 percent of the SPHR® exam. Because of its weight, it is the most important chapter to review for the exam. While there is some overlap with information in Chapter 1, the focus is quite different as senior HR professionals are responsible on a strategic level for decisions and for assessing the impact to the organization at a higher level.

Required Knowledge

It is important that we continually grow in our knowledge as we progress to become senior HR professionals. Knowledge comes from either personal experience or the study of the experiences and lessons taught to us by others. Human resources professionals preparing for the SPHR® exam must possess certain knowledge acquired from experience or study. In this chapter, the knowledge portion reviews business concepts practiced at the higher levels of an organization usually beyond the transactional.

Mission, Vision, and Values

Human resources professionals must know the mission, vision, and values of the company. In many of their tasks discussed later in the chapter, they function as the champion, interpreter, or arbitrator of these concepts to the employees. The mission of the company is usually expressed as a short statement sentence describing the purpose of the company's existence. It should be overarching and usually is an infinitive statement to do something. It answers the question, "Why?"

The vision of a company looks at the future and paints a vivid picture of what the organization will look like as it grows, develops, or changes over time. The vision considers where the organization is currently and describes where it wants to go. A vision must be able to be consistently repeated by employees to be effective. In other words, they are all able to describe the same picture. Vision statements should be simple to be effective and, in some instances, consist of only a phrase or a couple of words. Table 6.1 shows some mission and vision statements from familiar organizations.

TABLE 6.1   Sample mission and vision statements

Statement	Company
"The Walt Disney Company's objective is to be one of the world's leading producers and providers of entertainment and information, using its portfolio of brands to differentiate its content, services and consumer products." https://thewaltdisneycompany.com/about/	Walt Disney Company
"As a leader in the global steel industry, we are dedicated to delivering high-quality products to our customers and building value for all of our stakeholders." https://www.ussteel.com	U.S. Steel
"Empower every person and organization on the planet to achieve more." https://www.microsoft.com/en-us/about/default.aspx	Microsoft
"The mission of Southwest Airlines is dedication to the highest quality of customer service delivered with a sense of warmth, friendliness, individual pride, and company spirit." http://investors.southwest.com/our-company/purpose-vision-values-and-mission	Southwest Airlines

Values are the foundation of how a company is going to perform its mission and achieve its vision. From the HR perspective, a goal is to ensure that employee behaviors are aligned with the values of the organization. When behaviors are not aligned, the resulting issues and negative outcomes can impact performance management, employee relations, and human resources development, all of which are reviewed in later chapters. Values must be communicated and modeled consistently throughout the organization to be effective. It is always the values that are practiced, not the ones that are written, that define how the organization conducts itself.

Corporate Governance and Compliance

Knowledge of rules and regulations also relates to corporate governance procedures and compliance. Senior HR professionals are responsible for knowing current reporting requirements with respect to laws such as the Sarbanes-Oxley Act.

The Sarbanes-Oxley Act of 2002

The Sarbanes-Oxley Act of 2002, or SOX, was enacted following several public corporate and accounting scandals that occurred in the early 2000s. It set standards of corporate governance, oversight, auditing independence, and enhanced financial disclosure. To review the law, you can visit www.sec.gov/about/laws/soa2002.pdf.

Corporate governance procedures vary based on the type of company (private, public, not-for-profit) and the number of employees. In addition to federal statutes, the organization may be subject to state provisions depending on which states the company does business in. Also, international corporations have added compliance requirements throughout the globe, especially throughout Europe and Asia.

These are elements of corporate governance to review:

- Board composition and election of officers
- Corporate responsibility statements and ethics
- Conflict of interest policies and procedures
- Internal and external auditing practices
- Financial disclosure statements
- Whistleblower protection

Human resources should have working knowledge of the activities surrounding these elements and the input that is provided. For example, it is not necessary to know how to do a full audit of the agency. However, senior HR professionals will provide documents such as payroll records and personnel files to verify or validate parts of the audited reports. HR professionals must know how their functional activities are tied to others within the organization.

Beyond this specific law, senior HR professionals must evaluate the applicability of federal, state, and local laws to the organization. Often as organizations grow, new requirement thresholds are met that trigger compliance. For example, when a private company exceeds 100 employees, it is mandated to file the EEO1 report to the Equal Employment Opportunity Commission that evaluates the diversity of the company. Because senior HR professionals are the chief architects of HR-related policies and programs, they must ensure that these policies comply with the laws and regulations, including any regulatory findings.

Strategic Planning Process

The elements of the strategic planning process illustrated in Figure 6.1 include design, implementation, and evaluation. At each phase, senior HR professionals provide key input to ensure that the process moves forward and accomplishes the goals and objectives established.

FIGURE 6.1   Phases of the strategic planning process

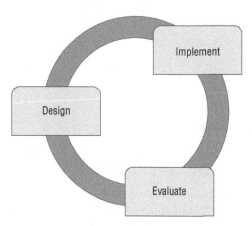

The key to a successful implementation is communication throughout the organization. Stakeholders must understand their role and contribution to the plan to have "buy-in." This is particularly important in overcoming internal resistance that exists in companies with long-term employees, long-standing practices, and traditions where change is imminent.

Remember, all strategy begins with the organization's most core elements: its mission, vision, and values. Key to any other aspect of this chapter is the understanding that without a clear mission or vision it is impossible to develop a cohesive, effective strategy. Part of the function of human resources is to ensure that every employee's behavior is consistent with the stated values of the organization and that their actions continually drive the organization toward the vision established by the executive leadership. Most dysfunction in an organization happens as a result of failing to align people to values, not understanding the mission, or having a murky vision that cannot be vividly seen by everyone.

Strengths, Weaknesses, Opportunities, and Threats (SWOT)

These four areas look at the positive and negative influences, both internal and external to an organization, that impact operations, strategic objectives, and the overall success of the company. Senior HR professionals must know how to assess these four areas accurately and honestly to make competent recommendations to the organizational leadership. Strengths and weaknesses refer to the internal capabilities of a company and how well (or not) it can meet its goals. For example, are there any unique skills that a company has that can set it apart in the market, or does it have challenges that are preventing it from reaching its maximum potential? By identifying strengths, the company hopes to exploit what it does well and find more situations that allow it to grow. Conversely, a company must identify weaknesses and find ways to minimize their effect on the company's mission.

Externally, the company should look for opportunities in the market, such as a new product line or innovation that improves a business process to increase market share or revenue to the company. These external events are often limited in time, so senior HR professionals should be aware of how to seize these moments when presented. In a similar manner, threats pose risk to the company through external influence by competitors, new products, changes in customer behaviors, or other influences that will decrease a company's ability to stay relevant and competitive. A great example would be Blockbuster video stores—once extremely profitable, they ultimately were put out of business with the advancement of streaming technology that allowed direct-to-consumer purchases.

Political, Economic, Social, and Technological (PEST)

As discussed with opportunities and threats in SWOT, political, economic, social, and technological factors can influence a business. Senior HR professionals must be aware of these environmental conditions to advise decision-makers in the organization. For example, political changes such as the regulatory environment or new laws with changes in political administrations can have a large impact on decisions concerning human capital. As the economy improves or declines, it often will have an impact on operational decisions and cash flow to the business. Customer attitudes, social pressure, and corporate responsibility are social impacts that might affect policy decisions or corporate strategy. In the example of Blockbuster, the technological advancement of the Internet and streaming video was the proximate cause of the company's downfall.

These areas are interrelated and therefore overlap. So, senior HR professionals should analyze how they intersect and where the company can take actions to minimize the severity with which they will impact the company's bottom line. It is difficult to predict future events, but to the best of their abilities, senior HR professionals must know how current events and items in the news could eventually reach the organization and be in a position to make timely recommendations to take advantage of the situation.

Management Functions

Senior HR professionals should understand four major management functions as part of business functions.

Planning   Planning involves all aspects of preparation, problem-solving, strategic assessments, and environmental scanning. This function looks forward to likely project outcomes and the necessary courses of action capable of meeting future needs. Tasks performed in the Planning function include forecasting, setting goals and objectives, and conducting assessments.

Organizing   As part of the Organizing function, a corporation will use available resources to design systems, procedures, and policies; structure their organization; and determine lines of authority and responsibility for conducting operations. Table 6.2 lists the most important methods and tools that assist this process.

TABLE 6.2 Organizing tools

Tool	Definition
Delegation	Process of management assigning authority and responsibility to subordinates to complete a task
Flow charts (Gantt and PERT charts)	A Gantt chart is a horizontal bar chart that shows several components of a project that flow simultaneously over a period of time; a PERT (program evaluation and review technique) chart organizes projects to reveal sequencing of events and decision points
Calendar	Long-range planning calendars that synchronize operations across divisions in an organization and are part of integrated master scheduling activities.

Directing   This function involves the active leadership needed to ensure that goals are met and employees' behaviors and performance align with the organization's mission, vision, and values. Continual assessments and review of performance metrics help gauge and direct the actions of managers to carry out daily tasks.

Controlling   This function serves as the check on progress for how the outcomes predicted in Planning match the actual performance and determining where gaps are and how they can be corrected or mitigated. As with Organizing, there are several tools and methods that can be used for this function, listed in Table 6.3.

TABLE 6.3 Methods used in Controlling

Method	Description
Audits	Internal or external evaluations of the business processes, controls, or systems to compare practices against industry standards or other qualitative or quantitative metrics
Internal controls	Measures developed and used by the organization that check the integrity or accuracy of a process designed to prevent loss
Project management techniques	A variety of methods or models that plan, schedule, and manage projects

Techniques for Forecasting, Planning, and Predicting the Impact of HR Activities and Programs across Functional Areas

Senior HR professionals do not come equipped with a crystal ball to foretell the future. However, predictive analysis based on available information is a required skill. Modern business planning uses historical data to build models that can estimate how certain activities will be affected by HR decisions. As discussed in Chapter 1, the HR strategy and plans must be synchronized with the organization as a whole. For example, human capital projections can look at how many employees will be needed over a time period based on growth of the company or the increases to salaries or benefits costs. Such projections might also be an indicator for the consumption of office supplies or demands for technology, such as information system user accounts.

The most common technique in modeling is to look at past historical data for trends that can be beneficial if the company is relatively stable or with a predictable growth. For a rapidly changing company or one that is leading an industry where no trends exist, this technique has a shortfall. In those cases, HR can develop a rapid, iterative process to assess accuracy of predictions and make adjustments more readily. In this situation, the HR team might plan separately in a parallel planning process to be unencumbered by other departments but still responsive to changes. The other option is to plan in series; here, HR waits on each department to submit its plans and then conducts an analysis and estimate based on what other departments provide. Workforce planning and human resources development are two functional areas of HR that require attention for predicting the impact across other functions of the company.

The end state of a comprehensive planning process is an effective service delivery plan showing how the company intends to provide HR services across all functional departments or divisions and to each employee regardless of location. This may be direct support or a combination of shared services, contracted from third-party vendors, and internal resources.

Handling Uncertainty and Unclear or Chaotic Situations

At the strategic level of an organization, situations are often fluid enough that senior HR professionals need the skill of adaptability in ever-changing situations. It is impossible to be 100 percent certain of any decision or outcome, and often situations can go from stable to chaotic rapidly. Senior HR professionals must be proactive in gathering available information and using their knowledge of the organization to make educated guesses and recommendations that allow the company to keep moving forward. The situation may not provide the clarity these professionals desire, but they must be comfortable in their knowledge of best practices and HR fundamentals to be confident in decisions even without the availability of certain information or in unclear circumstances.

Business Elements of an Organization

Senior HR professionals are expected to know more than the basics of HR delivery. They must have business savvy. They should strive to understand the components of the business in which they operate and how they are all linked together. More importantly, they must understand how HR impacts each function and element at the strategic level and be able to support executives with timely and accurate information to make decisions. Table 6.4 lists some of the business elements and key knowledge points about their function.

TABLE 6.4   Business elements of an organization

Element	Description	Role of HR
Products	Goods or services that a company produces for market that generate a stream of revenue	HR must know how to recruit and train labor to perform tasks that produce these products, and they must know how the production of various products impacts the company financially.
Competition	Other companies that produce a similar good in the same market as the organization	Competition will impact the availability and cost of labor for the market.
Customers	Individuals or groups who are consumers of the products delivered by the company	Awareness of customers is needed for soft skills and technical training and for the development of employees.
Technology	Includes all systems and automation that improves efficiency, quality, or capability of an organization, often leading to a competitive advantage	Technological requirements often demand a higher-skilled labor force with specialized knowledge, skills, or abilities. HR must be aware of these demands in workforce planning.
Demographics	The diversity of the organization in terms of gender, race, educational background, age, social status, or other grouping of people internal or external to the company	The intentional diversification of an organization is essential for the development of new ideas or products. Senior HR professionals must be familiar with programs designed to cultivate diversity.
Culture	The ethos of the company often defined in its mission, vision, and values and exhibited by its employees	Through the creation and implementation of policies and programs, the senior HR professional will shape the organizational culture and then model behaviors designed to support and enhance that culture.
Processes	Sequential actions that are documented and followed to execute tasks consistently to produce a desired outcome	HR will help the organization design and implement processes that meet the goals and objectives of the company.
Safety and Security	All elements that are designed to protect the well-being of employees and limit risk or liability due to loss within the company	The knowledge of how to design and implement programs and policies, compliant with laws and regulations, that create a safe and secure working environment is critical for senior HR professionals.

Technology to Support HR Activities

A variety of technology and tools are available to support senior HR professionals and accomplish the tasks to be performed. In general, human resources information systems (HRISs) are the electronic hub to store, access, and analyze HR data on employees in the organization. There are many vendors and programs that can be used to accomplish this, and the choice largely depends on the size and type of organization. These systems range from storing basic personal data all the way to massive databases with thousands of fields. Obviously, the more complex a system, the more training involved for its users, and the need to ensure data accuracy. Many systems have a self-service function that allows the individual employee to update certain elements to increase timeliness and accuracy of the data being stored. It presumes that an employee entering information such as home address is more likely to be accurate with their own information than someone performing data entry based on written information on a paper form that must be transposed and uploaded to a digital record.

In addition to storage of information, senior HR professionals must be familiar with systems for e-learning and learning management systems (LMS) that are available to train and develop employees in the organization. These systems have access controls and content management requirements that are controlled by senior HR professionals responsible for organizational development. Additionally, a company might use an applicant tracking system (ATS) as part of its recruiting structure to allow candidates for employment to complete applications online and then filter, sort, and evaluate the applicants in the digital space. There is often a communication module as part of the ATS that allows the HR team to communicate with an applicant to schedule interviews or request additional information to determine the best-qualified applicants and to make a hiring decision. These systems collectively improve processes and HR functions in the daily delivery of services discussed in Chapters 2–5, but they also have a significant impact on the reduction of risk associated with data loss and breaches by having standardized practices, backup, and storage of critical HR-related information for the company.

Change Management Theory, Methods, and Application

Change is a natural part of the growth of organizations. Failure to recognize change could prevent a company from adapting to new business conditions. Consider the last company to make horse-drawn carriages for wide use; they might very well have been the best maker of such transportation. However, with the creation of the automobile, their function today has changed to be for recreation or novelty in a niche market. Senior leaders must constantly review technology, public demand, and the availability of alternatives to meet the needs of the consumer. It is easy to accept that things change; however, in practice, the reality is that managing change effectively is difficult. Senior HR professionals must understand how to manage change as a process and function of the company.

There are numerous change management theories. Among them are Kotter's theory, Lewin's change management model, and the nudge theory, to name a few. For some examples and explanations, refer to https://www.process.st/change-management-models/. A senior HR professional should have more than a rudimentary understanding of these theories, because they are responsible often to be the change managers or work with employees and managers that are experiencing change. In general, the organization recognizes a need for change and a desired end state once the change is implemented. Next, the organization must prepare for the change and communicate the significance and importance of the change to the employees to gain support and momentum to adopt the change. Then the company implements the change and must include a process to evaluate how the change is being received and integrated into current operations. Finally, the company reaches a new stasis having fully accepted and assimilating the change. This process continues as the needs for change keep presenting themselves.

Types of Organizational Structures

Structure is important for a company, and senior HR professionals must understand how a company is organized to perform critical tasks essential to operations. Often senior HR professionals must know the various departments or teams and how they are interconnected to establish policies over personnel transfers, evaluations, promotions, and other routine HR actions. Each organization is different, so there may be slight variations in how the organizational structure develops as a company expands. Senior HR professionals examine how a company's structure will impact its human capital, management, and operational control. This provides them the ability to advise corporate executives as to the best approach when making structural decisions.

Two common approaches to organizational structure are the matrix and hierarchy methods. In a hierarchy, the structure resembles a pyramid; the chief decision-maker such as a chief executive officer, president, or chairperson is the ultimate head of the organization responsible for all actions and the accomplishment of the mission, vision, and values of the company. Below the organizational head might be division heads, then lower management, and finally teams of employees. In this kind of structure, there is a general stovepipe of information, and the flow tends to go up and down with little contact across. Figure 6.2 shows an example of an organizational hierarchy.

The other common structure is a matrix. This example is often shown as a series of groups or equal parts all sharing responsibilities for the execution of the company mission. In these environments, information can flow across as well as up and down. While it may seem that this would be a preferred method given the more open communication, it has its own unique challenges. For example, there can be too much information sharing or conflicting guidance based on different priorities or interpretations of the needs. People who work in a matrix environment must be more disciplined when resolving problems because of their access and ability to impact a far greater portion of the company with each decision. In Figure 6.3, you can see the differences in structure compared to the hierarchical organization shown previously.

FIGURE 6.2   Hierarchical organizational structure

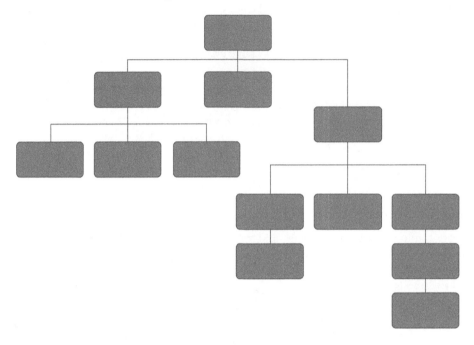

FIGURE 6.3   Matrix organizational structure

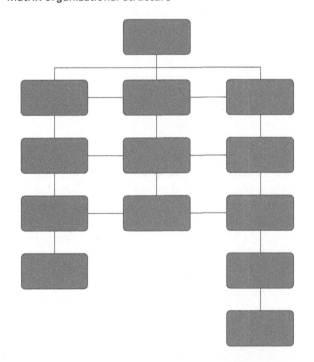

Third-Party or Vendor Selection, Contract Negotiation, and Management

Some shared HR support services that have been discussed in the book are sometimes better handled by an outside entity that specializes in the skills needed to perform the functions. This helps the organization streamline processes and focus on their core competencies. Senior HR professionals must be familiar with the steps and skills needed to determine which outside group or third party will be selected and must be able to negotiate the terms of a contract that will be beneficial to all parties involved. Once a contract has been established, senior HR professionals may be responsible for administering the contract and providing oversight on the vendor to ensure that the agreed-upon services are being performed according to the terms of the agreement.

A request for proposal (RFP) is a formal process whereby the organization that needs a service creates a statement outlining the work to be done, the terms and limitations of the requirements, and any other stipulations needed to perform the service in a satisfactory manner. The RFP is then announced publicly for outside vendors to submit bids or proposals that outline how they would complete the work. These proposals often have additional information, including previous work or other documentation that demonstrates their ability to do the job according to the specifications and the overall cost of the proposal. The company that receives the bids can then objectively evaluate and compare the proposals based on a set of determined criteria and choose the entity that best meets the needs of the company.

The acceptance of a bid generally constitutes a contract that both parties agree to. The contracting company then must manage and monitor the contracted services to ensure that they are being performed according to the terms. In cases where the services are not performed to the standards, this may constitute a breach of contract and would result in some penalties, usually outlined in the original RFP or as part of the agreement. Large corporations and government entities usually have a lengthy and formalized RFP process to protect the integrity of the overall work being produced and thus minimize the impact of any third parties whose inability to deliver as promised would threaten the continued productivity of the organization.

Outsourcing and Service Centers

Sometimes a corporate strategy will be to focus on only the core competencies of the organization. To do this, they will seek to remove all the areas in the business model that are not directly related to those competencies. In many cases, those functions can be done by other companies or service centers that specialize in niche capabilities and reduce overall costs. These cost savings can then go back into the core functions to develop or refine the products or services the company seeks to deliver to the public.

Cost-Benefit Analysis   Corporations when determining courses of action will often do a cost-benefit analysis that considers several factors related to the amount of capital expenditure required for a given result. It is important to note that some costs are not strictly monetary.

Vendor Selection and Alternatives   The process to select outside sources begins with identifying and evaluating alternatives to executing the work inside the organization. If the company has done a cost-benefit analysis and concludes that outsourcing an HR service or capability is best, the HR department will help develop the statement of work and/or the requirements needed for contracting outside vendors. They may help determine the suitability and completeness of proposals submitted and whether they meet technical qualifications. They may also be responsible agents for the company to monitor the performance of the vendors and assess whether the vendor is meeting its obligations under a contract or agreement.

Since many of the services that may be outsourced in human resources can directly affect the welfare of employees, senior HR professionals must be diligent in determining which functions can be transferred outside the company and which should remain in-house. Otherwise, something that may be a cost savings to the company could negatively impact morale if the quality or responsiveness is lower when outsourced.

Transitioning or Implementing New Systems   HR may sometimes take the role of project leader to oversee the transition and implementation of new systems, service centers, and outsourcing. Senior HR professionals will use project management techniques to plan, acquire, implement, and maintain these new systems within the company. Figure 6.4 shows steps for the implementation of a new service center by an organization.

FIGURE 6.4   Implementation of a new service center

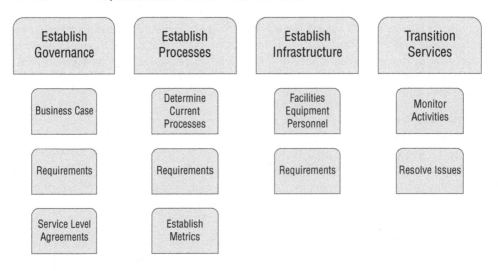

Consolidating shared support services across business lines or companies requires evaluation of the business case that is driven by cost savings and profitability. An organization determines what services will be shared, what processes must change with the support changes, what requirements are in terms of manpower and resources, and how the changes will be monitored through the implementation.

Tools for Measuring, Evaluating, and Analysis

Senior HR professionals must be proficient in the knowledge of how to design, measure, and evaluate strategic outcomes. There are a variety of tools available for project management, quantitative and qualitative analysis, and risk management. Proper analysis of the available data will help management formulate and refine strategic plans within the planning process.

Project Management Concepts and Applications

Project management is its own field of study and has its own certification and credentials similar to HR. Senior HR professionals will manage a multitude of projects that are related to HR and other business management functions. In general, project management begins with its foundation, defining the scope of the project and how it will be managed. From this point, a project is initiated by establishing the parameters including time, cost, risk management, and human capital. The project is planned, executed, and monitored throughout the project life cycle and is finally closed at its completion. The Project Management Professional (PMP) certification is reserved for those certified individuals in project management. For more detailed information, I recommend reviewing *PMP Project Management Professional Exam Review Guide* (Sybex, 2016). Project management provides a structured approach to solving complex problems and managing large events in a systematic method using controls and procedures that are generally accepted as best practices. While it is not necessary for senior HR professionals to also be certified PMPs, an understanding of the functions will be helpful in their daily work.

Budgeting, Accounting, and Financial Concepts

Senior HR professionals are not accountants, but understanding the most basic financial concepts is essential to being successful. The greatest shortcoming in our profession is our ability to understand budgets and the financial stability of the organization. Pay increases, training costs, company-paid benefits, and many other HR elements have a direct impact on the budget, so it is imperative that senior HR professionals communicate constantly with the finance department and maintain a fluid understanding of their issues and concerns.

One fundamental concept to understand is the general ledger, which maintains the record of all financial transactions of the organization. Accounting guidelines will group each entry into categories to organize the information and properly account for all expenditures, identify sources of revenue, and prepare required financial documentation and reports. In a similar manner, profit and loss (P&L) is a category of financial statements that show the profitability of the organization by comparing income to spending. The financial statement that shows the overall net worth of the organization by comparing assets to liabilities is the balance sheet.

With budgeting, the financial team attempts to program out, usually over a year, the projected revenues and expenditures. In HR, it is important to capture all the costs including payroll, recruiting, marketing, and training to determine how much money and resources need to be allocated to achieve the HR functions. In most cases, the available funds will have a limit, and HR must work within this constraint, so they must program crucial spending first and advocate strongly when resources may be cut. Simultaneously, they must understand that they are only one area of the company and not always the priority when money is tight. However, this should not prevent them from making the case to prioritize some of the available resources to human capital. Companies that do well have a balance between human capital needs and other elements of the business.

Qualitative and Quantitative Methods and Tools

Qualitative and quantitative methods and tools are needed for analysis, interpretation, and decision-making purposes. A simplified way of understanding these concepts is that qualitative methods answer the question, "How well?" and quantitative methods answer the question, "How much or how many?" Two important questions for HR to understand are the following:

Are we doing the right (proper) things?

Are we doing things right (correctly)?

To answer these questions, HR professionals have a variety of tools and measures they can use. These tools establish metrics with benchmarks to measure performance and effectiveness in core competencies throughout the organization. They use methods such as a cost-benefit analysis discussed in the book to determine whether a course of action will provide sufficient return on investment (ROI) to overcome any possible negative consequences to that same decision. Finally, senior HR professionals can examine and understand financial statements to measure recruiting costs, payroll expenses, benefits, and other costs that impact the profitability of the company and make recommendations or adjustments to improve the financial position of the organization.

Quantitative methods include mathematical sets such as statistical averages, regression analysis, or standard deviations. These formulas are tools for HR professionals to determine average salaries in a pay group, the relationship of variables such as education level to starting salary in statistical modeling, and the range and distribution of salaries in a pay group.

Risk Management Techniques

Chapter 10 discusses in depth the associated concepts of risk management as a responsibility of senior HR professionals; however, a core knowledge point is the understanding of the choices an organization has about risk in general. These risk management techniques define how an organization will proceed to address the risk once identified. The general choices are avoidance, mitigation, transference, and acceptance. Each choice seeks to address the risk in a manner that is acceptable by the company and is consistent with the organizational values.

In avoiding risk, the company elects not to pursue a goal or perform a task because the risk is too great and cannot otherwise be resolved. While this is an option, it comes with the loss of an opportunity to benefit from a positive outcome. Generally, however, the choice to avoid may come after a risk-reward or cost-benefit analysis and a determination is made that the risks far outweigh the potential positive outcome, which is not assured.

Mitigation is the choice most often agreed upon by an organization. The company seeks ways to reduce the identified risks through implementation of controls and measures and leaves a residual risk. It is impossible to remove all risk in this case, but with mitigation, the risk is now below the value of the positive result expected and can be supported in a business decision.

Transferring risk is not mitigation because the total risk is still present. However, the area exposed might be different and therefore have less impact to the overall organization. Insurance is an example of risk transference where a company hedges against loss by providing a premium to a provider that calculates the likelihood of loss. Workers' compensation insurance and employer group health coverage are examples of transferring risk to employees and the organization.

The final option is acceptance, which means that the executives responsible for decisions in the organization have underwritten the risk as a function of the work to be performed and are fully aware of the consequences of a negative outcome. Ultimately, any residual risk falls in this category regardless of the other three choices. It is imperative that senior HR professionals understand that they must identify risks to the organization related to HR actions but that it is a function of the executive to choose to accept that risk. The greatest danger is that they are often underwriting risk that they do not fully understand or are not aware of.

Exam Essentials

Know how the mission, vision, and values of a company interrelate. Companies exist for a purpose, usually to deliver a product or service to a consumer. When the company is organized, the executive team charts the course of the company defining these three elements. Often, they come in the form of a statement or summary, but what is essential to understand is that the actions of the company define these concepts, not what it says on paper. You should review your company's mission, vision, and values as well as those of other organizations and look at how each organization defines its own purpose.

Review the strategic planning process. The strategic planning process is a formalized way of defining a problem, developing courses of action, evaluating those choices, and selecting and implementing the best course for the organization. It is a continuous cycle looking at the big picture of the company, not the granular details, usually with overarching themes and goals. Some companies get caught trading off the important for the urgent and fail to look at long-term issues until they are too big or there is insufficient time to address them. Reviewing this process will help you effectively understand large-scale decisions made by the company beyond day-to-day operations.

Review core business concepts and functions. One of the greatest criticisms of senior HR professionals is that they lack common business competencies and view HR in isolated terms. It is important to review each of the functions of business and how they impact HR and, more importantly, how HR impacts them. Pay particular attention to those functions in business such as accounting that have mirror processes or are closely related to HR functions. The more general business knowledge you possess, the more fluent you will be in terminology and concepts.

Responsibilities

The SPHR® exam asks questions related to the responsibilities of a senior HR professional. These are the tasks that senior professionals in human resources *do* every day. In Functional Area 01: Leadership and Strategy, these tasks relate to the higher-order strategic and transformational functions. These tasks are specific only to senior HR professionals, so only individuals taking the SPHR® exam will have questions on those responsibilities.

Development of a Strategic Plan

Strategy refers to how an organization or individual thinks about the business model and what outcomes are desired. Business management is the practical application and end result of the strategy. Organizations develop and execute a strategy and then evaluate the results to determine whether the desired outcome has been attained. Senior HR professionals must have a clear understanding and knowledge of basic business concepts and processes beyond the HR functions. The more a senior HR professional can know about how certain functions work in a company, including operations, the more responsive they can be with timely and accurate HR support. This section will look at the elements associated with strategy followed by those associated with business management.

Gathering Information from Internal Sources

As a senior HR professional, you are part of a network within the organization that optimally should be working to achieve the same goals at the strategic level. Each department within the organization should be integrated and collaborate to ensure that tasks performed by the individual support the team, department, division, and organizational goals. When the executive or C-suite is developing these goals, it is important to get input from all elements of the company.

The departments provide quarterly reports and forecasts, business projections, budgets, new product information or programs, and other internally generated data and metrics that are indicators that drive human resources decisions. Each division has different functions and will bring different viewpoints to the meeting, which can help the organization grow.

⊕ **Real World Scenario**

Adding New Locations

A company has several stores throughout a geographic region and is expanding, adding new locations in new markets. The HR team is tasked with analyzing the markets to assess the availability of skilled labor in the area.

Additionally, other areas such as finance, IT, and operations are contributing to the planning process with reports such as cash flow, infrastructure and networking requirements, and processes and procedures flow. These functions are all brought together in one cohesive plan to help determine which of the possible new locations has the best return on investment for the company.

Each area contributes and brings key pieces of the puzzle, without which there could be unforeseen risks or gaps that could negatively affect the overall business. The outcome of an orchestrated plan supports the vision of the CEO and can be directly tied to the specific strategic objective of growing the company in the next 5–7 years.

The information that a human resources professional has access to within an organization can be used to interpret data and make recommendations and decisions that affect the company. HR uses information gathered from reports produced by the finance department, marketing, sales, operations, information technology, legal, and others. HR experts must know how the different business units fit into the overall organization. By understanding these internal customers' needs and objectives, HR can provide timely and relevant support that enables the company to achieve its mission. Often a company will perform a formal strategic assessment across the departments to look at its financial position, facilities and equipment, operations, information technology, and other internal factors that currently determine where a company is positioned. It can use internal audits, accountability reports, and production numbers as metrics to measure performance and effectiveness.

Gathering Information from External Sources

While a strategic assessment will help a senior HR professional know the internal starting point of a company, many factors are beyond the control of an organization and will over time greatly impact its success. These external factors come from a variety of sources, and as a senior HR professional, you are expected to know how to interpolate the data and make inferences about how it will inform practices and policies within the company.

A great example is to look at regulatory changes from the government. In 2016 the U.S. Department of Labor announced a final rule change to the administrative test for exemption to the overtime rule of the Fair Labor Standards Act. The previous rule had a salary threshold of $23,660, regardless of the type of work or position that would otherwise qualify an individual for exempt status under the rule. This regulatory change proposed to move the threshold to more than $47,000 and further benchmark the amount to

40 percent of the median wage of the United States, which would automatically place thousands of additional workers in a nonexempt status, thus making them eligible for overtime pay. This one regulatory change could have affected hundreds of companies across the country and would have ramifications on workforce planning, compensation and benefits, and policies and procedures, and it could alter strategic plans. If a company wanted to hire or expand operations as part of its strategic goals and objectives, this cost of labor change as a result of the regulation could impact that goal. While senior HR professionals do not have a crystal ball and cannot always know what external factors will change, they must be aware of and responsive to the potential for change. Staying informed and current on HR regulations, networking with other senior HR professionals, and following changes in industry practices will help ensure that such environmental changes don't disrupt the organization.

Here are environmental scan areas to consider:

- General business environment
- Industry practices (sometimes referred to as *best practices*)
- Technology changes
- Economic outlook
- Labor market
- Legal and regulatory environment

Credibility and Relevance of External Information

There is a plethora of information available to senior HR professionals and companies about the current operational environment in business. Some of this information is important and relevant, and some is not. It requires senior HR professionals to analyze the credibility and source of the information to make reliable recommendations to management. These are some specific types of information:

- Salary data
- Management trends
- Surveys
- Industry studies
- Legal cases

There are companies that specifically focus on collecting and analyzing industry data to publish trends and information to companies for a fee; the amount depends on whether the information is generic for the industry or is customized for the company. Salary data can be a good source of information to set hiring and pay scale ranges, while items such as management trends may have limited anecdotes based on surveys limited to an industry segment or region. Legal cases should be scrutinized because precedents may be related to certain states or regions depending on the ruling and jurisdiction of the court. It is advisable that any legal information be reviewed by the company's general counsel or legal support beyond the interpretation of senior HR professionals.

Some companies will send solicitations to individuals in an organization with an HR title offering a "free report" on HR-related topics. This information is generally a teaser or limited in scope or relevance. However, accessing these reports requires contact information to be provided. This almost always invites a direct sales call from a marketing agent who has very little experience with the HR function. They are attempting to sell you their product or services, which may or may not be useful to your organization.

Aligning the HR and Organizational Strategic Plans

The human resources department develops its own strategic plan. Like any other organizational segment, the HR team develops internal goals and objectives, implements action plans, and uses metrics to determine success. These plans should nest within and support the overall strategic plan of the organization, as depicted in Figure 6.5. If, for example, a strategic goal of the company is to develop its employees, HR might establish as its goal the development of an employee training program that furthers the overall goal of the organization.

FIGURE 6.5   Nesting goals

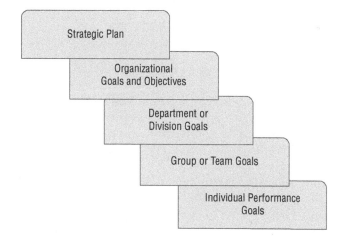

Code of Ethics

Many companies specify breaches of the values that the organization espouses when writing their code of conduct or ethics policy. They cover things such as fraud, waste, abuse, and conflicts of interest. Usually, there is an affirmative requirement that employees report any suspected violations to internal audit, human resources, or the legal division of a company. In the case of government-regulated industries, there may also be compliance entities within the government that impose reporting requirements.

Establishing Strategic Relationships

Human resources is concerned with maintaining positive, productive relationships through-out a company's life cycle. From the employee to employer, stakeholder to executive, or customer to company, the HR functions help build and maintain these relationships. Among the more critical relationships are those that are forged at the strategic level. These relationships serve a high-level purpose to provide insight, access, and ability for senior HR professionals to influence and shape the company's direction and maximize the human capital potential of the organization.

Influence Organizational Decision-Making

Senior HR professionals must build and maintain strong relationships within the organization. Decision-makers rely on you to have discretion and maintain confidentiality with sensitive information. Access to key leaders is essential for exerting direct influence over the organizational decision-making process. Senior executives are more likely to share their thoughts with someone observed to be technically competent, honest, and trustworthy. Integrity is essential for any senior HR professional.

- Be approachable and open.
- Maintain confidentiality.
- Actively listen to concerns and issues.
- Offer technically sound analysis.
- Stay within your scope of responsibility and expertise.
- Be professional.

Successful senior HR professionals have a high degree of skill with interpersonal communications. They understand organizational behavior and can evaluate personal motivations and emotions of others. They have strong emotional intelligence. This is not to say that all senior HR professionals are "nice" or "people friendly." In fact, there are several parts of HR that are certainly not "nice" (like having to terminate an employee). What they are is empathetic to the situation.

Senior HR professionals use referent or expert power to influence others. Managers and executives see them as subject-matter experts and rely on their judgment in situations involving the human capital of the organization.

Review the following observations to determine the strength of the relationship:

Access   Do you have access to the key individual(s) making decisions? If your information and analysis are going through a filter process and there are layers of bureaucracy or intermediaries between you and the key decision-maker, it is unlikely you exert a great deal of influence over their decisions.

Support   Do key leaders support your initiatives and decisions? Are recommendations made by you implemented? Or even better, are you given autonomy to implement certain decisions that have been delegated to you by executives? Good senior HR professionals will have great support from those making decisions. They will acknowledge your expertise and advise others to bring concerns and issues to you for advice and counsel. Your sphere of influence grows with more support by decision-makers.

Candor   Do you filter comments and advice to shape what you need to say because "the boss" isn't receptive to hearing it? Senior HR professionals must speak their minds but tactfully. Dissent, in most cases, does not equate to disrespect. Sometimes HR must tell decision-makers the hard truth about the situation from the human capital perspective. If you feel you cannot be candid for fear of the reaction or response, your ability to influence the situation will be diminished. Otherwise, you will second-guess what information to provide and when; over time this will erode confidence in what you are saying.

Communication   Closely related to candor, communication refers to the means of and frequency of the flow of information. Are items expressed in formal communications with memorandums and carefully worded emails? Is there informal, more frequent dialogue with influencers throughout the organization? What process is established to ensure feedback and accountability when information is transmitted?

Building Alliances and Networks

A key responsibility for senior HR professionals is to establish relationships with individuals and groups external to the organization. The field of human resources is complex and constantly changing. While certified professionals are expected to know much, they are not expected to know everything. Only through building relationships and alliances with others can you help the organization achieve its strategic goals.

Community Partnerships   Community partnerships are important for corporations, especially those that have a large impact to the economy, labor force, or environment. Even small companies can belong to a business coalition that seeks to improve a local community or neighborhood that supports and hosts those businesses.

These are types of community partnerships:

- *Civic*: Government leaders, law enforcement, civic groups, community organizations, local community colleges
- *Business*: Chamber of Commerce, business coalitions, job training centers, benefit providers (healthcare, retirement)
- *Nonprofit*: Charity organizations, religious centers of influence

Corporate Responsibility   Corporate responsibility is the self-control regulating mechanism by which modern businesses operate. There are many instances where although a corporation is permitted to (may) do something, its corporate responsibility dictates otherwise (should). There are several factors to consider, including the spirit of a law or regulation, the ethics of a situation, or the impact to a social compact or the environment. A company with a strong sense of corporate responsibility views itself as part of the community and understands that business decisions do not occur in a vacuum. It serves as an internal control that allows a business to function within acceptable social norms.

Developing and Managing Workplace Practices

As discussed in the previous paragraphs about ethics and corporate responsibility, an organization must demonstrate through action, not words, its commitment to the mission, vision, and especially the values of the company. By aligning practices with these key organizational statements, a company will shape and reinforce organizational culture. Companies may institute open-door policies to allow employees to bring concerns to the attention of management, sometimes outside of direct reporting chains, if they feel strongly that actions of middle managers or direct line supervisors may be in conflict with a company's values.

A growing trend in today's business culture is how companies respond to claims of sexual harassment or other discrimination. Most senior HR professionals approach these topics with a compliance attitude to minimize exposure or risk to the company, and so training and modeling reflects this approach. However, it may not actually address the underlying causes or prevent future occurrences. Instead, today companies are attempting to restructure how this important training is focused toward the root of a problem, which may be a passive culture or attitude among employees or management. In a passive climate, the response is immediate after an incident, but there is no prior work to identify potential problems with behaviors or attitudes. Training is compliance oriented about reporting, investigation, and adjudication of complaints. An active culture explores the motivations, behaviors, and experiences of employees in the workplace and builds practices and policies that are directly aligned to the values statements of the company.

Senior HR professionals have the responsibility to integrate these programs into the company's training plans and to reinforce them through the entire employee life cycle process. When areas of concern are identified, they must immediately offer options to managers to avoid incidents in the first place. This requires proactivity and is generally more difficult to achieve, but the results have a greater impact on the overall organizational climate and the long-term success of the company.

Measuring and Evaluating Outcomes

Having a great strategic plan isn't enough. You must measure the outcomes and constantly be on guard for changes in the operational environment that impact your plan. To do this effectively, senior HR professionals must be able to design and use various metrics that indicate whether the organization's human capital is being maximized and where improvements can be made.

Developing and Utilizing Business Metrics

Senior HR professionals use metrics to measure the achievement of strategic objectives and goals. Measures of performance tell you how the organization is performing according to the established standards. Measures of effectiveness determine whether the organization is evaluating the right things that can provide insight into how the organization performs. It is important to review the available data of the company in an unbiased manner to provide a realistic picture of the successes or failures of strategic plans.

KPI

Key performance indicators are generally those data points that a company reviews on a regular periodic basis to establish trends and look for patterns. Number of units produced, overtime costs, and net sales are just some examples of operational KPIs that an organization might use to determine how well it is meeting its goals. In the area of human resources, KPIs could be turnover, training costs, accident rates, or absenteeism. Over time this information could present a clear picture to decision-makers about the overall health of the organizational climate and how effectively the company is engaging its human capital.

Financial Statements

Financial statements such as profit and loss (P&L) statements provide the company with a snapshot of the financial stability of the company. The P&L looks at income and expenses of the business usually monthly or quarterly. It can also pinpoint trouble areas such as where costs exceed projections or estimates. EBITDA, or earnings before interest, tax, depreciation and amortization, is an effective way to evaluate a company's operating performance. It removes the accounting and external financial factors (such as tax rates) from the assessment and looks.

A balance sheet shows the accounting of the company, tracking all assets and liabilities to the company. When done correctly, these accounting entries are always equal and offsetting, which puts the company's books "in balance." For example, if the company purchased equipment for $5,000, the equipment would be an asset, but there would also be a liability in either a bill to be paid or in a loan amount due. A statement of cash flows identifies money coming into the organization and going out. It's important because not all money moves at the exact time. If a company has accounts receivable (A/R) or accounts payable (A/P), it generally has a period of time before they receive payments from customers or make payments to vendors and these need to be kept straight. If a company frequently has to pay money out before it gets paid by the customer, that can create financial stress on the organization as it waits to get back money it has already spent.

Budgets

Budgeting is an essential element of business, and for HR it is important to understand how to budget available resources to achieve certain objectives. The HR function is viewed as a cost center in a company, meaning that it does not generate revenue for the business. It doesn't produce widgets or sell services, so functionally any money it spends is usually going out without creating anything coming in. However, an effective HR team can be very valuable if its spending generates a stronger, more developed, and better qualified human capital base. For example, if an HR team spends $5,000 to recruit highly skilled labor technicians but those technicians are able to produce product more efficiently and with higher quality because of their skills, while reducing turnover, then that recruiting amount may be worthwhile in the long term.

To be able to determine how effective HR is in recruiting, training, or maintaining a company's staff, it must budget the costs for all services needed and to capture any costs in detail. As you develop reoccurring costs, you will begin to see that there is a need to forecast what HR needs to spend to operate effectively, and this can be given to the finance department to budget. If a retail company is opening new stores, the HR team should budget how much money is needed to recruit new hires, advertise for positions, and spend on training, as well as any new HR hires to support a growing employee population.

Designing and Evaluating HR Data Indicators

HR is a data-driven function. Business leaders are requiring that senior HR professionals have an understanding of available data and can evaluate and interpret the significance of information in trends or patterns that will impact the company over time. Some common indicators that are useful include the following:

- Turnover rates
- Cost per hire
- Retention rates

Turnover rates can show how often new employees are hired and how many employees leave the organization. Some turnover is natural and necessary. Retirements, promotions, or departures to move up when an individual has reached a ceiling in the organization are expected. However, poor management or training that results in employees leaving may be considered bad turnover that can be reduced by emphasizing better managers or more effective training. With higher turnover, more resources are needed to find replacements, and this impacts the bottom line of the organization.

Cost per hire takes all the costs needed, including recruiting, advertising, training, and onboarding, to bring one individual in the organization fully qualified to perform their assigned duties. It is expensive to find the right person, with the right skills, to perform the right tasks in an organization. Figure 6.6 shows the cost-per-hire formula.

FIGURE 6.6 Cost per hire

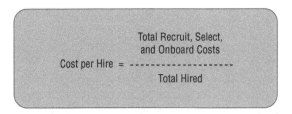

Figure 6.7 shows the average tenure time in months for all employees that departed in that month. If the average turnover is relatively constant, as the length of tenure changes, it is a direct correlation to the retention rate—how long people stay with the company. If a company must hire new employees every 12 months, it is unlikely to be recuperating the costs associated with hiring the individual before hiring a replacement. In today's business environment, most people don't stay in a job beyond 3–5 years, so companies must maximize the performance of those individuals and can measure longevity through retention rates.

FIGURE 6.7   Turnover

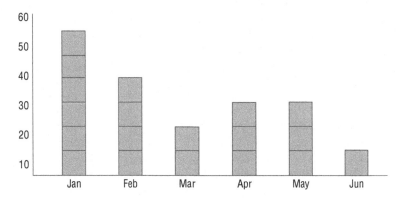

Design and Manage Effective Change Strategies

To align organizational performance with the organization's strategic goals, senior HR professionals must design and manage effective change strategies for the company. As discussed earlier in this chapter, change management theories discuss the motivations and methods of how individuals respond to changes in general, but specifically they apply to their work environment for the purposes of this review.

As the business environment changes with external factors, the company will respond with implementing new ideas or programs to remain competitive. While this might attract new employees or help the company grow, the executive leadership must be sensitive to how these changes will be received and ultimately implemented by long-standing, loyal employees.

 **Real World Scenario**

Changes to the Workweek

A successful collision repair company was expanding in its home area because of its reputation for quality repairs and exceptional customer service. As it added more stores, it still couldn't keep pace with the demand, without risking quality or burning the employees out with excessive hours. The company executives discussed new ideas to achieve the strategic goals.

One idea was to extend the current business operating hours from 5 days per week and 8-hour days to 6 days per week with 12-hour days. The extended hours would provide better customer support and improve the turnaround time for repairs to vehicles with more time each week. However, individual employee work schedules would need to be adjusted for these new hours to avoid overtime considerations and comply with existing wage laws. These longer hours would also potentially significantly impact the work-life balance of the employees. While some issues could be addressed such as ensuring that employees worked only 3 of the 12-hour shifts each week to avoid overtime and hiring more employees for the increased workload, there were still several other technical challenges to overcome. To decide whether this was a viable course of action, management chose to survey the entire company so that employees could be involved and provide important input to the decision-making process.

The survey was able to highlight concerns of employees that could be addressed and discussed with additional group meetings and by developing a frequently asked questions list for distribution. These interactions were well received by the employees and helped the executives adjust plans to account for potential problems. Overall, the method of introducing the ideas for changes, through implementation, facilitated the transition of selected high-volume stores to this new operating structure with minimal disruption to the company. By allowing the employees to be an integral part of the change process and allowing for transparency, there was a greater acceptance of changes.

Exam Essentials

Know how laws and regulations apply to practical situations.   Laws and regulations change often, and you are responsible for knowing current laws. What you may see is a scenario in which a rule change is provided and be given choices on how this rule might affect your organization.

Know types of metrics commonly used in business.

Key Performance Indicator (KPI)   A KPI is a measure of performance that is quantitative (has a number result) that can be compared against the actual results obtained during a period of time. In business manufacturing, this might be the number of errors in a process or the number of units produced per day.

Financial Statements   The financial statements, such as the profit-and-loss statement, balance sheet, and cash flow, are important indicators as to the financial stability and health of the company. They can often pinpoint areas that need attention because of inefficiency in operations or perhaps human capital.

Know the importance of values in practice.   The values of a company are those that are practiced, not the ones spoken or written on a document. Senior HR professionals must understand how ethical standards of a company relate closely to how practiced values match those expressed by an organization.

Know how to design and evaluate HR data indicators.   Senior HR professionals should know how to forecast new hires and determine turnover ratios as part of their responsibilities. Included in this function is the type of turnover (transfers, retirements, promotions, separations).

Summary

Be strategically focused on the mission of the company and in your approach to the delivery of HR support. Being an effective senior HR professional requires an understanding of basic concepts related to leadership and strategy. The SPHR® exam will test your knowledge and experience in business matters at the executive level. Mission, vision, and values are translated into strategic goals and objectives. These goals are the foundation for policy, programs, and processes throughout an organization, many directly tied to HR practices that will be discussed in the following chapters. As one of the organizational leaders, senior HR professionals must know and demonstrate the desired behaviors of the company reflective of the values it shares with employees. Senior HR professionals constantly evaluate the effectiveness of the organization through metrics and their own effectiveness as a leader.

Test-Taking Tip

Review your company's mission or vision statement and any related information on company values. Look for links to HR policies and practices that are directly attributed to these statements or values and the overall strategic impact they have. However, when looking at questions during the exam, read the questions carefully. Many times, answers to a generic question may not be exactly how your company chooses to operate, so be careful of the variations.

Review Questions

1. Which of the following is *not* considered to be a management function?

    A. Planning

    B. Controlling

    C. Implementation

    D. Organizing

2. When creating human resources policies for a company, they should be aligned with the company's _____ .

    A. Mission

    B. Management style

    C. Processes

    D. Values

3. What is the main purpose of a cost-benefit analysis?

    A. To provide an unbiased evaluation of the benefits of a decision against an alternative using the same scale for comparison

    B. To evaluate only monetary considerations in determining the value of a decision or product

    C. To determine the social impact of financial decisions by the company

    D. To choose products that a company can afford to produce over a given period

4. The Sarbanes-Oxley Act of 2002 established rules governing _____ in response to the public corporation and accounting scandals that occurred around that time.

    A. Board composition and the election of officers

    B. Reporting conflicts of interest

    C. Financial disclosure statements

    D. All of the above

5. A new HRIS is needed by the company. A senior HR professional might provide input on the vendor selection process *except* which of the following?

    A. Evaluating proposals

    B. Developing an RFP

    C. Monitoring the performance of a vendor

    D. Determining how to fund the purchase

6. Outsourcing is an example of _____ .

    A. Placing core business activities outside the organization to reduce costs

    B. Bringing new lines of business to a company

C. Shedding some important business functions to focus on core competencies

D. Keeping control of business functions that are routine

7. Audits and project management techniques are used primarily in which business management function?

    A. Planning

    B. Organizing

    C. Directing

    D. Controlling

8. When developing a business case for shared support services, which of the following might a senior HR professional do *first*?

    A. Address mitigation issues

    B. Determine roles and responsibilities

    C. Determine services to be moved

    D. Draft a service level agreement

9. An example of strategic performance expectations might be which of the following?

    A. The number of employees who quit last quarter

    B. Costs associated with a new benefit plan

    C. The start of a new financial wellness program for the company

    D. All of the above

10. When offshoring support services for an organization, which of the following is a consideration that should be made?

    A. The distance and time differences between the corporate headquarters and the consolidated facility

    B. The social perception of sending jobs overseas

    C. Differences in regulatory restrictions between the two countries

    D. The potential loss of core competencies

11. Human capital projections should do which of the following?

    A. Take into consideration turnover ratios only

    B. Only look at the number of available people to fill a job

    C. Take into consideration available talent in the market, turnover ratios, and types of separations

    D. Take into consideration talent in the market and an employee's reasons for leaving the company

Chapter

7

Talent Planning and Acquisition (SPHR® Only)

THIS CHAPTER COVERS THE SPHR® EXAM CONTENT FROM THE TALENT PLANNING AND ACQUISITION FUNCTIONAL AREA AND CONSISTS OF THE FOLLOWING RESPONSIBILITIES AND REQUIRED KNOWLEDGE. FOR PHR® EXAM CONTENT, REVIEW CHAPTER 2. RESPONSIBILITIES:

✓ 01   Evaluate and forecast organizational needs throughout the business cycle to create or develop workforce plans (for example: corporate restructuring, workforce expansion or reduction)

✓ 02   Develop, monitor, and assess recruitment strategies to attract desired talent (for example: labor market analysis, compensation strategies, selection process, onboarding, sourcing and branding strategy)

✓ 03   Develop and evaluate strategies for engaging new employees and managing cultural integrations (for example: new employee acculturation, downsizing, restructuring, mergers and acquisitions, divestitures, global expansion)

IN ADDITION TO THE PRECEDING RESPONSIBILITIES, AN INDIVIDUAL TAKING THE PHR® EXAM SHOULD HAVE WORKING KNOWLEDGE OF THE FOLLOWING AREAS, USUALLY DERIVED THROUGH PRACTICAL EXPERIENCE:

✓ 17   Planning techniques (for example: succession planning, forecasting)

✓ 18   Talent management practices and techniques (for example: selecting and assessing employees)

This chapter reviews the critical functions of talent planning and acquisition. This functional area covers 16 percent of the SPHR® exam. Many of the responsibilities and tasks associated with this chapter are most closely related to the strategic duties of senior HR professionals in forecasting the talent needs of the organization and developing methods of attracting and engaging new talent. This chapter reviews planning techniques, talent management practices, and employee engagement strategies. This functional area covers recruiting, selection, and retention strategies to attract desired employees and the processes, procedures, and rules that govern the associated tasks. It also reviews the process of successfully assimilating a new employee into the culture of the company.

Required Knowledge

In current HR practice, strategic talent management is still retained within the company. While the organization may outsource recruiting functions and have technology to support the acquisition process, it still requires an integrated strategic plan to maximize the human capital potential. This function is very much a core competency of a business model, though many organizations may, at least in part, overlook the responsibilities that are time-consuming and require specific knowledge. The required knowledge for a senior HR professional in the area of talent planning and acquisition will help an organization to forecast needs and strategically build a strong team of employees even if some of the tasks are conducted outside the company. Knowing how these functions work will develop depth within the HR team.

Planning

Senior HR professionals must know how to plan and forecast the talent needs for the future of the company. Knowledge of talent management practices and recruitment sources will support efforts to put the right individual in the right job and ensure that person is motivated to meet the goals and objectives of the organization. When practical, the use of staffing alternatives can benefit the company, and therefore senior HR professionals should understand the pros and cons of such alternatives that are available.

Planning Techniques: Succession Planning and Forecasting

Succession planning is not identifying a single person to take someone's job in the future when the individual leaves or retires. It is a comprehensive career development model that determines the required knowledge, skills, and abilities for a position and then plans how employees within the organization can learn and develop them through education, training, and experience. Ideally, the goal is to have a bench of potential successors to key jobs in the organization. It also means, as a corollary, that the organization identifies the key jobs in the company that either are low density and hard to fill or perform tasks deemed critical to the organization's core competencies. Through this technique there is a deliberate process to identify and groom quality employees with leadership potential. There is a risk, however, as there is no guarantee that these employees will remain in the organization or that anticipated openings will emerge when expected to allow timely promotions.

Forecasting looks at the demographics of the organization and determines things such as years remaining before retirement eligibility and turnover rates to project losses to the company. It uses skill inventories and surveys to determine the available talent to meet company talent demands. It then compares the available talent pool, examining graduation rates, market salary studies, skills, and geographic limitations for jobs. A geographic limitation might be something like the availability of affordable housing in the area for the workforce. This would impact a company's ability to hire employees, especially from outside the area needing to relocate.

Selecting and Assessing Employees

Techniques are available to conduct internal assessments of the current workforce in an organization and the available labor pool from which to draw talent. Some of the techniques are as follows:

- Skills testing
- Skills inventory
- Workforce demographic analysis

The skills testing and inventory are the parts of career development modeling that look at job positions and requirements in an organization and then systematically identify where the gaps are. In this gap analysis, the HR team may conduct assessments to quantify the skill level and knowledge and abilities of the talent. The goal is to determine the proficiency of the individuals with the skills and whether the skill is readily available. Beyond testing, the HR team must take an inventory of the required and available skills to perform the tasks needed to accomplish the organizational mission. Sometimes these are technical skills; at other times they are soft skills.

In some highly technical jobs in the United States, the skills inventory exists within an aging population. A *workforce demographic analysis* looks at the region and the available talent pool from which to draw the needed skills. This could include the number of people with college or technical education, years of experience, age of the workforce, and other statistics that can enable HR professionals to plan and understand how a talent pipeline is influenced by the available population. The Bureau of Labor Statistics has a website at www.bls.gov that consolidates and presents workforce data that can be used in this kind of analysis. Figure 7.1 shows an overview of available wage data from the website.

FIGURE 7.1   Bureau of Labor Statistics website

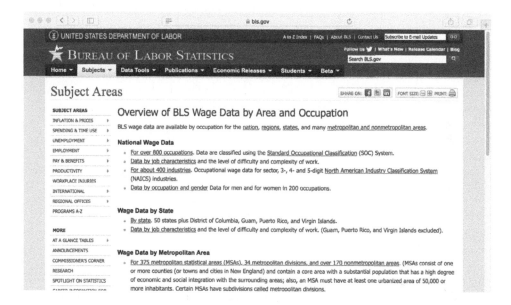

Recruitment Sources and Strategy

It is important that HR members responsible for talent planning know the available sources of talent and how to attract candidates. In many industries with highly skilled workers, there are limited pipelines, and companies will compete for a finite pool of applicants. Talent may come from the organization itself, which can be developed through formal and informal training development opportunities (which will be discussed further in Chapter 8, "Learning and Development"). These are known as *internal candidates* or *sources*.

External sources come from job fairs, college or campus recruiting, and online or web-based sites like LinkedIn, Indeed, or Monster.com. The company may also have a website that has a careers page to solicit and attract applications for available jobs. Social media sites are rapidly expanding to enter the job search market, allowing both employees and employers to match skills and needs. In some cases, where talent pools are limited, a company establishes cooperative training partnerships to develop a talent pipeline with the help of trade or technical schools to present apprentice or internship opportunities.

Active candidates are those currently looking for work. They may be unemployed or underemployed currently or about to finish school, or they may be currently employed but dissatisfied with their current work opportunity and looking for something else. In each case, the employee has taken the initiative to seek a new job and become available for the recruiter. Passive candidates may not be totally dissatisfied with their current opportunities, but they are likely unaware of potential offers and what is available. They are not "looking," but if the right opportunity presents itself, they now would consider a change in employment. As much as 70 percent of the available workforce is passively looking for employment. This number increases as the economy improves and the potential for finding a job increases; this phenomenon can be measured by looking at overall voluntary terminations or quit ratios, which increase with the perception that there are jobs and employers looking to hire.

HR may use databases or other means of direct marketing to attract passive candidates to generate leads and turn those leads into applicants for positions. Companies can use total rewards and intangible qualities such as culture and work-life balance to persuade candidates to leave their current employment for opportunities in the new company. Conversely, this same approach is being taken by others to lure talent away from your organization, so senior HR professionals must be aware of which employees are potential passive candidates and seek to retain quality talent essential to success. Consider people with experience in the three- to five-year range, those not afforded opportunities for upward mobility, and those below market value in compensation.

Global Workforce Planning and Employment

Senior HR professionals are responsible for knowing aspects of global workforce planning. For companies that operate overseas, hiring third-country nationals (those who are not U.S. citizens or are citizens of the host nation) and being aware of laws governing employment abroad are important. While the Global Professional in Human Resources (GPHR) certification is beyond the scope of this book, those preparing for the SPHR® must have a general understanding of the requirements and planning priorities for a global workforce.

 Real World Scenario

Cruise Line Industry

A few years ago I had the opportunity to take a cruise to Alaska. While the company was headquartered in the United States, the boat registry was from Australia, as many cruise ships operate under foreign flags visiting U.S. ports so that they are subjected to those nations' laws for, among other issues, employment. When I met with the HR director aboard the ship, she explained some of the challenges of having a diverse workforce among the crew representing multiple nations. Coordinating payroll, taxes, emergency notifications, and other basic HR tasks were much more complex. One specific point she mentioned was that the cruise line would ensure that an Australian citizen could not be permitted to work aboard the ships that were registered to that country. They could work for the company but aboard a different ship's registry because the citizen and the company would immediately be subject to the nation's employment laws as citizens and not as foreign nationals, creating an undue administrative burden to both parties.

Staffing Alternatives

Staffing alternatives are means to employ a workforce that may not be organic to the company. There are various techniques and resources that an organization can use to manage these available sources of talent. HR must assess alternatives and determine viability. Companies can choose to hire a talent management firm to provide temporary workers or temp-to-permanent hires in which an outside source is completely responsible for the recruiting, selecting, hiring, and sometimes training before the employee works for the company. In the case of staffing firms, even the management of payroll and benefits is handled externally for a fee usually calculated as a premium on the salary wage.

Outsourcing is where the entire function is performed by a separate company, eliminating the need for the talent or skills within the company. This is a good technique when the tasks are not the core competencies of the company. *Job sharing* is where two part-time employees can fill one full-time–equivalent position, reducing cost by reducing eligibility for full-time benefits. In some cases, this benefits employees that need more flexibility in their schedule or are not available for full-time work. Another staffing technique for longtime workers of the company is a *phased retirement*. In these circumstances, a senior worker transitions over a predetermined time (usually a year) and goes from a full-time worker to a part-time worker but maintains eligibility for benefits or is provided with an incentive. This allows upward movement in the company for highly qualified workers while providing business continuity, stability, and predictability for workers transitioning to retirement.

Selection and Retention

Planning for talent acquisition is the foundation, but senior HR professionals must be knowledgeable about selection techniques and good retention practices that keep employees engaged. In some sense, good selection practices are not just about hiring for the opening right in front of you but considering the growth, potential, and expansion for future opportunities within the company. The methods and best practices for motivating and keeping employees engaged are critical knowledge points.

Interview Techniques

One of the most important parts of the selection and hiring process is the interview. Ultimately, interacting with the candidate and understanding firsthand the qualities, knowledge, skills, abilities, and other attributes the individual is capable of bringing to the organization is a critical step. We too often bring our own lenses formed with the bias of experience into the process, so it is essential that senior HR professionals understand the limitations and restrictions that accompany this process and be able to train hiring managers and company executives to understand their own biases to improve the hiring quality and retention of applicants.

Behavioral Interviews

These types of interviews are common in the workforce today and are intended to give insight into how an applicant might handle a hypothetical situation that may occur by linking past actions or results to the future job. These questions may be structured in the manner "Give me an example of a time when . . . ," and the fill-in-the-blank would be related to the context of the new job, such as "had to deal with a difficult decision" or "made a mistake on the job" or "implemented a new program that employees needed help to understand."

While behavioral questions are popular, they have some challenges. First, most prepared applicants will have studied the types of behavior questions that will be asked and have prepared answers. These answers may or may not provide any more insight into the candidate's abilities. And because the questions are derived from a previous experience or hypothetical situation, they may not have relevance to the future position, and the employee may end up acting differently in that context.

Situational Interview

A situational interview is similar to the behavioral interview but does not look at past experience or actions; instead, it places the applicant in a scenario and asks them to describe the actions they might take if such an event were to occur. This allows the interviewer to perhaps set the stage for the conditions that the applicant might face in the job and how that individual might go about responding to the situation.

The shortcoming of this process is that the answer may be dependent on how well the scenario is described, and what facts are provided may affect the outcome of a decision. For example, if the situation called for handling a difficult employee who is being aggressive with co-workers, the applicant might respond with an answer to verbally reprimand the worker or choose some other disciplinary action. However, the situation changes if, in the situational example of handling this employee, other facts come to light, such as a lack of training, development, or involvement by the supervisor, that have contributed to such employee actions.

Group Interview

A group interview takes advantage of the multiple perspectives of different individuals evaluating the candidate at the same time. There are two types, panel and team interviews. In a team approach, all the members of the group are from the same work team and could be peers, subordinates, and supervisors. This is necessary because the team so heavily relies on cooperation among the group that input is needed from all levels. At the panel interview, there may be a representative group that comes from different departments in the organization. Each panel member may represent the areas that the position works with or may provide the subject-matter expert who can assess different competencies.

While group interviews allow everyone to get an understanding of the applicant, depending on the group size, the amount of time allotted might be split among the group members, limiting the amount of information that can be determined by any one individual in depth. The larger the panel, the more uncomfortable an applicant may be in answering questions. Finally, it is important to have a diverse panel if the intent is to gain more perspectives. Panels that are composed of all one gender, race, or ethnic group might inadvertently have bias toward some candidates.

🌐 Real World Scenario

Using a Personality Assessment with a New Executive Hire

The Guilford-Zimmerman Temperament Survey

When interviewing for an executive position, a company chose to conduct an assessment using this survey, first developed in 1948, to measure personality across 10 scales. The purpose of this test was developmental in nature and to gauge how compatible the candidates might be with the other executives who had taken the test and were aware of their results currently employed by the company. The results were shared with the candidates by an individual trained in the interpretation of the results and used as part of a larger series of personal interviews and reference checks to get a broad interpretation of the qualifications from both a technical and cultural fit.

The Impact of Total Rewards on Recruitment and Retention

Hiring and maintaining a quality workforce requires an effective pay strategy that considers the total rewards for the employee. While pay is often the strongest motivator, it is not the only reason employees seek employment nor is it the only reason employees stay with an organization. Chapter 9 discusses Total Rewards and is particularly focused on the role of senior HR professionals in depth, but it is worth noting here that a diverse workforce will have diverse motivations for working in a job.

Negotiation Skills and Techniques

HR professionals must be proficient in negotiation strategy and techniques to find a balance between the needs of the company in terms of costs of human capital and the need of the employee to feel they are treated fairly and respected for the talent they bring to the organization. When discussing salary and other negotiable elements of compensation, HR must know how to communicate effectively to determine the needs of the future hire and make an acceptable offer that meets the needs. As part of the interview process, HR should establish a range and may through the process ask if an applicant would be willing to accept an offer in that range. The salary range helps applicants know whether the organization can meet their needs early in the interview stages so the company does not waste time trying to hire an individual whose needs are above what the company can pay.

Termination Approaches and Strategies

At some point an active employee/employer relationship ends. The manner in which that relationship ends is dependent on the two parties involved and the circumstance. The term commonly used is *termination*, which denotes the official end of the employment relationship, but it may also be referred to as a separation from employment as well. The circumstances can be divided into two general categories, voluntary and involuntary. Senior HR professionals must understand the organizational impact of terminations, including how they affect morale, impact hiring, and relate to company culture.

Wrongful Termination

The term *wrongful termination* refers to certain terminations that are not permitted under the law or where courts have determined that such actions taken by the employer resulting in the loss of employment by the employee were improper. The "at-will" doctrine in the United States does allow an employer or employee to terminate their arrangement at any time for any reason. However, such reasons are subject to review if they violate any laws governing the protected classes of people previously discussed.

Constructive Discharge

This is a situation where the employee quits but only because the employer has made the working conditions so bad that the employee has no other choice. Radically altering the conditions of employment such that an employee feels compelled to resign can be considered constructive discharge.

Retaliatory Discharge

This situation occurs when the employer terminates an employee when the employee has engaged in some action that is lawful, even if it negatively affects the company. Examples include filing an equal opportunity complaint, participating in a legal investigation of the company as a witness, and taking an approved leave of absence under lawful conditions (such as under the Family and Medical Leave Act).

Voluntary Terminations

Voluntary terminations are initiated usually by the employee and are resignations or retirements. A resignation in lieu of being fired may not be considered voluntary under those circumstances. As previously stated, an employee can terminate an employment relationship at any time without cause. There may be some impact of such a decision, including the following:

- Ability to return to employment with the same company (rehire)
- Ability to seek employment with a rival company or a company that is in the same field (noncompete)
- Ability to obtain unemployment compensation
- Forfeiture of certain bonuses or incentives as part of an employment contract clause or separate written agreement

With retirement the employee leaves active service to the company usually to receive some pension or benefit tied to eligibility based on age and/or years of service to the organization.

In some cases, the company offers early retirement that has incentives to induce employees to separate from employment if the company is restructuring or needs to reduce its workforce. The individuals have a choice to leave or remain with the company.

 The Age Discrimination in Employment Act has provisions that do not classify retirement incentives as discriminatory based on age, provided that such retirements are voluntary and with the full knowledge of the rights of the individuals who are offered the retirement option.

Involuntary Terminations

Involuntary terminations are made by the company and usually are for three general reasons: performance, misconduct, or the result of a business necessity. In all cases, it is important to ensure that proper documentation regarding the decision to separate an employee is maintained by the company. This information may provide evidence in lawsuits alleging wrongful termination to be able to justify the decisions and actions taken.

In the case of poor performance, management should determine whether the employee was properly trained and aware of the tasks to be performed in the job. This can be demonstrated in providing the qualifications for the job and essential job duties discussed elsewhere in this chapter. Supervisors should document the specific deficiencies and corrective actions that the company has taken, such as in a performance improvement plan prior to termination.

Misconduct is another general category that encompasses willful or negligent violations of policy or law. Misconduct does not necessarily mean criminal. There are numerous administrative reasons that an employee can be terminated for such as misconduct including insubordination to management and ethical violations. As with poor performance, documentation is essential to limit a company's liability exposure. However, some companies have a progressive disciplinary policy where there is a proportionate corrective disciplinary action taken based on the severity of the infraction and the impact on the organization. Generally speaking, involuntary termination for misconduct is for egregious or repeated violations.

The third category of involuntary terminations is that of business necessity. Downsizing, organizational restructuring, and the outplacement of services are examples where the company makes a business decision that causes a decrease in the number of workers. A company that downsizes may be in decline or losing revenue and can no longer afford to maintain its current workforce size. As a result, some employees may be laid off to reduce payroll costs. In organizational restructuring, parts of a company may be eliminated or modified, requiring a change to the workforce. Workers who no longer have the necessary skills are separated from employment. Finally, some companies choose to outsource certain functions, as mentioned earlier in the chapter. That decision means that the employees performing those functions are not required.

In all cases related to involuntary separations, the HR professional must ensure that the company handles the notification to the employee in a consistent and professional manner.

The loss of a job is a significant emotional event to an employee, and there are a variety of reactions to this news. HR professionals must know how to handle outcomes and train managers to be sensitive to the employees who are departing the organization.

- Provide sufficient notice in a timely manner, such as in the case of layoffs.

- Discuss the circumstances with the employee directly.

- Focus on the specific reasons and provide them in writing.

- Complete the process quickly.

- Review with legal representation the circumstances if a wrongful termination claim is suspected or likely.

- Be consistent and follow a checklist.

Employee Engagement Strategies

A boss once told me that some employees quit and leave the company; some, however, quit and stay. While Chapter 8, "Learning and Development," includes some discussion of employee motivations and the impact on development, employee engagement influences retention and also the company culture. Engagement is the key to employees remaining with the organization. Over time, complacency or failure to motivate an employee will drive them to find new opportunities that meet their needs for growth and development. Companies must have comprehensive strategies to invest in their human capital or risk losing them to the market.

At the strategic level, senior HR professionals must be familiar with the various ways management can engage their employees. They review policies and practices that are designed to attract talent, motivate and inspire them while employed, and retain them as they grow and develop. Engagement strategies include the following:

- Rewards and recognitions programs for achievement, longevity, continuous improvement, industry success, customer service, and safety

- Engagement surveys that are in person (such as interviews) or online (on platforms such as SurveyMonkey or similar vendors) to assess the general climate of the organization or get answers to specific concerns

- Pay philosophy, best practices, and management's treatment of employees to make a lasting impact on the morale and the level of workforce engagement

Branding and Marketing

A goal of employers should be to differentiate themselves from their competitors as a preferred place to work for employees. As with the products that a company sells or manufactures or the services it provides, the company's brand should be consistent in the values it represents to employees. This means working conditions, total compensation, benefits, and management reflect how employees are treated by the company and should mirror how the customer is treated. Employees reflect the values of the organization to the customers, so part of the brand is how the employees' needs are met.

The HR team will work with marketing to share the brand identity in all recruiting products and services to ensure that prospective applicants know the benefits of being an employee of the company and will highlight some of the perks that appeal to the talent the company seeks to hire. This joint effort to demonstrate the company's values through the respect and caring of its workers will bring team members with the right fit from both a technical and cultural aspect.

Due Diligence and Assessments

At the senior HR level, knowledge of due diligence measures that protect the company from unforeseen risks in talent acquisition or divestiture processes is essential. The strategic understanding evaluates the human capital potential and costs when the company undergoes a transformation in the talent acquisition lifecycle. As a company is created and then expands to meet market demands, there are steps senior HR professionals must know for mergers and acquisitions. As the company changes or wanes, the same is true for divestitures.

Due Diligence Processes

Each major action in corporate reorganization has items to consider as the process relates to talent planning. Understanding these processes of due diligence will mitigate hazards in these complex corporate deals. Table 7.1 shows some considerations.

TABLE 7.1   Due diligence processes

Type of Corporate Change	Due Diligence for HR
Mergers and acquisitions	▪ Review employee records of acquired company including training, performance, and disciplinary records
	▪ Review financial liabilities such as pensions and benefit
	▪ Schedule interviews or meetings with each employee to discuss retention or separation options
	▪ Review any nondisclosure or noncompete agreements that restrict hiring talent prior to the completion of the merger or acquisition process
	▪ Develop or adjust policies to help blend the two corporate cultures as needed
Divestitures	▪ Notify affected employees in a timely manner
	▪ Determine the services or HR functions that will separate as part of the divestiture
	▪ Determine the core competencies of the new entity and the positions that will be required complete with job descriptions and requirements
	▪ Develop a transition plan for post-sale or separation

Transition Techniques

Senior HR professionals must know transition techniques for corporate restructuring, mergers and acquisitions, offshoring, and divestitures. Each type of corporate transition has a slightly different focus at the strategic level, and senior HR professionals must understand how to plan these changes and the impact to talent.

Corporate Restructuring

A company may restructure to meet changes in the market, such as the evolution of technology, environmental factors, or consumer changes. At the senior level, communicating the change to current employees, developing retraining programs, and handling any separations based on changes in job requirements are key knowledge points. Senior HR professionals must be capable of anticipating talent demands and plan to hire individuals where there is a skills gap in the company while also transitioning those individuals who are no longer meeting the needs of the organization.

Mergers and Acquisitions

When companies join or one purchases another, there is a series of transitions to integrate the company cultures and assimilate the employees that are retained. HR professionals should know how to rapidly assess the knowledge, skills, and abilities of all the available talent in the merger or acquisition process. They must also know how to identify any overlap or gaps in the talent pool.

Offshoring

In large companies, it may be necessary to shed some of the functions of the organization that are not core to the company's mission. Some of these functions will be performed externally from the company so the organization can focus on its core competencies. Senior HR professionals should already be familiar with the core competencies and plan to move nonvital functions and positions to external resources. At the global level, the HR team evaluates any issues with third-country nationals or geographically driven local support that are created when the company decides to offshore any function of the business. Because offshoring inherently causes a company to give up some control of the function, the HR team should evaluate the impact to the organization.

Divestitures

When a company decides to divest itself of elements of the organization that are no longer meeting its needs, senior HR professionals are responsible for the separation of the employees. The HR team must work with any organization that is acquiring the divested element to place affected employees or assist in establishing the organizational structure of a newly formed, independent business element. There are statutory and regulatory requirements for notifications to employees, and strict adherence must be followed to maintain compliance.

Methods to Assess Staffing Effectiveness

Figure 7.2 shows how to calculate a basic cost per hire. By determining how much a company commits in resources to hiring each employee and examining the turnover ratios, HR professionals can determine how effective their recruiting efforts are. The goal should be to bring on board the best talent in the shortest time possible for the lowest cost, while keeping new hires in the company productive beyond the time to recoup the initial investment.

FIGURE 7.2   Cost-per-hire calculations

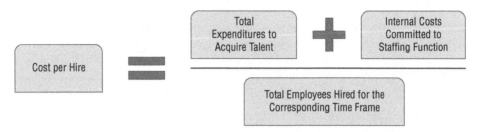

Another important metric is selection ratios. A quality hire comes from having a good pool of qualified candidates and finding the best fit from among those best qualified. HR should know how to track using a manual process or an automated applicant tracking system (ATS) the number of applicants, the number of minimum qualified applicants, and how many are interviewed to obtain a candidate to present an offer to. This process should also determine the numbers of minority applicants and women to ensure equal opportunity hiring practices and how this correlates to an affirmative action plan. Companies must be aware to prevent adverse impact in hiring because of internal practices that may have biases.

Exam Essentials

Know selection, retention, and termination strategies.   Be familiar with the methods and purposes of selecting, retaining, and terminating talent and the reasons that each is employed based on the life-cycle position of the company. Be aware of the biases that can be present with management based on historical practices or company policies and how to adjust them to meet changing talent demands.

Understand how to measure the effectiveness of talent management strategies.   Human capital is expensive and should never be wasted. You should understand the direct correlation between employee turnover and lost opportunity or productivity costs. By analyzing the effectiveness of talent management strategies of the company, you will be able to reduce turnover costs and keep a company performing at optimal levels.

Responsibilities

The SPHR® exam reviews a senior HR professional's understanding of the basic practices surrounding developing and executing strategies to attract and engage new talent. The key responsibilities cover forecasting organizational needs, developing recruitment strategies, and engaging new employees while overseeing cultural assimilation. The major tasks that senior HR professionals must accomplish are at the strategic and operational levels.

Evaluate and Forecast Organizational Needs

An important function for senior HR professionals is to evaluate and forecast the talent needs of the organization. Throughout the business cycle, they create or develop workforce plans to meet those needs. At the various stages the needs change, and the HR team must be responsive. Figure 7.3 shows the business life cycle and the key responsibilities at each phase.

FIGURE 7.3   Business life cycle

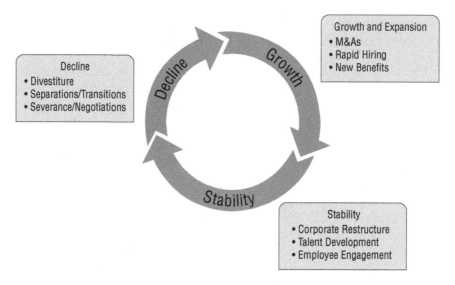

Identify Needs throughout the Business Cycle

As with strategic planning discussed in Chapter 6, recruiting should have short- and long-term goals that align with the company's mission, vision, and values. Senior HR professionals must identify the needs of the company and establish requirements for hiring based on where the company is in its business cycle. This might be skills or knowledge needed to develop a product or provide a service in an emerging market, or it might be talent to help the company divest some of its holdings that are no longer profitable as the market changes. Once the company knows what it needs to hire, HR sets goals such as the number of applicants for a position and establishes objectives to help reach the goal—for example, increasing the number of job posting views and hits to the company website careers page and generating the interest that leads to applicants.

Recruitment Strategies

It is the role of senior HR professionals to develop, monitor, and assess recruitment strategies to attract desired talent. You must conduct labor market analysis to evaluate the availability of talent in the market and then develop compensation strategies to draw the talent to the organization. This should be done as part of an overall branding strategy to align company values with the recruitment process. Once an applicant pool is available, the sourcing, selection process, and eventual onboarding process are all areas that fall in the realm of responsibilities at the senior HR level.

 Real World Scenario

Increasing Social Media Use in Recruiting

A company was attempting to increase the talent pool from which applicants for jobs were coming. The HR team began to redesign job postings and place them on social media websites. This reached a different audience that may not have accessed the more traditional venues previously used for posting jobs and might not otherwise have known about hiring opportunities. This also included more applicants from out of the region willing to relocate for jobs with the company. As a result, a more diverse, skilled workforce could be recruited and hired. The company increased the total number of applicants and improved the overall quality of the applicants.

Analysis

The analysis required for employment planning consists of looking at labor market trends, assessing the skills of the existing workforce, and examining duty descriptions and job functions to determine the criteria for hiring, retaining, and promoting qualified individuals.

Labor Market Trends

In the United States today there continue to be shortages of highly skilled workers with advanced training in technical fields. At the same time, with an education system focused on higher education as a goal, trade schools and craftspeople are at a premium. This imbalance in the labor market can make finding the right person with the right skills challenging. Senior HR professionals can create reports and extract data from state and federal websites that show how many jobs were in various sectors, the salaries reported, and other demographics. The purpose of these reports is to present a clear understanding of the available talent to fill jobs within the organization.

These reports can be used with knowledge about compensation and benefits to establish salary bands and ranges that are competitive and attractive to talent by being at parity or even leading the market in total compensation.

Assess the Skills of the Workforce

Talent demands are the needed knowledge, skills, and abilities of an organization to successfully meet its goals and objectives. Talent demands are determined first by examining the required tasks and then by deciding how to best accomplish those tasks. HR might complete a skills inventory through analysis of job requirements. When preparing and reviewing job postings, senior HR professionals must identify the minimum required skills for the position and any preferred skills to distinguish top-tier candidates who are best qualified.

In the case of internal talent pools, HR may use performance evaluations and recommendations of supervisors and senior managers in the organization to assess the knowledge, skills, and abilities of the workforce. Workplace assessments such as department exams or field tests are also possible methods. Personnel records or databases may also contain information on training courses, education, or additional skills such as language abilities that can be compiled and analyzed.

Third-party vendors such as recruiting firms or web services can be a repository for hundreds or thousands of prospective applicants' résumés. Usually for a fee for services or other agreement, companies may access these vast databases and search engines to find qualified matches that can then be targeted for recruitment through messaging directly or contacted through the vendor. In the case of recruiting agencies, their purpose is to conduct the initial search and assess the available talent pools with dedicated assets, saving time and resources for the hiring organization. HR serves as the point of contact for the external sources and communicates the needs of the company as determined by the hiring authority.

Compensation Strategies

Senior HR professionals have an important part at the executive level in developing compensation strategies. While Chapter 9 will further discuss the concept of total rewards in greater detail, it is important here to review the responsibilities associated with the strategy. While many will look to a pay scale or dollar amount as the defining characteristic of a compensation strategy, it really begins with a pay philosophy.

Developing a Pay Philosophy

The executive leaders of the organization must establish a pay philosophy for the company. How does the compensation and benefits offered by the organization support the mission and vision of the company by attracting and keeping the right talent? Are the values of the company reflected in this philosophy? When there are deliberate actions taken to develop the organizational compensation structure, it is a much more cohesive strategy. However, the intent is not to be restrictive or remove all flexibility or the company loses its ability to respond to market changes. For example, some positions may have a range of salary but more is offered to a new hire in an emerging market because of the limited availability of talent in that area. This is not a departure from the pay structure but a response to the market reality.

Lead, Match, and Lag

Senior HR professionals may recommend setting pay rates that lead, match, or lag the prevailing market to complement the company's pay philosophy. While some may think that it is imperative that a company always lead the market on pay, Table 7.2 shows that there may be more to examine depending on the situation.

TABLE 7.2 Compensation strategies

Strategy	Advantage	Disadvantage
Lead	Higher pay than competitors Can attract harder-to-find talent	Requires capital investment and more resources
Match	Keeps pace with the market	Requires continued assessment of the market
Lag	Conserves financial resources Most effective when there is an abundance of available talent	Limits flexibility in hiring the best talent Necessitates having other means of compensation or climate to retain talent

Sourcing, Selection, and Onboarding

Senior HR professionals are responsible for sourcing the talent of the organization. Sometimes this may be developing raw talent that may come from schools as entry-level hires, while other choices involve using external staffing agencies that use their resources to match candidates to requirements developed by the company. The HR team provides minimum and preferred qualifications for these job openings. Maintaining a steady talent pipeline is a required duty. The successful integration of recruiting sources, marketing, and the development of job requirements highlights a primary responsibility in this functional area.

The selection of qualified candidates is usually at the discretion of the hiring manager or supervisor. However, senior HR professionals establish selection procedures that should be followed to be compliant with laws and regulations governing hiring. They establish policies for the company to qualify and validate candidates. Senior HR professionals may be required to contract for background and screening services as part of the interview and selection process as well.

Onboarding is not just the first-day activities that are associated with HR. A successful onboarding includes integrating the employee into the culture of the company and ensuring that they are fully capable to perform their assigned duties. Senior-level HR practitioners usually do not conduct the day-to-day hiring processes but must be proficient enough in the details to monitor and synchronize. If there are multiple areas of a company each with HR support, at the senior level the HR director or manager will supervise the processes and ensure consistency among HR business partners or generalists who are performing the onboarding tasks. They may also provide status updates to organizational leadership about recruiting metrics and recommend any necessary changes to procedures. Onboarding may include initial training and assessment that the employee is trained and qualified to perform all assigned duties with the job. They must fully embrace the culture and values of the company. The more focus a company places on making an employee feel like a valued member of the team in the early stages of employment, the more likely the employee is to remain in the organization.

Branding Strategy

A company branding strategy includes determining how potential recruits and applicants view the brand and how that may support talent acquisition efforts for the company. A digital presence and the ability for applicants to apply to the company online can impact recruiting efforts as well. Senior HR professionals may work with the marketing team to have gift items and displays for hiring or job fairs and other community engagement opportunities. Company uniforms or attire for both on- and off-duty wear by employees "sell" the brand through awareness and visibility. Company sponsorships may also be part of the branding strategy. Senior HR professionals must work with the finance department to develop budgets for items specific to the branding of the organization.

Of course, one of the strongest brand representations is the employees themselves and the word of mouth on their job satisfaction. The company's reputation will be a strong indicator of the brand's value and how it can support talent management. The company needs to invest in its human capital to get a return in terms of engagement and long-term branding strategy.

Strategies for Engagement and Cultural Integration

Senior HR professionals are responsible for developing and evaluating strategies for engaging new employees and for managing their cultural integration into the company and throughout the various phases of a company's life cycle. Among the areas that this covers are new employee acculturation and periods of downsizing, restructuring, mergers and acquisitions, divestitures, and global expansions.

New Employee Acculturation

The faster an employee is accepted and integrated into the organization, the more their loyalty will be engendered, and the more likely they will remain committed to the company. Senior HR professionals are responsible for building programs and procedures around new employee acculturation. The Disney Company has a strong process in this regard. Its "Disney University" is designed to acclimate new employees to Disney's vision, values, and culture. The first "course" in this school is "Traditions" and is for every employee to learn the history of the Disney brand and why they do what they do. The United States military, which prides itself as being a professional and competent military force, has a basic training process that is as much about the acculturation of the service member and learning the ethos and value system as about military combat training. Even after the training phase, units receiving new members have a dedicated process to integrate them into the team and esprit de corps. Here are some key points for successful acculturation:

- Develop a history of the company that is communicated to each new employee.
- Discuss the mission, vision, and values of the company.
- Assign veteran employees to work with new hires to exemplify the work ethic and behaviors desired of employees.

- Include the employee's family as part of the welcome process when possible as part of the work-life balance.
- Design the process to be completed over time with specific events that reinforce the culture instead of a onetime event early in the onboarding.

Engagement Strategies and Practices

Senior HR professionals are responsible for the development and implementation of engagement strategies and practices that motivate and drive the talent of the organization to perform tasks and exhibit behaviors that facilitate the accomplishment of the goals and objectives of the company. These practices must align with the company's values, and senior HR professionals are responsible for communicating these practices to managers and employees throughout the organization. Rewards and recognition programs, engagement surveys, and basic company practices are some of the strategies senior HR professionals may explore.

Rewards and Recognition Programs

Senior HR professionals help design and implement rewards and recognition programs to positively reinforce employee behaviors that emulate the company's values. When implemented correctly, they will encourage employees to stay in the organization. The rewards can be large or small but should demonstrate how the employer values the contribution made by the employee. For example, if an employee's action saves the company thousands of dollars, providing a $5 gift card to a coffee shop doesn't say that the employee's actions are highly valued.

Training and opportunities to grow and develop skills are also a means of recognizing the achievement and potential of employees. The employer should dedicate resources to helping manage the talent so that there is a pool of available individuals who can be moved into leadership or supervisory roles and who are capable of performing those tasks and responsibilities successfully.

Engagement Surveys

Another effective retention tool is the *stay interview*. This technique allows supervisors or the HR team to engage employees and determine what needs are being met and which ones are not and helps understand the motivations of employees. Surveys, needs assessments, and one-on-one interviews will help senior HR professionals and supervisors understand clearly why employees want to stay in an organization. While not all employee needs can be met by an organization, the idea is to see where the company can invest resources to improve the chances that an employee will choose to remain loyal to the organization instead of deciding to transition.

NOTE Websites such as Glassdoor.com allow employees to anonymously rate their companies in a variety of areas including salary, climate, benefits, and the effectiveness of company leadership. Companies can effectively use this tool as feedback for the engagement of the employees, and senior HR professionals can make recommendations to adjust policies or practices that may have the effect of disengaging employees at work.

Basic Company Practices

Employees stay with organizations where values align. An employee has a reasonable expectation that they will be treated fairly, provided a fair wage, have effective leadership with clear goals and vision, be trained sufficiently to perform their job duties well, and have the time, equipment, money, and people required to complete the expected tasks. If these basic needs are met, the employee has no need to seek elsewhere. It is only when there is a large enough imbalance that retention becomes an issue because the fear of the unknown and seeking other employment options is outweighed by the perceived lack of support within the organization.

Engagement during Transitions

In organizations that are experiencing changes, a large responsibility of senior HR professionals is to develop communication practices that are as transparent as possible and engage employees who are affected by transitions. When a company downsizes or restructures, there may be anxiety and fear among employees about layoffs or other changes that would be significant to morale. There are often questions, unfamiliar processes, and decisions that are made that must be communicated.

When a company is involved in a merger or acquisition, the same concerns exist with employees who might now have to compete for positions with new workers added or learn new competencies; this could be difficult for some employees who have not kept pace with skills development in an emerging market. In general, employees will lose stability, and senior HR professionals must examine the expected changes and identify key employees and managers who can help with the transition or may need support. Managing the impact on employees requires a high degree of emotional intelligence. Communicating and being honest assures the employees of the intent of the organization and respects the concerns they may have. While ultimately a business decision must be reached on the merits of the business needs, being attuned to the attitudes of the workers will help keep them engaged in the process of change.

Exam Essentials

Know the various engagement strategies available to HR.   An organization can use several methods to engage people to achieve the company's mission. You should understand the different means and the pros and cons they present. Especially important is to review the organizational culture and choose options that have a direct impact on business decisions using methods that are available to the organization. Also important is to know the timelines associated with each choice because some engagement strategies can take time to mature and develop.

Understand data and statistical analysis.   Know how to extract information from tables on demographics, pay, numbers of jobs available, and how that information is relevant to where and how to recruit talent. Using data helps evaluate and forecast organizational needs.

Summary

Finding the right people at the right time and with the right knowledge, skills, and attributes is an ongoing challenge for any organization looking to maximize its human capital potential. Talent planning is an essential skill that senior HR professionals must possess. The added complexity of understanding the business life cycle and the demands on talent at each phase mandates the need to hire a diverse workgroup capable of meeting the needs of the company. Companies must select and retain the desired talent through a variety of strategies and successfully integrate new hires into the company culture. By using effective tools and resources, along with external partners, HR teams can become effective in delivering the necessary talent that meets the needs of the company to perform its mission.

Test-Taking Tip

Look at a company's website and their careers or employment page. Review the job application process and recall the steps to hire that you went through to get your current position. Review any checklists or onboarding packets that new employees are required to complete during the hiring process. Pay close attention to the mandatory disclosure statements about equal opportunity or other antidiscrimination hiring practices and policies.

Review Questions

1. When searching for passive candidates to employment opportunities, HR professionals should consider _____ .

    A. Internal candidates

    B. Candidates who submit résumés through an online application portal

    C. Individuals working for competitors who are being compensated at or below market

    D. An individual who has been in the same position for almost 10 years

2. When determining whether a test is reliable in selecting an applicant for hire, it is important that the test _____ .

    A. Consistently measures what the employer intends to measure during the test

    B. Predicts how the employee will perform in their new duties

    C. Is effective in measuring an applicant's qualities

    D. All of the above

3. When interviewing an applicant, choosing to have several technical experts conduct the interview is an example of what?

    A. Situational interview

    B. Behavioral interview

    C. Panel interview

    D. Working interview

4. Onboarding a new employee is the responsibility of _____ .

    A. The HR department

    B. First-line supervisors

    C. Senior management

    D. All of the above

5. Computing the cost per hire is a way to determine which of the following?

    A. HR's internal budget

    B. The time needed to onboard a new employee

    C. Staffing effectiveness

    D. None of the above

6. Voluntary quits tend to occur in the market _____ .

    A. As the economy improves

    B. As unemployment rates rise

    C. As the economy declines

    D. As companies announce layoffs

7. To assess the skills of the available workforce, an HR department could _____ .

   A. Use a timed, written exam not tied to the essential elements of the job

   B. Hire a third party or outside vendor

   C. Create a skills team to determine what job duties are needed in each position

   D. None of the above

8. Succession planning for an organization is _____ .

   A. Preselecting preferred employees to fill senior management roles in the future

   B. Part of a broader talent management strategy

   C. The first step of a gap analysis

   D. All of the above

9. A company located in Seattle, Washington, as part of the post-employment activities for a new employee residing in Boston, Massachusetts, may engage in which of the following?

   A. Contact references to verify employment history

   B. Assist the employee with relocation

   C. Use online teleconferencing technology to facilitate the interviews

   D. Offer a signing bonus

10. A critical aspect of retaining quality employees in an organization is _____ .

   A. Rigid management that is focused on achieving business results

   B. Limiting training to increase productivity of the workforce

   C. A strong socialization and onboarding of new employees

   D. Providing higher compensation or a raise in salary

11. An exit interview should be conducted _____ .

   A. To improve the organization by getting feedback on working conditions

   B. On every employee who is being involuntarily terminated

   C. By the immediate supervisor or someone in the employee's chain of leadership

   D. Only when requested by the employee

Chapter 8

Learning and Development (SPHR® Only)

THIS CHAPTER COVERS THE SPHR®
EXAM CONTENT FROM THE LEARNING
AND DEVELOPMENT FUNCTIONAL AREA
AND CONSISTS OF THE FOLLOWING
RESPONSIBILITIES AND REQUIRED
KNOWLEDGE. FOR PHR® EXAM CONTENT,
REVIEW CHAPTER 3. RESPONSIBILITIES:

- ✓ 01 Develop and evaluate training strategies (for example: modes of delivery, timing, content) to increase individual and organizational effectiveness

- ✓ 02 Analyze business needs to develop a succession plan for key roles (for example: identify talent, outline career progression, coaching and development) to promote business continuity

- ✓ 03 Develop and evaluate employee retention strategies and practices (for example: assessing talent, developing career paths, managing job movement within the organization)

IN ADDITION TO THE PRECEDING
RESPONSIBILITIES, AN INDIVIDUAL
TAKING THE SPHR® EXAM SHOULD
HAVE WORKING KNOWLEDGE OF THE
FOLLOWING AREAS, USUALLY DERIVED
THROUGH PRACTICAL EXPERIENCE:

- ✓ 30 Training program design and development

- ✓ 31 Adult learning processes

✓ 32   **Training and facilitation techniques**

✓ 33   **Instructional design principles and processes (for example: needs analysis, content chunking, process flow mapping)**

✓ 34   **Techniques to assess training program effectiveness, including use of applicable metrics**

✓ 35   **Career and leadership development theories and applications**

✓ 36   **Organizational development (OD) methods, motivation methods, and problem-solving techniques**

✓ 37   **Coaching and mentoring techniques**

✓ 38   **Effective communication skills and strategies (for example: presentation, collaboration, sensitivity)**

✓ 39   **Employee retention strategies**

✓ 40   **Techniques to encourage creativity and innovation**

This chapter covers the area of learning and development. This important topic composes 12 percent of the SPHR® exam. The topic is covered in the exam because senior HR professionals will be responsible for the growth and development of the talent in their organization. Additionally, HR must analyze the business needs for companies and must understand how this translates to training strategies. Employees learn and retain new concepts and ideas by creating training that is impactful.

The key skills to master in this chapter are developing and evaluating training strategies, developing a succession plan for key positions, and developing employee retention strategies. At the senior level, HR professionals must know techniques, theories, and practices related to organizational and professional development and how the successful implementation of training impacts overall retention.

Required Knowledge

The desire of every senior HR professional is to help their company's leaders be champions of continuous learning and development. Effective organizational leaders help employees to reach their maximum potential to grow and support the organization as they continue to improve the business. To do this, senior HR professionals must be proficient in assessing training and development needs, developing and implementing training, and determining the effectiveness of the training delivered. They must be fluent in modern instructional design principles and have knowledge of learning theory. They must master techniques of facilitation and delivery of instruction, as well as methods of coaching and mentoring to encourage learners in the learning process.

Training Program Design and Development

Senior HR professionals must know how to design and develop training programs that build the talent in the organization and enable employees with the proper knowledge, skills, and abilities to meet the organizational goals and mission while supporting the underlying values of the company. These training programs might be technical or behavioral and could be internally developed or externally procured to meet the needs and budget of the company.

A training program is more complex than just one course or class. It is a comprehensive system with delivery mechanisms, measures of performance, tracking of progress, and the means to adjust training as needs change in the company. The first step in design is to determine needs through a skills gap assessment—that is, what are the skills, points of knowledge, or abilities that are missing currently in the organization that are required to perform jobs? From there, senior HR professionals can determine the best method to deliver the training that will be most effective in closing the gaps.

Training programs must be systematic, progressive, and comprehensive in their design and function. Each level of learning should build on previous knowledge and follow a flow that enhances the retention of the material learned. Often senior HR professionals must coordinate between the instructional designer who creates the training, the subject-matter expert who has the knowledge that the course is founded upon, and the facilitator who will present the material. Generally, these are different individuals, and the synchronization can be challenging.

Adult Learning Processes

The classic adult learning theory was popularized by Malcolm Shepard Knowles (1913–1997), who developed these four concepts related to adult learning:

- Adult learners want to have a voice in deciding the content and method of delivery.

- Adult learners are most interested in learning about something that has immediate impact and relevance in their world.

- Adult learning is experiential, meaning that adults draw upon their own experience to learn new concepts.

- Adult learners use problem solving as the primary method of learning and retention of ideas and concepts.

In addition to Knowles's learning theory, Benjamin Bloom (1913–1990) defined what has become a standard taxonomy of learning. It has three levels of learning, based on senses, emotions, or knowledge. The cognitive level, based on knowledge, has six levels: Remember, Understand, Apply, Analyze, Evaluate, and Create (or Synthesize). This is important to understand for adult learning because it shows the levels of retention and ability to integrate new concepts from the lowest level (just understanding) to the highest (creation of new thoughts based on what has been learned).

A full dive into the adult learning process is beyond the scope of this guide, but a general understanding will help with concepts outlined in Chapter 3 for the PHR® exam and is equally applicable to senior HR professionals. For more information on this subject, I recommend the Department of Education information paper at https://lincs.ed.gov/sites/default/files/11_%20TEAL_Adult_Learning_Theory.pdf.

Instructional Methods and Delivery

Senior HR professionals will know how to train and prepare facilitators for training events. They must understand the adult learning model, taking on the role of group advisor or senior trainer/instructional designer to help the collective team discover and learn using their own experience and understanding. The material is available for the group to draw upon, discuss, and collaborate, and the facilitator keeps the team motivated and sets milestones and general guidelines to ensure that learning objectives are met.

Training can now be delivered in a traditional classroom presentation or through online content or blended using both methods. Senior HR professionals must know how to find the best methods to deliver materials and subjects to ensure maximum retention. Some complex tasks require hands-on experience to learn. Training on equipment, on complex machines, or in specific locations cannot be easily replicated in a classroom.

In a classroom, there can be interaction with the instructor. With e-learning, an instructor must anticipate questions that will flow naturally and prepare the response within the script. It is beyond the scope of the exam to know instruction design software for building online learning; however, it is the responsibility of HR to be able to review, evaluate, and select the platforms available to deliver the training.

Career Development and Leadership

Great organizations have intentional paths for how an entry-level employee grows and progresses throughout their tenure with the company. For example, in the United States Army, how does a new private who enlists today grow up to be a senior noncommissioned officer, an officer, or potentially a four-star general? Every career field has a career development model that is designed to plan the steps needed to advance and that includes experience, education (both formal and informal), and professional development. Not only the *what* but the *when* in the timeline of a career is essential.

This is equally true in civilian companies. It is important when an employee joins the company that they understand what they need to do to continue to grow and advance. Sometimes they may not seek increased responsibility or supervisory roles, so there should be consideration paid to how to enrich their current role to maintain engagement and keep the employee motivated to achieve the goals and objectives that support their role and the company's mission, vision, and values. A career development map can show which positions have similar skills or duties that facilitate an employee switching jobs or career paths. From this, an individual can create a personal career development plan that takes into account their goals and desires and the needs of the company.

It is not always possible for the employee's ideal work and the reality of the job requirement demands for the company to align perfectly. In these cases, it is necessary for the leadership of the organization to motivate, coach, and develop the employee to maximize their contributions. Leaders select leaders and must be involved in succession planning to identify future leaders. They intentionally plan for their development to assume roles of greater significance, determining how to close or minimize any skills gaps in these prospects.

Real World Scenario

Leadership Development Program

A company recognized that 40 percent of its organization was retirement eligible in the next five years. In addition, 60 percent of the individuals in leadership positions were retirement eligible. This risk of loss of institutional knowledge and expertise was significant to the company, and the executive director in conjunction with HR developed a program to identify high-performance potential employees and group them in cohorts to train in four core competencies that were deemed critical needs for leaders in the organization. This provided multiple individuals who had training and potential to perform at higher levels and were exposed to senior executives in the company to draw upon their knowledge and expertise in the field. This step allowed the company to prepare for the "Silver Tsunami" of baby boomers soon to retire without significant interruption to functions in the organization.

Instructional Design Principles and Processes

When designing instructional material, it is important to understand the basic design principles and processes. The general intent is to know how the adult human brain learns and design a presentation in such a way as to maximize the retention and comprehension of the information. Through the use of developed instructional design techniques, content material can be learned faster and more efficiently with greater simplicity.

The first step is a needs analysis. As discussed in other chapters about total rewards, talent management, or anything that requires HR input into business operations, a needs analysis clearly shows what the organization requires to meet its goals and objectives. A proper needs analysis in instructional design will reveal what needs to be learned and the best methods to achieve learning.

HR professionals should be familiar with such design models as Analysis-Design-Development-Implementation-Evaluation (ADDIE). This five-step process begins with analysis of the problem or objective, followed by intentional design and development of the training and its implementation. It then concludes with an evaluation of the results. This dynamic and flexible process provides necessary structure for learning development.

Another example is Robert Gagne's nine events of instruction, a model that attempts to capture the process of learning in concrete events as they occur in the instructional process. Figure 8.1 shows the events that were first developed by the American educational psychologist. The process begins with capturing the attention of the learner and flows through to practical use of the information gained, where the knowledge is transferred to long-term memory and can be recalled and used over and over.

FIGURE 8.1   Gagne's nine events of instruction

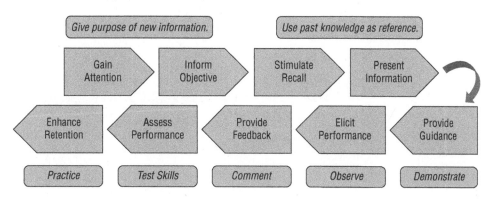

Needs Assessment and Analysis

Several functional areas require HR professionals to know how to conduct a needs assessment and then analyze the results. A needs assessment uses a simple technique of establishing a goal or objective state for a project or program within an organization, evaluating the current state, and then comparing the results. If there is a delta that shows a gap, the organization must create a pathway to achieve the desired results. The gap will often show what is needed to change the current situation, but in some cases, there may be different options or choices available. Courses of action can be developed, evaluated, and implemented. Time, resources, equipment, and people are all factors that may present needs or shortfalls, and from this the organization can plan how to overcome the need. In the analysis, the company compares the results with the planned actions to determine whether the gap has been successfully addressed, and if not, why not. Structurally, this is a cyclical event that continually reviews progress toward an end state until it is achieved.

Needs assessments are conducted for workforce planning, recruiting, human resources development and training, compensation and benefits, and risk management to determine whether the company has the right workforce, whether sources of recruitment are providing the right talent mix, whether training is preparing employees to do the work, what benefits employees need to maintain a good quality of life balance, and whether safety measures can be improved for the company. Using the techniques to assess and analyze the needs of the company allows the organization to plan, manage resources, and prioritize efforts to accomplish the goals of the company.

Process Flow Mapping

When a process is created in the organization, process flow mapping allows the steps in the process to be visually displayed so that the learner can review the process and have greater understanding and comprehension. It allows the learner to identify steps that don't add value, facilitates teamwork and communications, and keeps everyone on the same page. There are standard graphics used in modern process flow mapping. Figure 8.2 provides an example of a basic process shown in a flow map. Creating the map is often part of the instructional design process so that the employee can learn visually how the process is to be followed.

FIGURE 8.2   Process flow map

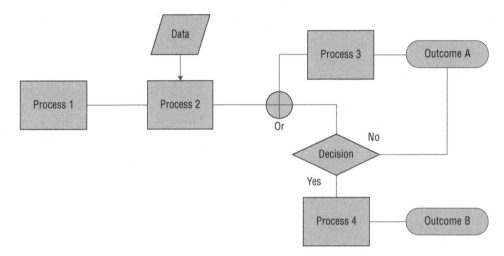

Content Chunking

Content chunking is the process of breaking down material in a learning environment into smaller components that are easier to process mentally and allow for greater understanding and retention of the information. As an example, this book uses specific formats, fonts, and visual cues to show the content in a manner that the learner can process quickly and absorb. You've probably noticed that the text does not flow sequentially based on the exam content outline at the beginning of the chapter. Instead, the information is covered in groups of like ideas, concepts, or function. The knowledge section is presented first because HR professionals must know first before they actually do. All of these elements are done intentionally in the design as a means of content chunking.

Training and Facilitation Techniques

Senior HR professionals must be proficient in the various techniques related to training and facilitation. The Association of Talent Development (ATD) is a professional organization that supports training and instructional design professionals and is a great resource for the HR community to have greater depth in this area. For more information, visit www.td.org.

Training Techniques

Senior HR professionals are often responsible for training other trainers, senior managers, and executives in a variety of subjects. It is required that they understand different training techniques and how to instruct others in the use of such techniques. With the availability of modern technology, there are now more options available including simulations and virtual environments, along with more traditional classroom methods or on-the-job (OJT) training. OJT offers a unique opportunity for hands-on learning in the actual environment where the work is performed under real conditions, but it doesn't allow for many mistakes or errors. The classroom works when learning theory or basic concepts related to the job but does not lend itself to realistic training because the environment doesn't account for real working conditions. A virtual environment is helpful when communicating and learning across distances or with multiple learners, but again it may not be the optimal learning environment for real conditions. In those situations, it also limits the amount of direct interaction between the learners and the instructor. All HR professionals must contemplate the training that will be conducted and determine the best technique to use to achieve learning. These techniques are used in combination with other core elements discussed, including the adult learning process and motivational concepts.

Facilitation Techniques

Senior HR professionals will know how to facilitate training events as well as develop master trainers who can improve courses and the platform skills of others. As part of the adult learning model, the lead trainer is not an instructor providing all the knowledge and information but instead takes on the role of group advisor to help the collective team discover and learn using their own experience and understanding. At the senior level, these groups often consist of executives or individuals with a great deal of experience and knowledge, so the focus is on keeping the group working toward a collective goal and remaining on task. The material is available for the group to draw upon, discuss, and collaborate, and the facilitator keeps the team motivated and sets milestones and general guidelines to ensure that learning objectives are met.

Training can now be delivered in a traditional classroom presentation or through online content or blended using both methods. HR professionals must know how materials and subjects are best presented to ensure maximum retention. Some complex tasks require hands-on experience to learn. Training on equipment, on complex machines, or in specific locations cannot be easily replicated in a classroom.

In a classroom, there can be interaction with the instructor. With e-learning, an instructor must anticipate questions that will flow naturally and prepare the response within the script. It is beyond the scope of the exam to know instruction design software for building online learning; however, it is the responsibility of HR to be able to review, evaluate, and select the platforms available to deliver the training.

Evaluating Program Effectiveness

Senior HR professionals are responsible for evaluating the effectiveness of employee training programs. There are several methods for establishing the metrics and collecting data to compare the program results with the desired results. Surveys are a comprehensive method for quickly collecting results and depending on the type of survey can measure various levels of responsiveness. Table 8.1 shows examples of surveys, the information they solicit, and how that information is used by an organization.

TABLE 8.1   Surveys

Survey Type	Information Gathered	Allows Measurement of
Immediate reaction	Responsiveness/quality of instruction or instructor	Initial response to training format and delivery
Short-term follow-up	Check on learning/implementation of instruction	Utilization of knowledge obtained in training
Long-term follow-up	Determination of incorporated practices	How much the information from training has improved the process output or results

Using Metrics to Evaluate Training Effectiveness

The cost for training and the retention of information in post-learning surveys or tests are two metrics that companies commonly use to measure training effectiveness. It is important that HR professionals know how to capture all the costs associated with learning and development. These costs include not just paid courses external to the company but also those of the internal resources committed to building in-house learning. Senior HR professionals can also develop tests that are administered after a short period of time following training to reinforce and measure retention of information of the class provided.

Organizational Development

Organizational development (OD) theory looks at both processes within an organization and the implementation strategy. A learning organization is one that continually assesses its situation, determines what it needs to improve, and develops a plan to make those improvements. It then evaluates the results at the end and starts the process again. As part of this theory, senior HR professionals should know change management and the variety of quality and control improvement methods that exist. Table 8.2 lists some common methods and their key points.

TABLE 8.2   Quality improvement methods

Method	Key Aspects
Total Quality Management	▪ Find issues that affect quality
	▪ Identify stakeholders in the process
	▪ Eliminate wasteful steps
	▪ Establish conditions that support continuous improvement
ISO 9000	▪ Benchmark standards that define quality processes in a company
	▪ Implement continuous improvement
	▪ Focus on reducing defects

Method	Key Aspects
Cause and effect	■ Establish major factors in defects to process and what elements cause them
	■ Create a visual map to improvement
Lean process	■ Establish principles on which to do work, such as the 5S methodology (Sort, Set in Order, Shine, Standardize, Systems)

In addition to quality improvement methods, senior HR professionals oversee the implementation of desired changes in an organization and reporting results to the executive leadership. There are three basic areas: people, technology, and structure. Figure 8.3 shows their relationship and how they may interact within an organization. It is important to know and understand how each type of change affects the other areas and how to adapt these changes over time.

FIGURE 8.3   Organizational development change theories

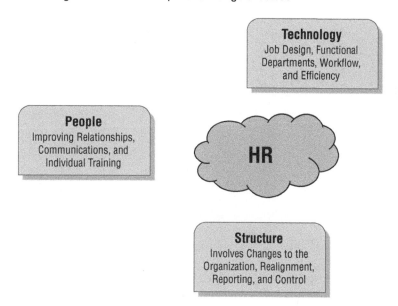

In all cases, senior HR professionals must know how to act as the change champion, embracing the continued growth and development of the company and reassuring its human capital that to be successful companies must continually change to meet the current demands that are informed by the current operational environment. They must communicate with leaders, employees, and other HR professionals about how people are accepting and adjusting to the reality of change within the company.

Motivation Concepts and Applications

A key point of knowledge for senior HR professionals is an understanding of motivation for employees and its relationship with organizational behavior. There are many different models and academic studies on this topic, each with a different variation on what compels people to behave in certain ways and how to use that knowledge to lead and inspire others to perform in a manner consistent with the desired values and behaviors of the company. It is not necessary to study every single motivational method in detail, but senior HR professionals should be familiar with the concepts and how to train and develop other HR professionals in this important functional area.

Maslow's Hierarchy of Needs

Probably the most popular motivational structure is Maslow's hierarchy of needs, first developed by Abraham Maslow in his research published in 1943. This model lists six levels from the basic physiological to self-actualization and explains that individuals move along the hierarchy only after each lower level is satisfied. Figure 8.4 shows the hierarchy model. It is important for HR professionals to understand these basic needs to help the organization provide for their employees and allow them to develop. For example, according to the hierarchy, physiological needs (such as food, shelter, and clothing) are well below esteem (accolades, rewards, and recognition). Therefore, it is logical that an employee's basic compensation so that they can buy those items to meet physiological needs is of greater importance than a certificate of appreciation for their quality of work. However, for an employee to progress to self-actualization, those points of recognition are also needed.

FIGURE 8.4 Maslow's hierarchy of needs

Theory X and Theory Y

Motivation of employees is important to their development and continued effective performance in an organization. Developed by Douglas McGregor at MIT in the late 1950s and 1960s, the two competing philosophies known as Theory X and Theory Y reflect on the nature of the generic worker and the corresponding management techniques that should be applied. Theory X views workers in a generally negative light, holding that they are not motivated to work and when given a choice will choose not to work and be generally lazy.

The management technique that is required under this theory is one of punishment and reward to constantly motivate employees to meet the demands of the organization and segregate those workers unable to perform from those who can. Managers focus on tasks to be performed rather than the workers who perform such tasks more often in this scenario.

The converse to this is Theory Y, where the employee is motivated internally to succeed and do the necessary work, and it is obstacles or restrictions that limit the performance of most employees. Therefore, the manager's role is to eliminate barriers of performance by communicating with the employee and help find ways to help the employee. These managers are more proactive and people-oriented than task-oriented. In the first theory, the relationship is more transactional, while in the second case it is more transformational. In Theory X management, the results last only as long as the desire for reward or punishment is greater than the consequences of not completing the task in the mind of the employee. However, Theory Y will have a longer effect if the known barriers are removed and the employee is free to develop.

Problem-Solving Techniques

An eight-step problem-solving method is an example of a practical series of actions to take when solving complex problems. There are many versions of this method, but not all problems require a formalized step method. Many small issues are solved without the need to address each step. However, for difficult issues, HR professionals should be aware of the following steps:

1. Define the problem.

2. Gather facts and assumptions.

3. Define the goals and objectives and establish success criteria.

4. Determine root causes and develop possible solutions.

5. Analyze and compare the solutions and choose the best option.

6. Implement the proposed solution.

7. Evaluate the results.

8. Continue to monitor progress of results and recommend any changes or future action.

Mentoring and Executive Coaching

Senior HR professionals must have knowledge of mentoring and executive coaching. This is not the same as being an instructor or a supervisor, as the relationship between the senior HR professional and the individual is based on *referent power*.

That is, senior HR professionals through their competence and extensive knowledge demonstrate their ability to be subject-matter experts and so derive power from their position to influence key members of the executive, supervisory group, and general employees. Their influence extends only to the point that these groups value and respect the information and abilities they provide. When fulfilling the role of a mentor, it is important that senior HR professionals help with discovery and exploration of competencies, behaviors, actions, and results, as well as the causes and effects from each exchange with employees and management alike. As all employees are different, there will be different dynamics and results with each pairing. Providing honest feedback in a manner that is respectful and focuses on the outcomes, without judgment, creates a climate of trust, making it more likely the individual will accept recommendations and counsel.

At the executive level, this can be even more delicate. In many situations, senior HR professionals report directly to a member of the executive team, and yet they are responsible for the human resources development and talent management of the organization, which includes top executives. As the company grows as a learning organization, so must the leadership. Great leaders understand this principle and will often seek the advice and counsel of HR professionals to provide direct assessment of the status of the human capital in the organization. HR must have working knowledge of influence, organizational behavior, emotional intelligence, and leadership principles to be effective as an executive coach. This is difficult in part because leaders often feel vulnerable addressing their shortcomings or needs for development with anyone perceived to be a subordinate. It takes time to build this important relationship to earn the trust required to be effective in this capacity.

Coaching Managers

Senior HR professionals must work with supervisors and managers throughout the human resources development process. Often they will be responsible for developing new managers and helping them understand their new role as an organizational leader. Managers often are highly skilled and knowledgeable about technical processes, but that doesn't necessarily mean they are able to teach and groom others or can identify untapped potential performers in the group. All HR must use interpersonal skills to build relationships with managers to help them develop all their employees to constantly and consistently achieve the goals set by the company. HR professionals use their role as advisors to coach managers to have deliberate discussions about employees' desire for progression, career goals, and development plans. Both HR and management develop training to provide the needed skills for employees to advance and improve. HR must also ensure that managers understand their internal biases and ensure equal opportunity for all high-potential performers. HR professionals should routinely meet with managers to discuss their teams and the best course of action to develop them that meets the goals and objectives of the company.

Encourage Creativity and Innovation

Senior HR professionals should encourage creativity and innovation within the culture of the organization. In a similar manner to those techniques employed by coaches and mentors, encouraging creativity allows for the free flow of information and newly generated solutions to problems that can negatively impact the organization. To truly be innovative requires the removal of fear of failure. This does not mean removing consequences for poor performance or bad actions, but rather that when mistakes are made in the learning process, the focus is on correction and growth, not shame and blame. An organization that inspires dialogue and continuous improvement in the learning process will see the results in innovation.

Turnover is very costly in organizations. The company commits time and resources to the learning and development of its employees and expects a return on that investment. When an employee departs the company, that loss has a financial impact and affects the morale of others. A company that is constantly in training mode for new employees cannot move forward or grow; it stagnates. Therefore, senior HR professionals must know employee retention strategies to keep their engagement high. They must possess strong interpersonal communication skills and be able to relate to the working conditions of the employees and have influence where needed. These are some areas that should be considered in the strategies:

- Rewards and recognition programs
- Training opportunities and continued development
- Career progression
- Job enrichment and job enhancement

Communication Skills and Strategies

Communication is a critical skill in HR. Senior HR professionals must be especially well versed in the variety of strategies available to send and receive information and provide feedback. Communications consist of verbal and nonverbal cues that an individual interprets through the filter of their experience and can sometimes distort through prejudices or biases that may exist. How the communicator presents the information can also have a profound impact on the reception. For example, a message sent by email is received differently than one communicated by telephone or face to face because those methods include nonverbal and visual cues that are not conveyed in text. A written communication often conveys none of the emotion or timbre that is more apparent in direct visual or auditory communication. The following are some other considerations for communication:

- The ability to collaborate with a group and share complex ideas across a multitude of media
- Presentation styles and how they can affect the message being delivered
- Sensitivity because certain topics require a different approach and it's imperative to understand how the audience will be impacted by subject matter
- Language barriers, especially in multinational or multilingual environments, which do not create a good environment for idiomatic expressions or paraphrasing
- The ability to communicate clearly and concisely

Exam Essentials

Understand organizational development theory. While it is not required to know every theory in detail, exam participants should know the basics and be able to identify more commonly used theories.

Know how learning and development translates into real-world organizations.   Almost every organization has some kind of learning and development system. The components, the various measuring methods, and how the system is used to advance employees in the company are important knowledge points for HR professionals.

Responsibilities

The responsibilities associated with the functional area of human resources development are critical to a successful organization, but often in smaller organizations some or all of the key tasks are outsourced. The tasks of other functional areas tend to have immediate impact on employees, support the immediate needs of employers such as payroll, or have compliance requirements that mandate work for HR such as record keeping. Because these short-term needs can overwhelm even the most efficient small HR teams, companies often view human resources development as a nice-to-have, not a need-to-have, function. Unfortunately, this is common, so senior HR professionals must strongly advocate for the continued development and training of the organization's talent or risk stagnation and complacency throughout the company.

Develop and Evaluate Training Strategies

At the core, learning and development are investments in an organization's human capital. Like any investment, they grow fundamentally based on how they are supported. If the company strives to be a learning organization, making efforts to improve its culture and its people regularly through intentional training strategies designed to align to the company's mission and goals, then it will sustain success. Otherwise, the company will plateau and then sharply decline over time as the conditions and people change.

Developing Training Programs

The purpose of training programs is to improve individual and organizational effectiveness. After evaluating the results of a needs assessment and developing courses of action for training, senior HR professionals will be responsible for the acquisition, design, and implementation of training and facilitators. There are numerous third-party vendors that provide training content, and the HR team will select and coordinate the training to be conducted. A curriculum is developed that determines the courses that will be required to meet the training goals. These courses vary based on time, content, and method of instruction but usually have a similar theme.

Training always demands resources, so part of the development is determining which training is a priority and will have the greatest impact to the organization. This does not always mean that those courses with the highest attendance are truly the most important. It is possible that for a critical function in the organization there may be only a few people responsible, but those few must have mandatory training to complete their assigned tasks correctly. Therefore, this training becomes a more urgent priority in situations where there could be a sudden transition from experienced to inexperienced individuals. HR professionals are responsible for recommending training focus and priority and monitoring the completion of the training.

Improving Organizational Effectiveness

Training should be tied to the overall goals and mission of the organization, and each individual position in the company should have required training to sustain and improve the team. As part of the training needs assessment, HR should look at the critical tasks performed by each employee and the necessary skills or behaviors that an employee should possess to perform the tasks properly. Using performance appraisal methods discussed later in the chapter, supervisors and management can determine where an individual employee needs to improve, and training can be matched to meet the needs. Surveys and assessments are conducted post-training to see whether there are changes in performance, improved efficiency, or other tangible results because of the training. Training the individual must align with the needs of the company to improve organizational effectiveness. The training must be balanced so that the employees' improvements are related to the areas the company needs to remain successful.

Succession Planning

Senior HR professionals must help the organization to grow and meet the ever-changing needs of its employees, stakeholders, and customers. As companies transform, there must be systematic plans that ensure continuity of core competencies and that knowledge is retained in the company. Key positions that have a large impact on the overall operations must have functional succession plans that identify potential replacements as vacancies are created over time through transition such as retirements. As a skill, senior HR professionals must know how change disrupts an organization and are responsible for minimizing the impact of those disruptions or mitigating the potential negative consequences that often follow change in succession.

Performance Management Systems

Development of an employee performance management system (EPMS) is a key responsibility of the HR team. As discussed earlier, HR attempts to align employee behavior with the desired behaviors needed to meet the company's goals and objectives. To measure the success of this, a key metric is an EPMS.

Several different systems can be used for this purpose, from comparing employees' performance to one another to using a scale that rates an individual against an established standard. There is formal feedback that can be given using a written format that includes required submission timelines and is completed periodically. There are also informal sessions, which allow a manager to be more of a coach and mentor to guide an employee to discover their potential and bring out characteristics that support the organizational mission, vision, and values.

Senior HR professionals are responsible for working with managers and executives to determine the best system that supports the culture while meeting the needs of objectively measuring the alignment of the employees with the company.

Performance Appraisal Processes

Senior HR professionals will develop policies that govern the instruments used for evaluating performance and the metrics for determining ratings. Policy should establish specifics including the time periods, standards for documenting or justifying exceptional or substandard performance, and how poor performance is handled by the company. Generally, there is a due diligence process to verify the required skills of a poorly performing employee and some period of remedial training before ultimately the employee is terminated for cause.

The most common type of appraisal is a forced ranking system in which employees are measured against one another to determine who the best performer is. If a numerical scoring system is used, the results tend to be a bell-shaped curve that has a small percentage at the top and bottom with the bulk of employees in the middle of the range. Figure 8.5 shows an example. Senior HR professionals should counsel managers and executives to be aware of the limitations with any appraisal method and be sure that evaluations are comprehensive to provide the best understanding of an employee's job performance.

FIGURE 8.5   A bell curve

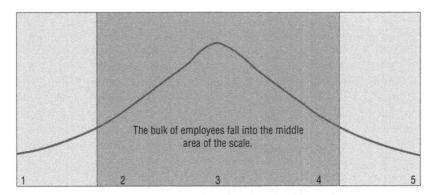

Other appraisal methods include narrative statements that quantify performance objectives and compare actual outcomes to goals or objectives established at the beginning of the rating period. Supervisors will meet with their employees to discuss performance periodically. Senior HR professionals are responsible for ensuring that there is an effective process and procedure to ensure that reviews are completed and documented. In the event of claims of wrongful terminations, they will work with legal counsel to provide detailed information to justify separation.

At the senior level, HR helps the organization develop general performance objectives that raters can use so that employees may provide input in a collaborative process to agree on the performance standards. Doing this allows the employee to "buy in" to the evaluation and take responsibility for the outcome.

Training for Evaluators

Senior HR professionals are responsible for providing training at the managerial and executive levels on how the evaluation process works for the organization. They will also train other HR generalists to understand the nuances to specific evaluations. Technical training, including the specifics of how any instruments are completed and submitted and the time frame to do so, is one form of training that senior HR professionals may delegate to other HR practitioners. The other, often more beneficial training requires helping supervisors develop clearly defined performance success criteria. Evaluations cannot be arbitrary, but often tasks are hard to measure from a quality standpoint. In manufacturing jobs, production numbers compared to goals are straightforward, and comparisons can be done from rating period to rating period. However, it is harder to measure qualitative results for manner of performance.

Supervisors must measure both technical and behavioral competencies in the evaluation to provide a comprehensive look at an employee's performance. Technical competencies are connected to what tasks are being completed and to what degree. Behavioral competencies seek to show how an employee is performing. Too often employers will overlook one side in favor of the other. Having someone who produces great results but has a negative attitude can still be a performance problem, as is someone who struggles to meet goals but is positive and gets along with co-workers. Senior HR professionals are skilled at navigating difficult conversations and can develop this skill in managers and supervisors.

Conducting a Needs Assessment

Senior HR professionals responsible for the development of the organization start with a needs assessment. Figure 8.6 shows the critical steps of the process. The results of the needs assessment will be a training plan or outline for a training event, such as a class or online course.

FIGURE 8.6   Needs assessment

The critical step in the process is obtaining a sponsor, usually someone with authority and ability to commit resources in which the return on the investment of training will improve a process; increase the knowledge, skills, or abilities of employees; or provide a better service or product as a result. Without "buy-in," it is unlikely that a company will fully embrace the training.

Additionally, the needs assessment ensures that the training solves the deficiency identified. For example, a manufacturing company has assembly technicians who struggle to meet their quota each day. If a needs assessment is conducted, it may reveal that the employees lack an understanding of the proper process, which is causing defects and delaying production. However, it may also reveal that there is a motivational behavioral problem that can be solved only through better leadership. In the second case, the proximate cause demands a different course of training.

Employee Retention Strategies and Practices

The responsibility a senior HR professional has regarding employee retention strategies and practices is to assess the talent in the organization, develop career paths that allow for progression in roles and responsibility, and manage the job movement within the organization. In performing these duties, senior HR professionals provide guidance and influence executives, managers, and employees to find the right balance of career experience, technical knowledge, and organizational roles for each individual in the company to maximize the human capital potential.

Talent Management

Senior HR professionals must help leaders manage the talent of the organization and continually invest in the employees to ultimately benefit the company. They build career development models and methods to identify high-potential employees to ensure that those employees are managed more closely. The goal is to groom them for positions of increased responsibility or complexity and to provide training at the right time in a career timeline to possess the right skills needed to do the work. Finally, senior HR professionals develop job enrichment opportunities for dedicated workers whose performance is aligned with the behaviors desired by the company to keep them engaged and performing at a high level.

Building a Career Development Model

Senior HR professionals must know how to chart the career progression of all the critical positions in the organization. It requires an understanding of the knowledge, skills, and abilities required of each position and how those positions might be developmental to other more senior positions such as supervisors or executives. Career development models also show HR planners where skills of positions overlap to enable cross-training or suggest lateral transfers across the company.

Ideal models can clearly demonstrate to new employees the career progression of a job within the organization and provide guidance as to how an employee can grow and develop their skills over time to advance in the company over an entire career. A career development model will show a combination of experience, education, and professional development that someone must possess to advance. It is important to note that while this process may show what is required, it doesn't evaluate the potential or performance of an individual. So, it is possible that an individual's career is limited by how well they are able to reach some of the milestones determined by a career development model. Figure 8.7 depicts a career development model for an administrative position within a human resources department in a company.

FIGURE 8.7   Career development model

CDM for HR Generalist
- Promotion potential to HR Lead or Supervisor
- Specialization as Benefits Administrator; Labor Relations Specialist;
     Organizational Trainer; Recruiter

Educational requirements: High school diploma, preferred two- or
four-year degree from accredited institution

Technical progression: HR training; certification (PHR)

Experience: Exposure and relevant work in HR subject areas of
workforce planning, HR development, employee relations, and
compensation and benefits. Firsthand knowledge of company
procedures and practices governing HR delivery.

Managing High-Potential Employees

As the term suggests, high-potential employees are those who have shown the ability to perform high-level tasks and are capable of management or supervisory responsibilities. Senior
HR professionals have a duty to help current managers identify, select, train, and advance
these individuals to help the company sustain its corporate leadership over time. Senior HR
professionals have oversight of the techniques and tools used in the organization that measure the potential of certain employees and then assist supervisors to cultivate skills. They
might require the use an individual development plan (IDP) to coach talented individuals
and assist their leadership in determining the areas that may need attention. Figure 8.8
shows a potential versus performance matrix, commonly referred to as a *nine-box*.

FIGURE 8.8   The nine-box model

Potential			
	High Potential Low Motivation	High Potential Moderate Motivation	High Potential High Motivation
	Moderate Potential Low Motivation	Moderate Potential Moderate Motivation	Moderate Potential High Motivation
	Low Potential Low Motivation	Low Potential Moderate Motivation	Low Potential High Motivation

Motivation

For high-potential employees, you are looking at those employees who would be categorized in the far-right column but not necessarily in the top-right corner. It is the job of management along with the assistance of HR to determine what limitations are preventing those employees in the spectrum to the right of the matrix from being placed in the upper right and how to overcome them.

Creating Job Enrichment Opportunities

In some cases, employees have reached their potential for advancement through either desire or capability but are still competent in their role and have a strong desire to perform their job functions well. Senior HR professionals must assist managers to creatively find opportunities to enrich the jobs these skilled individuals already have. In some cases, training on new technology or processes will better equip employees to do their job. Adding depth to their understanding of the role, which may include increased knowledge or control over certain aspects, can be considered enrichment. For example, an employee who is highly competent may be given a lead role for their job but not supervisory responsibility. They may instead be responsible for training new team members initially or perform quality control checks because of the quality of their work and knowledge of the right processes.

Developing Programs to Meet Changing Needs

As organizations grow and mature, HR professionals at a more senior level will identify changing needs in the organization and develop or implement programs to meet those changing conditions. For example, as a company's technology infrastructure grows and work can be performed remotely, a company may offer the opportunity for employees to do telework from an alternate work site. This simple concept involves many tasks for HR professionals, including coordinating with information technology and procurement departments on equipment needs for telecommuting and procedures for accountability of organizational equipment outside the normal place of work. Policy and procedures will change when new programs are implemented, and HR professionals have the responsibility to ensure that they are updated.

Senior HR professionals will evaluate new programs to determine whether the needs of the employees and organization are being met. Programs such as diversity and inclusion or apprenticeships are detailed and have significant impact across multiple domains in a company. Senior HR professionals must integrate these programs while keeping executives informed of the results.

Exam Essentials

Understand the correlation between training strategies and retention of employees.   An organization can use several methods to find and hire the right people to achieve the company's mission. You should understand the need to have a training strategy that positively impacts the retention of those hired. Especially important is to review the costs associated with each option, as that may have a direct impact on business decisions as to what methods are available to a particular organization. It's also important to know the timelines associated with each choice, because some training strategies can take time to mature and develop.

Understand how to perform retention analysis.   Human capital is expensive and should never be wasted. You should understand the direct correlation between employee turnover and lost opportunity or productivity costs. By performing analysis on the effectiveness of retention strategies of the company, you will be able to reduce turnover costs and keep a company performing at optimal levels.

Summary

Learning and development, or the effective management of talent within an organization, is a critical function for HR professionals to master and understand. They must be able to assess needs and meet business demands by developing comprehensive strategies that cover the opportunities for employees to participate, the design and creation of the training, and the performance assessment of employees.

Training development is the responsibility of the HR team by either creating the necessary training to improve performance or determining what available training may be outsourced to reduce costs and time to deliver. Understanding generally how the training cycle runs from need to design to implementation to evaluation is part of an HR professional's knowledge base. Senior HR professionals have the added responsibility for program development and coaching and mentoring at the executive level.

Test-Taking Tip

Talk with the individuals responsible for training in your organization and ask them about their important functions and daily job duties. Get a sense of what priorities they have to create and deliver effective training and how those priorities relate to the overall company mission and strategic goals and objectives.

Review Questions

1. Three basic areas of organizational change in a company are with its _____ .

   A. People, technology, and structure

   B. People, mission, and purpose

   C. Mission, vision, and values

   D. Technology, equipment, and finances

2. When selecting training programs for an organization, an HR professional should consider the following *except* which one?

   A. Number of employees to train

   B. Time to implement

   C. Method of delivery

   D. ROI

3. When conducting surveys to assess the effectiveness of training, the best results are with surveys that _____ .

   A. Measure the learners' immediate feedback on the class

   B. Collect data on learners' performance changes over time

   C. Test short-term retention of the material covered

   D. None of the above

4. High-potential employees are _____ .

   A. The primary focus of training within companies

   B. Easy to identify within the organization without any additional resources

   C. Critical to identify within the organization for succession planning

   D. Immediately capable of management or supervisory positions and should be promoted

5. What is the primary purpose for a performance appraisal system?

   A. As a developmental system to align behaviors of employees with the values of the company

   B. As a compliance tool

   C. As a mechanism to document poor performance to terminate unproductive employees

   D. As a method to compare different employees across different divisions of an organization

6. What is forced ranking an example of?

    A. A rating scale of a performance appraisal system

    B. A method to compare all the employees of a company

    C. A way to identify employees in the top and bottom percentage of the company

    D. All of the above

7. To ensure that consistent and effective evaluations are performed throughout the company, an HR professional should do what?

    A. Ensure that evaluators are properly trained in the process and understand how to use the evaluation tools

    B. Contract third-party trainers to instruct supervisors on the evaluation process

    C. Develop policies that establish guidelines and governance over the evaluation system

    D. Both A and C

8. A key responsibility of a senior HR professional in the human resources development is to do which of the following?

    A. Monitor the attendance and use of training classes by employees within the organization

    B. Teach customer services classes to employees

    C. Implement programs to meet the changing needs of employees and the organization

    D. Both A and B

9. Succession planning is best described by which of the following?

    A. A systematic approach to identify, assess, and develop talent for leadership roles in an organization

    B. Predetermining employees within the company to fill management roles

    C. Planning the career path of entry-level employees to fill different roles in the company

    D. None of the above

10. Organizational development (OD) theory has which two general categories?

    A. Change process and implementation

    B. Technology and personnel

    C. Design and implementation

    D. Quality control and execution

11. A company has a proprietary process using unique software and a custom-designed procedures manual. Preparing employees to work in this division successfully may require which of the following?

    A. Behavioral analysis

    B. General training

    C. Process redesign

    D. Specialized training

12. An HR professional should understand executive coaching as part of their role in human resources development. Which choice shows how this is best demonstrated in a company?

   A. An HR professional helps the chief operating officer develop a strategy to improve time management for all supervisors and managers.

   B. An HR professional delivers training on performance management to all supervisors in the company.

   C. An HR professional counsels an employee who is having difficulty performing tasks that a senior manager requires them to perform.

   D. An HR professional meets with the chief financial officer to understand the company growth plan for the next five years.

Chapter 9

Total Rewards (SPHR® Only)

THIS CHAPTER COVERS THE SPHR® EXAM CONTENT FROM THE TOTAL REWARDS FUNCTIONAL AREA AND CONSISTS OF THE FOLLOWING RESPONSIBILITIES AND REQUIRED KNOWLEDGE. FOR PHR® EXAM CONTENT, REVIEW CHAPTER 4. RESPONSIBILITIES:

✓ 01 Analyze and evaluate compensation strategies (for example: philosophy, classification, direct, indirect, incentives, bonuses, equity, executive compensation) that attract, reward, and retain talent

✓ 02 Analyze and evaluate benefit strategies (for example: health, welfare, retirement, recognition programs, work-life balance, wellness) that attract, reward, and retain talent

IN ADDITION TO THE PRECEDING RESPONSIBILITIES, AN INDIVIDUAL TAKING THE SPHR® EXAM SHOULD HAVE WORKING KNOWLEDGE OF THE FOLLOWING AREAS, USUALLY DERIVED THROUGH PRACTICAL EXPERIENCE:

✓ 41 Compensation strategies and philosophy

✓ 42 Job analysis and evaluation methods

✓ 43 Job pricing and pay structures

✓ 44 External labor markets and economic factors

✓ 45 Executive compensation methods

This chapter covers the important topics of total rewards for the SPHR® exam. *Total rewards* is the term referring to all policies, programs, compensation and benefits, recognition, and rewards designed to attract and retain the necessary talent to meet the organization's goals and objectives. It represents 12 percent of the total exam content. The functional role at the senior HR level, with respect to total rewards, is to monitor the effectiveness of compensation and benefits strategies for attracting, rewarding, and retaining talent. Senior HR professionals who understand the full details of such programs are much better equipped to analyze and develop strong programs that benefit all the employees of the company. Fairly providing compensation and benefits to company employees is critical to all successful organizations.

This chapter focuses primarily on analyzing and evaluating compensation strategies that support the company's mission, vision, and values. The process begins with the development of a compensation philosophy that meets the needs of the organization. Emerging companies that are growing do well to invest in a strong senior HR professional with knowledge of compensation and benefits to oversee the programs involved.

Required Knowledge

This chapter has among the most complex knowledge requirements of all the topics in this book. Because this is a review guide, the intention here and throughout is that individuals preparing to sit for the SPHR® exam already have a base knowledge and are reviewing the content as a refresher. However, I highly recommend that even individuals with experience and in-depth knowledge spend a little more time with this chapter. The knowledge areas of compensation and benefits can be viewed in different ways: strategy, methods, and responsibilities.

Compensation Strategies and Philosophy

In conjunction with the overall corporate strategy and aligned with the HR strategy, senior HR professionals must help the executive leadership establish a compensation and benefits plan that meets the needs of the organization and its valued employees. They are required to know and understand the factors that impact compensation and benefits within a market. Senior HR professionals should be familiar with the company's mission, vision, and values to know how to design a compensation and benefits strategy that matches them. Organizational culture and a pay philosophy from the executive leadership will impact the strategy as well.

Total Rewards Strategies

Senior HR professionals must know how to establish a total rewards strategy to attract and retain the right employees capable of performing the duties required to accomplish the goals of the organization. It begins with the company's pay philosophy, which determines how it will structure its compensation plan and the types of benefits that can be offered. The strategy must take into account the available resources and consider when and under what circumstances increases will be given.

The strategy first looks at external factors, which include the industry in which the company exists. Industries that have a shortage of qualified talent, such as emerging technology or information age companies, will have higher wage demands. Higher technical and skilled craftspeople will elicit a higher compensation scale as well. As a result, even the support functions and roles may have some pay affected by the other core occupations of the organization. Finally, where the company is located will also impact the compensation plan. Geographic distribution may have variations in labor costs, and this is magnified in international markets.

Senior HR professionals must know the market and the company's competition and with this knowledge make a decision about where to place the company's pay. If the organization matches the market, it will strive to be in balance with what others pay for talent. It will use metrics to establish the median salary point and try to target employees' salaries in a band on either side of this target. Companies with more available resources or seeking to be an industry leader will seek to lead the market by paying the highest salaries and providing the best benefits to the employees. The objective is to pull the best talent from the market to the company. However, it is important to be careful with this methodology as the highest paid is not always the best qualified; employees can be under- or overvalued. However, bringing in higher-paid employees should result in a more productive workforce, increasing profitability. Finally, a company may choose to lag the market wages because of costs or an availability of talent that allows the company to pay less and not fear loss of employees. It is also possible that any or all of these strategies may be employed at one point in the company's history or even at the same time with different occupations within the organization. Figure 9.1 shows the relative position of the wages in the market and their pros and cons.

FIGURE 9.1   Comparative wages

External Labor Markets and Economic Factors

Pay rates and the benefits offered cannot be exclusively controlled within the boundaries of the company. There are external factors that will impact decisions regarding compensation and benefits provided. Senior HR professionals must know how to review these external factors and estimate their impact on the company. Two significant areas to understand are the external labor market and other economic factors.

The external labor market consists of all the available talent external to the company that could be readily employed in the organization. Factors that affect this variable include the complexity of the work and required skilled labor needed to successfully complete the assigned duties. In cases where there is a shortage of qualified applicants, it will inflate the cost of human capital by the laws of supply and demand. Conversely, if there is an abundance of labor, companies will have an advantage when it comes to salary ranges. In states where there is a strong organized labor presence, the expectation is that negotiating wages will result in higher costs to the employer.

 In 2017, the Trump administration supported legislation that would alter the nation's immigration policy, which would impact the composition of immigrants entering the United States. This decision could potentially have consequences on the talent pool traditionally filled by immigrant labor and increase labor costs as a result.

The economy also plays an important role in the compensation and benefits strategy of a company. In times of economic recession, wages and costs are compressed in response to the slowdown. In 2008, the housing market bubble resulted in a significant economic downturn. Because the housing sector has such wide-ranging secondary effects, it ultimately put strain on certain industries that caused jobs to be lost, which created a spiral effect feeding on each other. While it is not the job of senior HR professionals to be economists, they must understand how the economy flows, especially in the United States, and how this ties to wages and unemployment.

Executive Compensation

Senior HR professionals must know and understand the difference between executive compensation packages and other pay structures for the rest of the organization. Executive-level compensation is usually reserved for those at the highest managerial and leadership positions within the organization. This is sometimes referred to as the *C-suite* as it includes the chief executive officer (CEO), chief financial officer (CFO), chief operating officer (COO), and other such designated positions that bear the responsibility and authority for the creation, execution, and sustainment of the company's mission, vision, and values. Because these positions have such a mantle of responsibility, including the professional lives, welfare, morale, and development of the company's entire workforce, it is difficult to determine a valuation for such positions.

There are two components to executive compensation. The first is the cash value, which consists of the base salary and any incentives that are paid annually, and the second is the noncash compensation offered by the company. The second is usually tied to the outcomes of the actions undertaken by the executive. It is important to note that the combination of both should align with the overall values of the company in terms of adequate compensation and reflect the values of the company. As discussed later in this chapter, there is an ethical component to pay for executives that must be considered when establishing the pay parameters. The cash portion is easier to calculate with a base salary and is set based on the knowledge, skills, and abilities of the executive, along with the experience and gravity of the job. Added to the base would be cash incentives that are a direct result of the outcomes of the executive's contributions to the company. These could be as much as twice the base salary depending on the company and the executive compensation structure.

Noncash Compensation

A large portion of the compensation at the executive level is the noncash part, which can consist of a variety of offerings depending on the organization. While there may be a cash value, there is often a conversion that is required to realize the full monetary potential of the compensation provided. Perks are those select items that are provided for executives and have some intrinsic value. A company car, for example, has some value, as does a company expense account in the form of a company credit card. Other items might be event tickets, passes to amusement parks, exclusive fitness club memberships, or any other item that is not available to the general employees but reserved only for executives to recruit and retain their commitment to the organization.

Another portion of the noncash compensation is the written consideration to provide an amount of money if a top executive were to lose their job as a result of the company being sold or acquired by an outside entity and they would otherwise have difficulty finding a similar job and compensation elsewhere. Designed to lessen the burden to the individual from the fall from the executive level, this is more commonly known as a *golden parachute*. Such items might include early access to benefits or the company contributions of a retirement account.

Stock in the company is the most common component of the noncash compensation. There are a variety of methods for companies that senior HR professionals should be aware of and understand the requirements of each. While it is not necessary to be a stockbroker to be in the HR field, knowing the implications and rules, or where to find them, is beneficial for educating executives who may be new to such structures or advising boards, directors, or pay committees that are developing plans or hire offers to executives. There are many tax implications that must be considered for each of the choices, but they are beyond the scope of this book. Some companies may choose to offer stock options; that is, they provide the executive with the opportunity to obtain stock in the company when the value of such stock is higher than would be the purchase price. By doing so with the options, the executive does not need to commit large amounts of personal funds to the deal, essentially ensuring a payout at the fair market value of the stock. Because this leverages certain invested amounts, there are restrictions and tax implications that should be considered for both the company and the executive.

Another stock program would be the purchase of stock itself. The stocks could be a diversified package that is managed to provide returns as dictated by the market but also could be portions of the company stock itself. In the second choice, federal law and regulations place restrictions on company executives, especially those who have responsibility over the financial performance of the organization where they might be in a position to manipulate the financial decisions in such a way as to increase the profitability and therefore the value, which would inflate stock prices. Legal limitations created under Sarbanes-Oxley in 2002 and Dodd-Frank in 2010 have greatly restricted the practices of stock purchase plans in publicly traded companies. There are other stock choices that closely resemble the ones previously mentioned but take a different form to meet different situations that can be advantageous to both the company and the executive. Figure 9.2 shows some comparisons of two common miscellaneous stock plans that an executive might receive.

FIGURE 9.2   Miscellaneous stock plans for executives

Phantom Stock
Similar to stock plans but for entities that are not publicly traded. Aligns executives to the owners by creating similar desired outcomes.

Restricted Stock
Requires no purchase from the executive. Has significant restrictions on when this can be optioned, keeping the executive engaged to collect the full value.

Methods

Having an overall strategy for how a company will provide compensation and benefits for its employees is only the first step in the process. There are several methods of executing the plan, once developed, that senior HR professionals must have knowledge of to be successful. These methods cover examining the jobs themselves and the pay structures that result. The pay and benefit programs that include executive compensation are the direct results of the methods discussed here.

Job Evaluation Methods

A job evaluation determines the relative worth to the company of any particular position. An HR professional can rank the positions in degrees of importance to the company or can compare each job to another using a predetermined value scoring. When we compare jobs in an organization, it can sometimes be difficult to determine the more important job when the jobs vary significantly. For example, it is challenging to compare the controller's value with that of an area HR manager or the IT supervisor. All are critical, but how they are paid compared to each other could be different in different companies.

A technique that can be used simply is to compare each job, one by one, with another in the organization in a matrix. That will result in a one-to-n list, where n is the total number of different jobs in the company in order of value. This process looks at the whole job, not individual skills or competencies required. Determining skills and competencies is the fastest method, but it isn't useful in knowing why one job is favored against another.

Another method is the classification of jobs into a set number of grades, such as in the federal or state government systems. These job classes group common knowledge, skills, or attributes (known as essential job functions) needed for the successful execution of the jobs in that category and may have common work done by all. In many cases, the HR function may list example jobs, or benchmarks, that fit in the category. This is a highly effective method for grouping large numbers of jobs such as would be required by the federal government. The downside of such a system is that by its nature it is general and broad. A company may have two unrelated job functions in the same classification. As you will see later in this chapter, when those jobs in the same classification are banded together for pay purposes, it highly restricts certain positions from being paid at a higher wage.

A quantitative approach as shown in Figure 9.3 uses established compensable factors to score each job in a point comparison. Compensable factors are value added to the organization. To ensure compliance with the Equal Pay Act and Title VII, the following factors should be considered:

- Skill
- Responsibility
- Effort
- Working conditions
- Supervision

These factors take into account the actual work performed, documented in a job description, and supporting the organization's mission, vision, values, and goals. They should be reviewed periodically and be valued by the stakeholders of the company.

FIGURE 9.3   Quantitative approach

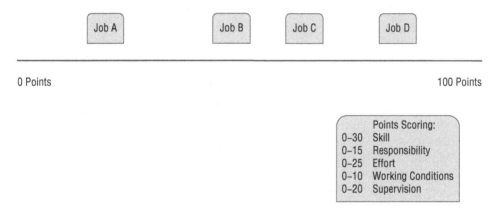

Job A   Job B   Job C   Job D

0 Points   100 Points

Points Scoring:
0–30   Skill
0–15   Responsibility
0–25   Effort
0–10   Working Conditions
0–20   Supervision

Senior HR professionals may choose to examine the jobs in their organization and conduct higher-level analysis with other similar jobs in the market and around the nation to benchmark relative value. This takes external factors into account such as the availability of qualified individuals and what competitor organizations are willing to pay for the same knowledge, skills, and abilities. The comparison can be scaled on a local area, at the state level, or nationally. There are several companies that specialize in doing pay studies that can help by analyzing large quantities of data to refine market-based pay. It is important to know the pros and cons of using external market values. For example, a company may value a particular position or job skill as more important than other companies and therefore have a higher pay value. Or it may be part of an emerging industry that does not have a lot of useful data yet, meaning that its market is not mature enough to price-compare.

Job Pricing and Pay Structures

Senior HR professionals must know the proper valuation of job categories and specific jobs within that category. It is a critical skill to find a competitive wage to pay for the right skilled talent that will further the company's mission without losing profitability. To do this, senior HR professionals rely heavily on data including information obtained from surveys, regularly published information from the government, and historical trends recorded over time. While no single survey can capture all the information, the combination of various data points helps to create a picture of the target pay area that can help when making decisions. The data when collected should capture a range of salaries and a time frame to determine how current this information is. For instance, if salary information in the company is reviewed once every four years, there could be significant economic changes that have impacted the organization during that time. As a result, the data will be harder to compare and make a determination of the right range. Likewise, if the information is new, it may be the result of a spike with no other data trend for comparison.

When the information is collected, senior HR professionals must know how to use analytics to determine trends, averages, and outliers in given pay categories. The goal should be to find the midpoint of a range of comparable salaries to have a target from which to base offers and set salary ranges. The pay structure is created by analyzing the data and creating either graduated steps or tiers from the lowest salary point to the highest. There is no specific rule on how to create structures for companies, and it is largely determined by the characteristics of the company itself. However, within the structure there will be pay grades and pay ranges that are established, and this will be the foundation for determining the salaries of the employees.

Pay grades band together jobs that have a similar value to the overall company. They may not be closely related in terms of duties or job function, but they have the same worth to the bottom line of the company. Pay grades will differ between larger or smaller organizations where the total numbers of employees being grouped are different. There may be different levels in the company from line employees to leads, supervisors, department managers, senior staff, or executives. The more complex a hierarchy in a company, the broader or more numerous pay bands needed. How people advance and grow in the company also will impact pay grades. If certain promotions carry increases in salary, it is possible that someone would need to move to a different band with promotion or risk reaching the upper ceiling of a pay range.

Pay ranges are the limits of pay for any employee who may have their pay determined by being in a pay grade. As shown in Figure 9.4, these upper and lower limits bracket the salaries within a pay grade, but that does not necessarily mean that there is no overlap between grades. The determination should consider how often a company moves individuals across pay bands and how an employee whose salary is at the maximum level of one band would be shifted to another band based on an increase in salary.

FIGURE 9.4   Pay ranges in a company

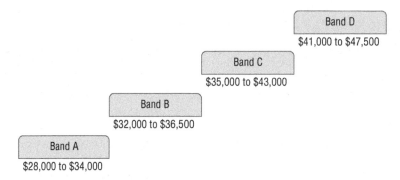

HR professionals should calculate the range spread by subtracting the minimum pay in a band from the maximum and then dividing the results by the minimum. In larger organizations, the midpoints of the pay grades may become compressed, and the result is an unmanageable system. In those cases, a company may choose to broadband the pay bands, putting multiple grades inside one band for the purpose of simplification.

Benefit Program Strategies

Businesses must compete every day for a limited supply of human capital. Benefits that are offered by companies have become much more than government-mandated offerings that are common among all employers. Instead, senior HR professionals, in conjunction with the executive leadership of a company, develop benefit strategies to attract and retain key talent. In many circumstances, employees will seek out employers that offer comprehensive benefits in addition to their base salary.

Health, dental, and vision insurance are common offerings along with supplemental disability insurance. Additionally, there are other critical care and catastrophic insurances for critical and acute illness such as cancer or heart attacks. This category of benefit usually has some costs shared between the employer and employee. Retirement benefits such as a pension plan or 401K can have a company match to employee contributions and are managed by the company for the benefit of employees. Finally, perks such as employee discounts, financial planning assistance, fitness and wellness, and educational benefits can attract talent that require more work-life balance as motivation for continued engagement.

Senior HR professionals must be knowledgeable in the rules and functions of each type of benefit offered by the company. They must assist in determining the percentage of the company's contribution toward the overall cost of these benefits and evaluate third-party vendors for both cost and offerings to match the needs of the organization. The average age of the workforce and the overall health, financial stability, and educational level are all factors that impact the decision of what programs to offer and to what level. Employers are limited only by the creativity of what they decide to offer and the financial resources they are willing to commit to benefit their talent.

Fiduciary Responsibility

HR professionals may be chiefly responsible for the administration and execution of the company's retirement plan. As previously mentioned, there are already numerous laws that govern this important benefit for your employees. However, beyond the compliance factor, the fiduciary obligations are critically important points of knowledge for HR professionals. The basic rules set forth in ERISA also provide the standards of conduct for those individuals charged with managing the benefit plan and its assets.

HR professionals should be familiar with these four elements:

- A written plan that outlines the benefits structure and general standard operating procedures

- A trust fund to hold the plan's assets

- A means of recording and tracking the cash flow of the plan

- Documentation that is provided to the employees (and regulators when required) with information about the plan

All those who are responsible for the management and day-to-day operation of these plans and who have discretion to make decisions about the plan are considered to be the fiduciaries. It is the functions that an individual performs, not their official title or position in the company, that determine the level of fiduciary responsibility the individual has.

In some decisions regarding a retirement plan, corporate executives may be making a decision in terms of the best interests of the business (what plan to have, the features, or when the plan is canceled). When making these decisions, they are not acting on behalf of the plan (and by extension the beneficiaries of the plan), so are not considered to be making fiduciary decisions. However, the execution of these decisions and how they are carried out can be fiduciary when doing so requires the individual to work on behalf of the plan.

The fiduciary, therefore, must act solely in the interest of the plan's participants with the purpose of providing the benefits, acting in a diligent manner in accordance to the standard operating procedures, maintaining a diverse investment portfolio, and paying only reasonable expenses.

Employer-Provided Benefits

As discussed previously, there are as many types of benefits as there are employers, and all have distinct features. It is impossible to detail each single type of program within the scope of this review, but HR professionals should be familiar with the general types and examples from each. In general, there are deferred compensation plans (often viewed as retirement or savings plans), health plans (such as medical, dental, and vision), and supplemental plans (including short- and long-term disability, life insurance, leave, employee assistance, and wellness). Table 9.1 shows these various examples and important knowledge points for HR.

TABLE 9.1   Employer-provided benefits

Benefit	Examples	HR Professionals Must Know
Retirement plans Education plan	▪ Defined benefit plan (pension) ▪ Defined contribution plan 401(k), 457, Roth, 403(b) ▪ 529 plan	Plans in these categories allow the employee to save money either pre- or post-taxes and make scheduled regular contributions with a cap amount and withdrawal restrictions or limitations. All have significant tax implications.
Healthcare	▪ Managed care ▪ Dental ▪ Vision ▪ Prescription drug ▪ Health savings accounts	These plans usually have employer and employee portions and offer many choices based on the needs and population of the employees; insurers may provide incentives to lower costs with wellness exams and fitness opportunities.
Supplemental	▪ Disability ▪ Other insurance ▪ Employee assistance programs ▪ Leave programs ▪ Tuition assistance	Employers choose from a variety of options based on the needs of the employees; many employees may elect to not have some of these options or may choose the minimum benefit provided.

Motivation Concepts and Applications

As discussed previously, numerous factors determine what kind of compensation and benefits packages will attract the desired talent for a company. Senior HR professionals must be capable of understanding the motivation of groups of individuals that comprise the talent network from which employees are drawn. Younger individuals who may not have families, for example, may desire low-cost healthcare with high deductibles and catastrophic coverage because they are generally healthier individuals. They may be drawn to educational benefits and growth opportunities, being eligible for performance raises and bonuses. Conversely, older, established employees may seek stability with retirement benefits, consistent pay security, and life and health insurance to sustain and support their families. While these are generalities, analysis across demographics can reveal common trends and needs by these groups that can then be offered by the organization. Senior HR professionals must evaluate the workforce population and apply an understanding of the needs of these groups to address what motivates them to remain engaged with the company. These various levers across the total rewards spectrum do not operate independently; they all impact in varying degrees on the motivation of employees. Only through adjustment and often trial and error will a company find continued positive results.

Benchmarking Techniques

Senior HR professionals should know how to benchmark both compensation and benefits for the organization. They must know how to conduct assessments, track utilization rates, and compare pricing from providers. Each year third-party administrators and brokers will desire to compete for business. This is especially true for growing and successful organizations.

Senior HR professionals should meet with brokers well before the open enrollment season and review data from the previous year. They must analyze the effectiveness of the coverage, usage, and cost and must consider any feedback from the employees. A good broker will bring several proposals to the company with competitive rates to compare. The company should be prepared to evaluate and measure the provider's proposals and make a decision. Performance history, reputation, and similar clients can all be indicators of how effective the provider will be.

In a similar manner, senior HR professionals look at the internal compensation structure and across the industry or at local competitors and determine whether the pay philosophy and compensation plan meet the needs to attract and retain talent. Number of voluntary separations, requests for increases, and history of previous salary adjustments are metrics that can be used to determine patterns related to compensation. It is important to look not at individual cases as the benchmark or trend but in the aggregate.

Exam Essentials

Understand compensation strategy and pay philosophy.   Familiarize yourself with the pay philosophy of your organization and how pay decisions are made. What is the compensation strategy for the company and how is it executed? Are there discrepancies in how pay is done, and how would an organization resolve those issues? The company should be able to identify the methods used in determining job demands that drive pay.

Understand the role of the fiduciary and their responsibility.   This is an important function within the organization, and those who hold this responsibility must place the needs of the employees and any benefits programs above the company in some instances. They are truly the honest broker in determining what is best in terms of management and decisions on the benefits programs.

Understand how job evaluations inform compensation structures.   As an organization defines the roles in the company, each job must be evaluated to understand its relative worth and importance to the performance of the company's mission. Once these roles are established, you should be able to evaluate the compensation structure to ensure that individuals are paid properly based on the role and duties associated with their job. You should look at objective measures that are used in determining a pay scale and compare them to the difficulties of the tasks a certain job performs. Review job descriptions and essential job functions for some key roles in your organization, and if you have the ability, examine the relative pay.

Responsibilities

Ensuring that employees are paid and receive the benefits to which they are entitled is one of the most critical responsibilities of an HR professional. The timely compensation for the hard work rendered by workers shows that they are valued and respected and demonstrates the ongoing commitment of the organization to see that their employees' basic needs are met. Senior HR professionals will analyze and evaluate the effectiveness of compensation and benefit strategies and make recommended changes needed to remain competitive in the market to attract and retain the required talent.

Conducting a Needs Assessment

As discussed in Chapter 6, "Leadership and Strategy," needs assessments are useful tools to plan for the organization by surveying the stakeholders and determining what actions can be taken to meet their needs. This is applicable to total rewards as well. Senior HR professionals can analyze surveys of the company's employees and determine what benefits are deemed most important. Certain benefits are governed by law, but others are discretionary, so there is a great deal of latitude in choosing which ones to provide. Because part of the goal of compensation and benefits programs is to reward employees who align to the values of the organization and keep them engaged, it follows that good organizations are responsive and attentive to their employees. Benefit programs align with the pay philosophy of the company. The HR team collects data on benefits programs and their relative importance, and it discovers any gaps that indicate where needs are not met.

When reaching a decision to provide a benefit, the HR team is responsible for understanding what kind of benefit is needed and for building a business case that supports inclusion of such a benefit program. Included in the recommendation is how the benefit will be delivered and who will manage it. They work closely with the company finance department to determine the feasibility of the cost and whether employees will cover a portion. Finally, it is critical that the company effectively communicate with the employees its decision to deliver a particular benefit and how it will impact the company. Many benefits are impacted by governing regulations, so this may be a factor in the company's ability to deliver certain benefit programs.

Analyze and Evaluate Compensation Strategies

A key responsibility for any senior HR professional is to evaluate and analyze the compensation strategy for the company. Determining the pay strategy is not a onetime event, but a continuous process to meet the changing needs of the organization. As a company grows and develops over time, the need for pay structures changes, and senior HR professionals are responsible for crafting the philosophy and evaluating direct and indirect compensation, bonuses and rewards, equity, and executive compensation that attracts, rewards, and retains talent.

Pay Philosophy

Senior HR professionals should meet with the corporate leadership and establish a pay philosophy for the organization. The pay philosophy aligns with the organizational values and company ethos. It often will become part of the brand identity as employees and applicants to the company factor pay as part of their motivation to seek and retain employment with a company. While pay is not the sole motivation for any employee, a fair and responsible pay structure is critical to maintain.

As part of the responsibility for implementing pay programs, the HR team is responsible for conducting the analysis of pay structure. Using either an external source or company resources to validate current pay, they can examine pay ratios to revenue, productivity, or other operational metrics. It is worth noting that sometimes external sources do not have a complete understanding of the scope and responsibilities of positions inside a company, possibly because it has nonstandard job titles or unique duties and scope of responsibility. The external reviews are only as accurate as the data provided to make a determination and are only a recommendation. The company must make the final decision, so the role of the senior HR professional is to be the arbitrator of all the various sources and provide counsel to the decision-makers of the organization.

Pay Range Spread and Increases

When determining pay raises for the company, there are some factors to consider to ensure that pay ranges are moderated. When the company uses a percentage increase, pay ranges expand because the total amount is less at a lower pay. This increases pay gaps over time. Conversely, a flat amount compresses pay ranges because as salary grows, the gap is unchanged but decreases as a percentage of the total salary. Figure 9.5 demonstrates these concepts.

FIGURE 9.5 Pay range spread

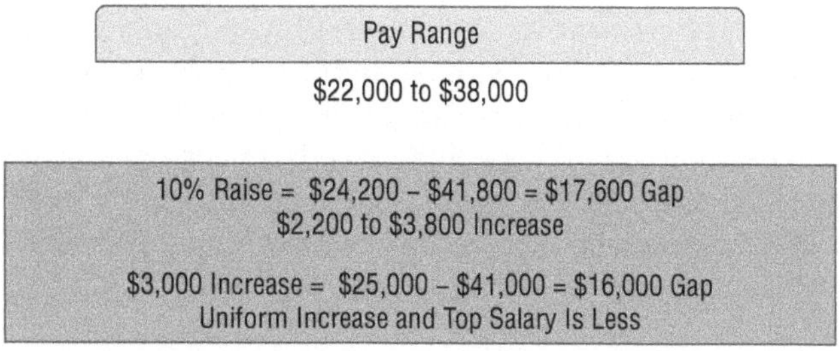

Pay Range

$22,000 to $38,000

10% Raise = $24,200 – $41,800 = $17,600 Gap
$2,200 to $3,800 Increase

$3,000 Increase = $25,000 – $41,000 = $16,000 Gap
Uniform Increase and Top Salary Is Less

Bonuses and Equity

A company with a strong commitment to employees as part of its corporate values should be concerned with pay equity within the company. Senior HR professionals are responsible for ensuring that pay equity is maintained with periodic adjustments. Sometimes a newly hired HR professional will discover through analysis that the company's pay equity is out of balance and may take some time to recover. It is important to realize that pay inequity that has occurred over the course of years should not be attempted to be corrected immediately as this could have negative consequences to employee morale.

Adjusting Pay Gaps

Determining the highest-paid and lowest-paid employee in the same job classification will show the pay range spread. For example, if the lowest-paid person earns $30,000 per year and the highest earns $50,000, it represents a $20,000 difference. This could be based on longevity or the fact that the higher-paid person has additional duties or skills adding value to their position. They could be classified as a lead or supervisor, justifying the increase in pay. However, more often than not, it may be that one was hired when the company was seeing high profits and the market supported that pay, and the other was hired at a different point. It's hard to determine in those cases what is the right targeted pay point and even more difficult to correct. It may not be feasible to raise all pay to the higher level, but cutting pay can also have a negative impact.

Cost of Living Adjustment

In some cases, a company may choose to apply a cost of living adjustment (COLA) to wages. Generally, the COLA is a percentage added to the base wage and is a onetime adjustment. The intent is to make periodic corrections based on significant changes to living costs, but if carried out continuously it could result in perpetual rising wage costs that could be detrimental to a company's profitability. HR professionals are responsible for recommending these adjustments because it has impact to all eligible employees and isn't connected to individual performance.

Bonuses

There are several types of bonuses that can be provided by a company. Monetary rewards based on performance or meeting certain criteria can be ongoing. Others may be onetime, on-the-spot awards for achievement. Senior HR professionals are responsible for ensuring that bonuses are awarded consistently, with established metrics and justification that is fair and equitable. Some bonus structures have legal considerations with respect to wage laws or taxes and should be discussed with the finance department and executive leadership to evaluate any unintended consequences or financial obligations to the company or employee. The advantage to giving bonuses is that they are not a continuing obligation year to year and can be adjusted as the company's needs change.

Most bonuses are taxable and also require that certain payroll taxes be withheld on the money earned. When giving a set award amount such as $500, the actual net to the employee may be less based on withholdings. Some companies will "plus up" the bonus to cover these taxes, making the net amount the intended award.

Analyze and Evaluate Benefit Strategies

As most companies grow and become more profitable, they will have the ability to offer benefits to remain competitive and retain top talent. What benefits are offered depends on the needs assessment discussed earlier and what the company can afford to provide. Companies will provide certain benefits such as health and dental early in the company's growth life cycle, and then other benefits follow depending on the company demographics and needs. Senior HR professionals are responsible for helping corporate executives decide which programs meet the needs of the company at an affordable cost. Over time, they analyze and evaluate the effects and benefits that the program produces and make change recommendations as needed.

Senior HR professionals will often review offers from third-party providers that consolidate services to broker benefit plans from a variety of providers. In many circumstances, these plans are highly subject to compliance laws and regulations. Because HR professionals are not legal advisors, it is recommended that these service providers be used, as they have the legal foundation and support to ensure that all regulatory requirements are met in providing these programs. This is especially important for organizations with limited internal HR resources that may not have the breadth and depth of experience in benefits administration.

In addition to reviewing offers from providers, Senior HR professionals are responsible for assessing the programs periodically and working with the executives to determine when changes are needed. They may solicit new proposals for services to be provided, developing the evaluation criteria and reviewing proposals from vendors. When a suitable program is found, they become the primary point of contact for the company and keep the company informed of the pending changes. If the program is new, then senior HR professionals develop an implementation plan with start dates, communication plans, and other necessary actions to ensure a smooth start. If, however, this is a change in providers or a new benefits program replacing an existing one, then they are responsible for the transition plan, which may include facilitating new registrations, updating any employee information, and monitoring the changeover.

Finally, Senior HR professionals will develop policies and documentation for the benefits programs for new employees as part of the onboarding process and to inform current employees. They may schedule and conduct information briefings on the new plans and their costs to employees and be available to answer any questions. They must work with employees to validate data so that benefits providers have the most accurate employee information when beginning the delivery of the services and benefits program.

Ethically Sound Executive Compensation Packages

In today's world of global information and the influence of social media on corporate reputation and corporate responsibility, a hot topic continues to be the relative compensation of executives. It is the senior HR professional's responsibility to help the company develop, implement, and maintain an ethically sound executive compensation plan. This is certainly a challenge in that, on one hand, it is important to compensate high-level executives fairly for the role they play in making or keeping a company successful; but on the other hand, they must guard against perception of excess. In all cases, senior HR professionals should always put first the mission and values of the company. This will serve as the guideposts for decisions and help with consistency.

Executive Compensation and Performance

What often seems right and fair is tied directly to the results produced by the executive in question. Senior HR professionals will work with a board of directors, executive committee, or key leaders of the organization to develop the objective evaluation standards for an executive entitled to executive compensation packages. Generally, it should be assumed that executives work to the best interests of the company and are doing their best to make timely, accurate, and ethical decisions.

Several regulations that govern compensation directly apply to executive compensation. For example, the provisions of the Dodd-Frank legislation cover public companies to ensure that underperforming executives are not entitled to certain compensation. However, the company must make the ultimate decision as to the manner that this portion of compensation is restricted. This is especially true when it comes to the separation or retirement of an executive whose departure triggers additional compensation in the form of stock liquidation or other severance. Senior HR professionals are responsible for monitoring these actions and carrying out the decisions of corporate leadership.

Senior HR professionals must remember that the intent of these stipulations is not to handcuff an executive from making hard decisions or cutting costs where appropriate for the betterment of the company. Again, it ties directly to the values of the organization. This applies equally in the public and private sectors, for profit and not for profit. These restrictions are safeguards to ensure that an executive is committed to the successful accomplishment of the goals and objectives of the company.

Health and Welfare

Senior HR professionals are responsible for the health and welfare programs that support and take care of the employees of the organization. Ensuring the well-being of the workforce is a critical task and significant responsibility. They must ensure that policies and procedures such as safety and workers' compensation and programs such as benefits and wellness are robust and well designed to keep the human capital healthy and functioning.

Work-Life Balance

The term *work-life balance* defines a concept that examines the employee as a whole person and seeks to balance their personal needs with the professional requirements the company must have to achieve its goals and objectives. This change recognizes that human capital in today's business environment is a limited resource, and the company cannot demand that an employee remain engaged and functioning in the job without risking burnout, if some consideration is not paid toward meeting the employee's needs for growth, development, and personal life. Some companies may not be concerned with employees beyond the workday, but research suggests that a lack of understanding of an employee's personal life situation will have negative consequences and manifest as a decline in the employee's performance. Companies that seek to understand each individual's personal situation will have more loyal and dedicated employees. Predictable hours, strong leadership, transparent communications, fair compensation and benefits, and a commitment to employees and their families are some of the ways a company can help achieve this necessary balance between work and home.

Employee Wellness

An employee's performance is impacted by more than just knowledge, skills, and abilities required for the job. Their mental, social, and spiritual well-being all have an impact too. Senior HR professionals are responsible for establishing programs and making recommendations on behalf of the employees that improve wellness throughout the organization. Stress management is important to a company. Some stress, like the need to finish a project on time or deliver great customer service, is needed to inspire growth and achievement. However, an abundance of unnecessary stress negatively affects performance and is detrimental. Some sources of stress could be the following:

- Financial issues
- Health problems
- Family problems
- Substance abuse
- Anxiety

Senior HR professionals should seek to adopt programs that can help employees in these life areas. Depending on the social structure and demographics, different practices can be implemented to meet the needs of the group or individual.

Rewards and Recognition Programs

Going hand in hand with employee wellness is the employee's need to feel appreciated for the work they contribute to the organization. Senior HR professionals are responsible for designing, implementing, and managing an effective rewards and recognition program. Such programs must be timely and seek to reward those behaviors that consistently align with the company's values and vision. For example, if a company values a commitment to the customer, then customer service will be highly valued in the company. Therefore, the company should have a method to recognize and reward those employees that are exceptional at customer service and spotlight those specific behaviors of employees that are tied to that performance. All recognition programs should be of some value that is at least equal to the value provided by the employee's actions or attitude being considered.

Retirement

Some employees will serve the organization to a point where they are eligible for retirement benefits. Some companies have pension plans that provide a defined benefit. This means that an eligible employee will receive a set amount based on criteria met, such as length of service, salary, and age. These programs carry liability to the future because the amount of resources needed to completely fund the liability may be unknown. The defined contribution retirement method allows for employees to set aside a portion of their compensation that may also be matched in part by the employer. This plan relies on investment vehicles that grow and provide a rate of return to have more value than the contributions when the employee becomes eligible for the benefit. While there is more flexibility in this option, the total amount set aside is unknown and not guaranteed. Senior HR professionals are responsible for evaluating the pros and cons of these two options and for determining which method and vehicles will be used to have the needed resources to meet the retirement funding obligations of the organization.

Exam Essentials

For SPHR, understand executive compensation packages.   These areas are important from an ethical and corporate responsibility standpoint, but most often HR generalists have limited interaction with these topics unless they work in this area specifically. Reviewing these sections will help trigger reminders about scenarios that might exist in larger corporations where the determination of a corporate executive pay program might exist.

Understand the responsibilities associated with analyzing and evaluating compensation and benefits strategies.   In addition to managing these programs, the knowledge of the roles and responsibilities when the function is distributed to third parties is also critical. The key points include the ongoing communications, notifications to employees, coverage, and compliance. Any outsourced function should reduce the burden of the HR team. You should review how programs are created out of needs that arise to address human capital demands in the company.

Summary

Total rewards will continue to be a core competency of senior HR professionals, but the landscape of the strategies to deliver these important services continually changes, impacted by legislation, the market, and the changing workforce population. The needs of workers should be evaluated and analyzed on a continuous basis to ensure the alignment of compensation and benefits and to meet the burden of taking care of the lifeblood of any organization—its people.

For additional information on this topic, candidates for the exam should visit the Department of Labor website at www.dol.gov, the Social Security Administration at www.ssa.gov, and the Internal Revenue Service at www.irs.gov. At these websites a key-word search of the topics discussed in this chapter will provide regulations, guidance, and rulings to review for a more in-depth understanding of the role these federal agencies play in compensation and benefits for employees.

Test-Taking Tip

The SPHR® exam is now available year-round at testing centers. In the past, these exams were offered only two times per year, which meant having to adjust preparation and study time to those windows, which may not work with an HR professional's busy sched-ule. Take your time in the preparation of this comprehensive exam. Review the material in the book including the references to ensure that you have a good practical base of knowl-edge prior to test day.

Review Questions

1. An HR professional is designated as a fiduciary for a company's benefits plan. They are required to do all of the following *except* which one?

   A. Have a written plan for the benefits program

   B. Establish a trust for the assets of the plan

   C. Make decisions in the best interest of the company that might reduce the valuation of plan

   D. Maintain records of the cash flows in and out of the plan's accounts

2. A company that is looking to conserve resources and reduce costs when there is an abundance of available talent may choose to _____ the local market with comparative wages.

   A. Lag

   B. Lead

   C. Match

   D. Lower

3. A company's systemic evaluation of jobs in the organization may result in the establishment of which of the following?

   A. A comprehensive benefits program

   B. A performance improvement plan

   C. A general increase in pay

   D. A grade system

4. When taking a type of quantitative approach to a job evaluation, which of the following compensable factors are included in the Equal Pay Act or Title VII?

   A. Skill

   B. Effort

   C. Working conditions

   D. All of the above

5. A board of directors of a publicly traded company is deciding on compensating senior executives with options to buy stock in the company. This is considered to be what?

   A. A noncash compensation package

   B. A company perk

   C. Unethical conduct in violation of the Dodd-Frank Act

   D. A portion of the executive's base salary for tax purposes

6. As a company grows and expands, the desires of employees may change, affecting the types of benefits the company provides. To determine what to do, HR may take what action?

   A. Recommend changes to pay scales

   B. Provide a cafeteria plan

C. Conduct a needs assessment

D. Consult an outside provider

7. When establishing a performance-based pay plan, HR should ensure consistency in the evaluation process by helping supervisors understand the importance of developing which of the following?

A. Metrics and success criteria

B. The amount of money used for increases

C. Noncash compensation options

D. None of the above

8. Which is an important consideration of a COLA?

A. It can be made available only to executives.

B. It is a onetime adjustment that does not have lasting impact to the payroll budget.

C. It is an annual increase that will create ever-increasing labor costs.

D. It is generally used for expatriates to adjust salaries in foreign countries to be commensurate with their parent nation.

9. In general, when evaluating a health plan for the company, factors to consider include which of these?

A. Types of coverage in the plan

B. The breakdown of employee and employer costs

C. The reputation of the benefits broker

D. Both A and B

10. A defined benefit plan has what advantage to a company?

A. The amount of the benefit to each employee will vary depending on the investment vehicle they choose.

B. The benefit has no tax consequences to the individual because taxes are taken with each contribution.

C. Employees can plan on a benefit amount based on eligibility rules such as age or salary history.

D. The overall obligation of the company may be unknown, creating a financial liability in the future.

11. Work-life balance in an organization seeks to:

A. Solve a variety of problems with employees including substance abuse

B. Allow a company to be more transparent with employees and improve communications

C. Recognize that employees are impacted by events outside the workplace and to remain effectively engaged must have balance between work demands and personal needs

D. All of the above

Chapter 10

Employee Relations and Engagement

THE SPHR® EXAM CONTENT FROM THE EMPLOYEE RELATIONS AND ENGAGEMENT FUNCTIONAL AREA COVERED IN THIS CHAPTER CONSISTS OF THE FOLLOWING RESPONSIBILITIES AND KNOWLEDGE AREAS. RESPONSIBILITIES:

- ✓ 01 Design and evaluate strategies for employee satisfaction (for example: recognition, career path) and performance management (for example: performance evaluation, corrective action, coaching)

- ✓ 02 Analyze and evaluate strategies to promote diversity and inclusion

- ✓ 03 Evaluate employee safety and security strategies (for example: emergency response plan, building access, data security/privacy)

- ✓ 04 Develop and evaluate labor strategies (for example: collective bargaining, grievance program, concerted activity, staying union free, strategically aligning with labor)

IN ADDITION TO THE PRECEDING RESPONSIBILITIES, AN INDIVIDUAL TAKING THE SPHR® EXAM SHOULD HAVE WORKING KNOWLEDGE OF THE FOLLOWING AREAS, USUALLY DERIVED THROUGH PRACTICAL EXPERIENCE:

- ✓ 51 Strategies to facilitate positive employee relations

- ✓ 52 Methods for assessing employee attitudes, opinions, and satisfaction

- ✓ 53 Performance management strategies

This chapter focuses on developing and monitoring strategies impacting employee satisfaction and performance, including diversity and inclusion, safety, security, and labor strategies. Treating employees with dignity and respect and building positive relationships throughout the organization is a critical function of senior HR professionals. Senior HR professionals have the responsibility to ensure working conditions that balance employer and employee needs and rights in support of the organization's goals and objectives. This functional area is 20 percent of the SPHR® exam. While employee and labor relations may not take up as much of the daily duties at the senior levels, senior HR professionals still execute some significant responsibilities in this functional area that are vital to a company.

While the other chapters focus on knowledge and responsibilities that impact the talent of the company, the topic of this chapter is more the organizational climate and its relationship to how employees behave. Risk management covers a wide array of threats to the organization from internal and external sources and the necessary actions to mitigate potential outcomes. In this chapter, we also review the knowledge and responsibilities required for developing, implementing/administering, and evaluating programs, procedures, and policies to provide a safe, secure working environment and to protect the organization from potential liability.

Required Knowledge

The general practice of employee relations is a vast subset of an HR professional's responsibilities, and there is a great deal of information to understand. In much of business today, companies often seek out specialists who are entirely focused and experienced on this topic. Being a successful senior HR professional requires knowledge of labor practices, employee and employer rights, and how to foster a strong organizational climate.

Senior HR professionals should be familiar with the strategies that improve employee satisfaction, promote diversity and inclusion, and ensure safety and security that are typically found in a company and how they should be administered and developed. HR professionals will often develop or execute the procedures across several different areas that impact risk management, including organizational response, business continuity, and investigations.

Employee Relations

Employee relations (ER) is a broad area that involves the attitudes of employees, their behaviors, the relationships between employees and management, the culture and climate of the organization, and how employees are recognized. However, many companies and senior HR professionals make the mistake that ER is just the "complaint department" for HR to handle disgruntled employees or discipline those "problems" within a company, which is often a manager's desire to fire an employee who is not behaving according to the company's established values.

This is a limited view and presupposes that the root of the problem always begins and ends with the employee. In fact, experience teaches HR professionals that ER problems are some of the most complex challenges they handle, and the knowledge required to successfully resolve them is significant. My favorite statement about ER cases is that the best ones are the ones that don't ever materialize. This simply means that the company has the foundation and proper training for managers to recognize early signs of concern and has the ability to take proper action that prevents an employee from entering a downward spiral to eventual separation from the organization. A senior HR professional who can develop programs and policies that promote a strong workforce is highly valuable to an organization.

Facilitating Positive Employee Relations

Senior HR professionals must be familiar with the strategies necessary to facilitate a positive environment for employee relations. These strategies can be placed in two groups. The first are those strategies and capabilities that seek to mitigate or avoid tensions and conflict prior to an event. These are all preventive in nature and involve direct communication with the employees to get a sense of the climate and where hot spots may exist. The second group involves post-conflict actions that seek to remediate problems that may be at the root cause and foster communications going forward. In both types of facilitation, HR senior professionals must understand both communication and conflict resolution theory.

Employee Attitudes, Opinions, and Satisfaction

It's important in building positive employee relations that senior HR professionals know methods of gauging employee attitudes, opinions, and satisfaction. Engagement surveys are used to measure the satisfaction levels and attitudes of employees across the organization. Recognition programs are an important tool for the organization, and HR should be familiar with strategies to implement them. It is a good idea to get feedback from employees about what would be of value in a recognition program. There are opportunities for managers or HR to solicit input through surveys or other communication means to determine the effectiveness of these kinds of programs. It is also important that the recognition be proportionate to the act or measure that was the result of the employee actions. For example, if an employee is recognized for implementing an energy-saving conservation program that resulted in the company saving more than $10,000 a year, a $25 gift card would not be appropriate. Table 10.1 provides examples of types of recognition events and examples of rewards or recognition that might be given as a result.

TABLE 10.1   A sample rewards and recognition program

Type of Program	General Award
Spot awards	Small cash award for onetime recognition usually for exceptional customer service or a single act.
Employee of the month (quarterly, annually)	A nominative award from supervisors or peers selected by a committee after evaluating based on established metrics. Usually recognized with a plaque or name recognition.
Longevity/service award	Given for completing service of 5- or 10-year increments to increase and reward loyalty to the company.
Operational excellence/ cost savings or other functional recognition	Awarded to employees who recommend or implement operational measures that result in improved efficiency, increased profitability, or saved money. The award should be proportionate to the financial savings enjoyed by the company as a result.
Special event recognition	Birthday, anniversary, or other life event of an employee recognized by the company.
Employee appreciation events	Parties, celebrations, or dinners that are covered in part or whole by the employer for the employees and may include family members to demonstrate appreciation.

Collective Bargaining

Senior HR professionals must have extensive knowledge of the process, concepts, and strategies associated with collective bargaining. At its core, it is the successful negotiation of an employment agreement between the management of a company and the union representatives that are authorized to negotiate on behalf of the company's employees. This collective bargaining agreement is a contract that governs the working conditions and employment settings for the employees along with the responsibilities of both management and the workers. These agreements take into account many factors, including the labor skills, overall economy, prevailing wages and benefits, and accepted practices of employers.

The agreement covers both mandatory and voluntary subjects. The voluntary subjects include areas such as retiree benefits for members of the union or processes for handling unfair labor practices. These may or may not be subject to negotiation. The National Labor Relations Act sets out which category a subject falls under, including those items that cannot be discussed under any agreement (illegal items such as requests that would violate other laws or regulations). The mandatory subjects include the following:

- Pay and Overtime
- Terminations
- Disciplinary and Grievance Procedures
- Reductions in Force
- Promotions and Seniority
- Holidays, Vacations, Time Off
- Promotions, Demotions, Transfers
- Safety Procedures

Collective bargaining can be done by first negotiating with one company in an industry, such as an industry leader or one a union feels will create the best deal for workers, and then attempting to promulgate the agreement with other competing companies in the industry. While this was a prevalent method in the past, it is less common today because industries now have standard practices that cover most of what would be negotiated by a union and offer no competitive advantages to either side. A second option would be for a group of employers to negotiate with the union seeking to represent employees at the companies. In industries where there are multiple unions represented (such as the airline industry), the unions can coordinate their bargaining processes with the employer to maximize their negotiation power. Finally, the process can be broken up to discuss complex details in a variety of committees to reach a consensus.

A collective bargaining agreement will have several articles that discuss each mandatory area and any voluntary area that is agreed to by the union and management. Within the agreement there will be provisions for who will be members and the dues and the rights of the union to exclusively represent the interests of the employees. If they work in a right-to-work state, senior HR professionals must understand that there are additional restrictions and provisions that limit a union's ability to collect dues or fees for the union to represent them. The largest difference is that in the right-to-work states, union shops are illegal, which means a union cannot require new employees to pay dues and become union members. While the employee's employment is protected, they cannot attend union meetings or have a vote concerning the approval of an agreement without being union members.

Senior HR professionals must understand how contracts are administered and how various provisions are handled, such as grievance procedures and arbitration. They must understand what actions should be taken in cases of litigation or allegations of unfair labor practices, as well as how to handle inquiries by the National Labor Relations Board if management is not negotiating in good faith as part of the collective bargaining process. They must also understand the protected activities that sometimes are the by-product of negotiations or failure to reach an agreement. Table 10.2 discusses some of these items and the role of senior HR professionals.

TABLE 10.2 Activities related to collective bargaining

Activity	Example	HR Considerations
Lockout	Management shuts down a plant to prevent workers from entering the facilities.	Works with management to control access to the facility; informs secondary managers of policies and procedures
Strike	Workers refuse to work as required to include slowing down processes or throughput.	Works with management to find temporary workers to maintain production; some strikes may not be authorized by a union or may not be allowed by contract making them a ULP
Picket	Employees exercise free speech usually at locations in proximity to work sites to protest management actions.	Ensures that management responses are compliant with regulations and continues efforts to reach negotiated settlement on contract; may arrange for additional company security

Performance Management Strategies

Senior HR professionals must be familiar with performance management strategies to help managers and supervisors develop their human capital talent. To maximize the organizational capabilities, senior HR professionals develop means to deliver feedback, evaluations, corrective discipline, and coaching. Informal feedback done on a frequent basis provides for the best communication and helps direct employees. When needed, corrective discipline should be meted out fairly but firmly to provide the minimal action necessary that results in a change of behavior. Coaching requires knowledge of mentoring and motivation to properly align behavior with desired results.

Human Relations Concepts and Applications

Senior HR professionals are experts at relating to people and understanding their needs at a personal level. They must leverage this knowledge and capability to ensure the optimal performance of employees as a collective group. They must be astute at recognizing elements of emotional intelligence in themselves and others. Emotional intelligence measures how well an individual perceives their own emotional state and that of others and also how the emotions of others affect them and the impact of their emotions on others.

Teaching others to be self-aware of their emotions is an important skill for senior HR professionals. They must show how emotions impact judgment and decisions and then provide strategies to enable others to manage these emotional states. Being aware that you are angry and being able to manage that anger are two different skills to consider. People with a strong emotional intelligence can predictably understand why certain emotions that they exhibit affect others in certain ways. Once someone can master these emotional intelligence concepts, they can improve and be more impactful to the organization.

The concept of organizational behavior is important because the organizational dynamic is largely based on how the group behaves and responds to leaders and conditions that exist in the company. A senior HR professional who can accurately predict how the organization will respond to decisions, policy changes, accomplishments, and setbacks is valuable to modern business models. They can help senior leaders maximize the human capital potential in the organization through their understanding of human relations and organizational behavior.

Ethical and Professional Standards

Senior HR professionals have access to a wide variety of sensitive and personal information in the conduct of their jobs. Senior HR professionals must maintain the highest ethical and professional standards. The HR Certification Institute certification process requires every applicant to adhere to a code of ethics to maintain their credential. In general, they must not use their position and privilege for their own personal benefit. They must strive to protect sensitive HR-related information about others in the organization and must avoid conflicts of interest. Those holding the SPHR® must acknowledge the ethical and professional responsibilities in six areas:

- Professional Responsibility
- Professional Development
- Ethical Leadership
- Fairness and Justice
- Conflicts of Interest
- Use of Information

I recommend that any applicant preparing for the certification exam review the code of ethics and professional responsibility at https://www.hrci.org/docs/default-source/web-files/code-of-ethical-and-professional-responsibility(1)-pdf.pdf.

Diversity and Inclusion Concepts and Applications

Senior HR professionals should strive for a diverse and inclusive organization to draw from different thoughts and experience within an organization. They should know concepts about diversity and how those apply in their company. Diversity and inclusion are not just about the protected classes discussed throughout the book related to Title VII of the Civil Rights Act. They go beyond those limits to look at differences among generations, cultures, and even learning styles.

We are at a unique point in today's business world with as many as five generations in the workforce. This unusual dynamic plays a crucial role in the introduction of technology to a company, the values the company espouses, and the general work ethos of each generation. The younger generations are more globally connected and have access to much more information in a shorter period of time. They will be challenged by synthesizing such vast data and being able to discern the reliability of the information available. At the other end of the timeline, older generations are more traditional and will have a harder time embracing new concepts or ways of doing business. While this doesn't seem new as there is always generational overlap, the fact that people are working longer and life spans have increased, combined with the exponential advancements in technology, has greatly affected organizations.

Senior HR professionals must also be attuned to cultural competencies and understand the impact of globalization in the marketplace. Being aware of the role that culture can play in a company will help develop diversity and inclusion programs that reach out to all cultures and respect their contributions to the company. These programs enhance an organization's capabilities with respect to employee relations. These slight differences in all employees will impact how they each assimilate information that is learned by the organization. Senior HR professionals must know how to lead this process and ensure that no group is marginalized or not allowed to contribute to the growth and development of the organizational culture.

Strategies for a Safe and Secure Workplace

Senior HR professionals must have extensive knowledge of the variety of strategies that protect employees from occupational illness and injury. Other programs also reduce the company's overall operational risk. While the structure and execution of these kinds of programs are very different, they are both a means of reducing risk to the organization with the goal of maintaining a strong and capable workforce.

There are several types of risks that companies are exposed to in the course of conducting business. Senior HR professionals must familiarize themselves with the variety of potential risks and how they can be mitigated to protect the organization. Properly identifying the risk to an operation is an essential skill that should be practiced. The risk is mitigated when proper procedures are established and followed, proper safety equipment is installed, and personnel are trained on incident prevention and response. In general, risks can be to the safety or security of the organization.

Occupational Injury and Illness Prevention

General safety programs seek the reduction and elimination of hazards that cause injury or illness. Table 10.3 provides some examples of creating the conditions to prevent incidents. Senior HR professionals must know how to develop these programs and evaluate their effectiveness. In some cases, senior HR professionals in conjunction with managers will create additional duties where an employee is the responsible agent for safety in a particular department or division.

TABLE 10.3   Prevention methods

Example	Result
Safety suggestion program	Allows employees to present ideas on how to improve safety practices
Proper equipment training and fitting	Ensures that employees exposed to hazards know how to use proper personal protective equipment (PPE)
Universal precautions	Industry standards in the medical, health, and food services industries that prevent transmission of bacteria or viruses
Safety equipment	Eye wash stations, first aid kits, fire extinguishers, safety showers to reduce or minimize injuries

In addition to individual appointments, senior HR professionals should understand how to design and manage committees with the task of promoting safety practices and general awareness of risks that employees are exposed to within the organization. They can help with policies that implement incentives that are awarded to individuals and teams that are safety focused and have solid practices that result in a reduction of preventable illnesses and injuries in a company.

 Real World Scenario

Explosion on Set

A licensed pyrotechnician on a movie set was working to rig explosives on cars for a scene to be filmed outside a warehouse. As the individual was carrying the charge to the place where it would be attached, it detonated, causing injury to the individual. Fortunately, the individual was following all of the established protocols for handling the explosive cord including proper distance from the body and location. While the injury sustained was severe, it was not fatal. An investigation was conducted to examine whether the individual missed a procedure or created an unsafe condition. This included other witness statements and a review of the area. It was ultimately discovered that this particular remote location was a former factory with iron filings scattered in the soil surrounding the building. These filings happened to create sufficient static charge when walking across the lot that the explosives ignited. This was unforeseen by the production crew or the very experienced technical expert. It shows that even with procedures and trained personnel, incidents can still occur. However, it also is worth noting that the severity of the occurrence was mitigated precisely because proper practices were being followed.

Workers' Compensation

Senior HR professionals must know how the workers' compensation program works and how premiums are determined. They must ensure that policies are created that govern procedures associated with the workers' compensation claims of employees. They must evaluate claims and look for trends that indicate gaps in safety practices. These claims usually have a medical component for any treatment, along with any rehabilitation and a portion of wages lost. These packages can be several thousands of dollars, so each claim will have a significant impact on the resulting premium increases.

Workplace Safety

Safety protocols are intended to reduce accidents and the extremely high costs associated with workers' compensation and other financial liability. However, these safety points work only if they are implemented and followed by the employees. Generally, safety risks are those specific risks that come from hazards that result in physical illness or injury and subsequent losses in work time, productivity, efficiency, or resources (such as money). Hazards such as those that cause slips, trips, or falls can be reduced. Table 10.4 gives some examples of hazards, the possible losses that they cause, and the prevention or risk mitigation method.

TABLE 10.4   Hazards and risk

Hazard	Potential Loss	Mitigation
Wet floor	Fall causing injury with loss of work days	Wet floor signs or other barriers to alert employees
Dust particulates	Inhaled by employee causing respiratory distress and lost days	Breathing respirator or other similar PPE
Blood-borne pathogen	Illness or sickness resulting in lost days	Universal precautions like latex gloves, gown, and face shield or mask

Certain safety risks, as shown in Table 10.4, require different means to reduce the threat. The necessary measures needed to protect employees against tripping are quite different from the measures to protect against blood-borne pathogens, but the steps to identify these hazards and implement controls are the same.

Security

Senior HR professionals should be familiar with a variety of security risks, from both physical and virtual aspects. Theft is a large risk that can create loss for an organization if access controls are not present; it's also a risk if there are situations where employees or outsiders perceive an opportunity to steal, if the consequences are low, or if there is a low chance of being caught. Without proper standards, some employees may feel entitled to take company property or feel that it's acceptable behavior. Senior HR professionals must ensure that the company clearly defines the disciplinary outcome if a theft occurs.

In addition to general theft, corporate espionage is a specific kind of theft that involves trade secrets and insider information about a company and its activities. This is an intentional act by someone who intends harm or damage to a company by stealing proprietary information that can be used to damage an organization's reputation, market share, or products. This person seeks for an outside entity to gain a competitive advantage over the company by using deceptive means to gain access and use the information. In a similar fashion, sabotage doesn't seek to take information out of the organization but to take action that harms the company from within. Sabotage is a deliberate act to disable, destroy, or break equipment that is needed for operations to delay or stop production or delivery of service.

Senior HR professionals should know how to reduce physical risk, by controlling access and establishing procedures for who may perform certain tasks in the company. For example, suppose a company that uses a direct deposit system for payroll transposes an account, causing an employee to go unpaid. To correct the situation, the finance department generates a handwritten check to be issued to the employee. Without proper controls, the check could be approved for any amount. The accounting department, without knowledge of the transaction, could improperly report the payment as an error, resulting in a stop to payment. These controls ensure that the right individual is approving money movement, and if there are any changes to procedure, that they are communicated throughout the organization to individuals who need to know this information to properly fulfill their duties.

Emergency Response, Business Continuity, and Disaster Recovery Plans

Like general emergency preparedness plans, business continuity and disaster recovery plans have components that senior HR professionals must know. Specifically, they must know the ways that their organization chooses to back up and protect sensitive data. This may include using a cloud service or third-party vendor to store data off-site. By having a backup of information stored at a separate location, the company reduces the risk that may be caused if an incident happens whereby the primary storage location is destroyed (fire, tornado, flood, and so on). Senior HR professionals must take care to develop and know the parts of a disaster recovery plan, which includes items such as alternate work locations. In some situations, especially with companies that have multiple locations, it may be possible to re-establish work in another place while waiting for recovery operations to restore primary locations.

> ### 🌐 Real World Scenario
>
> #### Hurricane Katrina
>
> In 2005, Hurricane Katrina devastated the Deep South of the United States and specifically was responsible for causing a catastrophic flood of New Orleans. The United States Military Entrance Processing Command (MEPCOM) is responsible for the accession and qualification of individuals joining the U.S. Armed Forces. It has 64 military entrance processing stations (MEPSs) around the United States, including New Orleans. At the time of the disaster, the personnel needed to evacuate themselves, along with files including hard copies and vital records such as birth certificates for those candidates who were in processing to the military and headed to basic training from that region. They successfully stored and secured thousands of files and moved them to alternative locations, including Atlanta and two other MEPSs to continue operations. These alternate work sites were able to take the increased workload and displaced workers until operations in New Orleans could resume. This is a great example of preparedness and planning in a short time to respond to a disaster.

Internal Investigation, Monitoring, and Surveillance

Senior HR professionals must know both the capabilities and the limitations of techniques for monitoring employees in the workplace and surveillance. This includes internal investigations of employees suspected of violating policies or those whose behavior may pose a risk to the organization. In the modern workplace, the most readily identifiable example of this type of activity is email monitoring and website visits. The IT department has the capability to track and store data elements that are transmitted across company equipment. Senior HR professionals must understand how to notify employees that they may be subject to this kind of surveillance as a condition of having access to and using company computer systems. Senior HR professionals must ensure that managers understand that communications transmitted in the conduct of work should not be considered private or personal and therefore may be accessed as part of routine work operations. It should be clearly communicated with active acknowledgment by each individual employee that they may be monitored while working. While a company should respect the privacy of its employees, it has an affirmative responsibility to protect its IT infrastructure, and any risk imposed by employees disregarding policies is too high.

Data Security and Privacy

Data security and privacy ensures that the digital information a company collects and stores is authenticated and secure from intrusion. Modern organizations store much of their information digitally on servers located within the company or externally maintained by third-party vendors. In all cases, senior HR professionals should know common practices to reduce the risk associated with data breaches and how to report incidents if they occur. The greatest risk to a company's data is the personnel who work for it. In most cases, the problem is not malicious actors from within but complacent employees who do not follow proper procedures and are unaware of threats to data integrity.

Data transmitted across email or the Internet can be stolen. It is important that senior HR professionals know which critical data should be encrypted. Personally identifiable information (PII), such as social security numbers, bank information, and credit card data, should be protected. Files that are stored on servers should be restricted for access to those individuals with a legitimate business interest. Shared folders, therefore, should be routinely checked to determine whether people have appropriate credentials for accessing the data contained in the files. Most files and computer systems are protected by passwords. It is an important practice in HR that passwords should not be shared to prevent unauthorized access or disclosure.

Because employee complacency or negligence poses the greatest risk to data integrity, data hackers will exploit this vulnerability. One successful technique is called social engineering. This is a construct where someone attempting to gain access uses a variety of practices that take advantage of the human nature to help or assist others. For example, someone may pose as a customer and ask questions in an attempt to get an employee to reveal sensitive information. This approach relies on good customer service standards and the employee's desire to answer the client's questions. Employees can be tricked into giving away passwords that can be used to gain unauthorized access to the data being protected. Senior HR professionals must be aware that training and vigilance are the best risk mitigation strategies for the organization.

Exam Essentials

Review methods for assessing employee attitudes, opinions, and satisfaction.   Know how to conduct and deliver results from employee engagement surveys. You should understand how to take survey information and create action plans on how to improve conditions for employees to improve their attitudes toward work and management of the organization.

Understand disaster recovery.   Know the parts of a disaster recovery plan and how the HR team contributes in an organization. Review any previous incidents that may have caused a disaster recovery plan to be implemented and how the organization recovered after an incident. Review what essential information must be saved, backed up, or protected in a company and how that task is being done. How are incidents reported that could cause a disaster recovery plan to be executed, and who makes the decision?

Responsibilities

The responsibilities of senior HR professionals for employee relations and engagement can greatly impact the overall climate of the company and therefore the organizational effectiveness. Senior HR professionals must diligently execute these duties as part of their jobs.

Often these responsibilities are neglected because the negative impact of neglect is not readily apparent. However, the consequences can be severe and long-lasting for inattention to this important role.

While safe practices must be part of a company's everyday operations, senior HR professionals must understand the importance of the responsibilities they have in this area. The proper development and implementation of a workplace safety and security program is paramount. However, it's not just about documentation and compliance; it is about developing and encouraging a culture of safety throughout the company. Effectively managing risk to prevent illness and injury will help the organization reduce loss and liability. HR professionals can demonstrate through their actions a continued commitment to the organization's employees and their health and safety.

Engagement Strategies

Employee engagement describes the level of workers' satisfaction with organizational policies and practices. Senior HR professionals are responsible for developing strategies that are designed to improve employee attitudes and motivate them to perform at optimal levels. Some techniques include the implementation of recognition programs, the design of career development models, and the use of performance management. To improve engagement, senior HR professionals must also examine the company's commitment to diversity and inclusion, seeking feedback from employees, improving hiring practices, and delivering effective training that celebrates diversity in the workplace.

Strategies for Employee Satisfaction

Because each employee is different, there is no universal solution for making them happy. In fact, senior HR professionals will realize through experience that attempting to make each and every employee "happy" is ultimately a self-defeating task. Gauging employee satisfaction is not about "happiness" as much as it is about fulfillment of their desires and goals by matching skills the employee is good at with tasks that must be accomplished to meet the organizational goals. When this alignment is accomplished, the employee feels they are a valued member of the team by having tangible results that reflect their contributions and efforts. Therefore, senior HR professionals must devise a variety of strategies that match skills, recognize contributions, and better align an employee's efforts to the goals of the company.

Recognition

A recognition program that is executed in a timely fashion and is fair and equal in its recognition for similar contributions between employees is necessary to maintain employee satisfaction. Senior HR professionals are responsible for the design and implementation of recognition programs and for training managers to know when and how to recognize employee contributions. As mentioned previously, each employee is different, so each may respond to different types of recognition. Some examples include monetary awards, noncash awards, honorary awards, and informal recognition. Motivations of individuals will help managers and HR professionals identify and meet their needs for recognition.

Career Development Models

Creating career paths and models that show potential developmental steps by which an entry-level employee can grow and advance over time is a key responsibility for senior HR professionals. Each position in the organization has job specifications and qualifications. By determining the necessary experience, education, and training, the company identifies how an employee might progress over the course of a career. The model may point to lateral moves across divisions or upward mobility based on potential. Senior HR professionals can then use these road maps in conjunction with managers to identify gaps, develop training plans, or find activities that build the necessary knowledge, skills, or abilities required for the next level.

Performance Management

To align behaviors of employees with the organizational goals, senior HR professionals develop and implement evaluations, corrective action, and coaching to identify an employee's strengths and weaknesses and, more important, strategies and suggestions for improving performance over time. Performance management is the entire process and includes the tools, such as formal reviews, and the procedures, such as one-on-one coaching sessions to discuss expectations and outcomes related to an individual's performance. Senior HR professionals must train managers and executives in the uses and limitations of performance management systems. There are a multitude of options available in the modern business environment, but there is no one-size-fits-all solution. However, if you view the ultimate goal of performance management as alignment of employee and organizational goals, then the required performance management is the system that most effectively accomplishes this task.

Strategies to Promote Diversity and Inclusion

In 2015, Vernā Myers addressed AppNexus's inaugural Women's Leadership Forum with a talk titled "Diversity Is Being Invited to the Party; Inclusion Is Being Asked to Dance." This analogy is very fitting and describes the strategies HR professionals can use to ensure that all employees are given opportunities in the organization and then to promote those opportunities to encourage participation. Among areas that senior HR professionals must focus on are hiring, employee feedback, and training.

While senior HR professionals are responsible for ensuring that hiring practices are compliant with existing equal opportunity laws, the strategies for diversity and inclusion go beyond minimum requirements and standard practices. These strategies should actively promote opportunities for talent pools that may not traditionally participate in the company's business sector—for example, targeting traditional women's colleges with training for careers that are historically male-centric, such as engineering. Another mechanism is using employee feedback on how to expand opportunities and increase participation. Finally, senior HR professionals work in conjunction with management to implement training that promotes awareness and counters residual biases and prejudices that may exist throughout the company.

Safety and Security Strategies

Senior HR professionals are responsible for the safety and security of the human capital of the organization. This includes emergency response plans, access controls, and data security and privacy. The goal with these programs is to protect the organization and mitigate risk. Among the more notable responsibilities of senior HR professionals is to develop and implement strategies to protect employees from the threat of workplace violence.

Protect against Loss and Liability

Senior HR professionals must help the organization protect against loss and liability. They work in conjunction with the safety personnel, legal, privacy, and information technology specialists to develop and execute emergency response plans in part to prevent but often to respond to incidents within the organization.

Prepared for a Catastrophic Crisis

The attacks of September 11, 2001, on the World Trade Center and the Pentagon killed nearly 3,000 people. A clear tragedy in American history, it has changed the face of emergency response and business continuity to prepare for the absolute worst conditions and destruction of an organization. However, there were almost the same number of lives saved by one individual, named Rick Rescorla, who was director of security for Morgan Stanley, whose headquarters were located in the World Trade Center. His actions on that day, along with preparations, planning, rehearsals, and communications, have been widely credited with saving the lives 2,687 of Morgan Stanley employees who safely evacuated the towers before they fell. We must all take the lesson that we must plan for the worst and be prepared to handle and respond to a crisis because it is impossible to prevent catastrophic events 100 percent of the time. It is not a matter of "if" but "when" it will occur.

Emergency Response

Emergency response plans are, in part, the responsibility of senior HR professionals. As new employees are hired and integrated into the organization, they must be familiarized with the plans to protect employees' safety and the assets of the company. Senior HR professionals develop plans and keep them current. They are also responsible for coordinating and developing training on the various topics covered by these contingency plans. Senior HR professionals play an integral part in maintaining business continuity and recovery to normal operations following any catastrophic event.

Preventing and Responding to Workplace Violence

One of the most critical risk management tasks that senior HR professionals are responsible for is preventing and responding to workplace violence. Just within the past few years, there have been high-profile violent events, in places of business or commerce, involving employees and bystanders. The term *active shooter* has become the general term to indicate an armed individual with the intent to inflict mass casualties through an intentional violent act. These acts are usually short in relative duration but inflict a great deal of damage, physically and emotionally, on the victims.

Not all workplace violence events are active shooter or mass casualty situations. Consider a domestic dispute between two individuals, one of whom works for the company. There may be a threat or possibility of risk should the other party attempt to cause an incident at the place of work of the employee. At that point, the business has an important role to ensure the safety and security of their employee. This may take the form of an escort to the employee's vehicle or verifying visitors at a reception station by checking valid identification. Table 10.5 shows some examples of workplace violence and prevention or response techniques that senior HR professionals might use.

TABLE 10.5   Workplace violence responses for HR professionals

Threat or Danger	Response
Domestic abuse	Counseling for the victim
	Increased security presence
	Escort of the victim at work to parking area
Bullying	Zero tolerance policy
	Bystander training to identify bullying behavior and scenarios
Angry/belligerent customer	Response and incident training
	Facilitate means to elevate complaints to supervisors
	Proper access controls to employee-only areas

Developing Security Plans

Senior HR professionals help the company develop security plans to protect unauthorized access to and disclosure of critical information or physical areas of the company. By doing so, they reduce the risk that the company undertakes in its operations. Security plans may include determining appropriate levels of access in information systems or in areas of the company. Senior HR professionals develop procedures and practices to maintain rosters or digital controls, issue security identification badges, and write policies governing access to vital operational information.

Business Continuity and Disaster Recovery

In theater, they say "The show must go on!" It's no different in business. Even if there has been a successful attempt to disrupt operations by outside entities or an incident has occurred resulting in serious injury or even the death of an employee, there is an expectation that the company must continue to function and perform its mission. Not to do so threatens to impact a much larger community of workers, stakeholders, and customers. Business continuity looks at the short term to keep operations running and to quickly assess what gaps may have occurred as a result of an incident. It is worth noting that when testing business continuity plans, the greatest risks are those where a loss creates an operational gap that is difficult to overcome, expensive, or time-consuming. Disaster recovery is an internal function that restores damages to a pre-incident state if possible or rebuilds a lost capability to offer the same or greater level of service than was provided prior to a disaster.

Senior HR professionals play a key role in developing, monitoring, and testing business continuity plans. They are responsible for identifying critical HR business processes that must continue to function and essential data that should be backed up or otherwise secured in the event of an emergency. Additionally, they are responsible for coordinating with executive management to identify essential personnel in the organization who play a critical role in disaster recovery and ensure that those individuals are properly trained and aware of their duties and responsibilities. Often senior HR professionals will be responsible for providing public relations or communications departments with information that has been properly screened to protect individual privacy but otherwise may have a public interest.

 Real World Scenario

Ransomware Recovered

A company that I worked for was hit by ransomware, a specific type of malicious software that allows computer hackers to gain access to electronic data and seize it, preventing any legitimate users from accessing it. Usually this is done through social engineering and an employee unknowingly giving access to an unauthorized party who is then free to plant the ransomware. The data is not erased or damaged; it is simply made inaccessible. To recover the data, the company is instructed to pay money to an untraceable account, and doing so will get access back. The goal of the hackers is strictly to make money, so having control of the data is just a means to an end.

In the case of this company, the organization has a strong disaster recovery plan and maintained continually updated backups of the data at an off-site location that was not affected by the ransomware. The company IT team was able to restore the data from the backup without any significant loss (other than time) without having to pay the ransom, and additional focus was placed on training employees to be aware of social engineering attacks.

Senior HR professionals also must communicate with employees to keep them informed of changes in operations that result from an emergency situation as well as serve as a point of contact for employees attempting to communicate with the company when normal operational channels are unavailable. For example, a retail chain that has stores in a hurricane evacuation zone must be prepared when a hurricane forces an evacuation of the area. Workers for the store may be displaced and have limited ability to communicate their whereabouts to the organization. Senior HR professionals may establish contact points to assist and provide a means for employees to reach out. If there is a significant loss of power or communications, it becomes increasingly difficult to reach employees to let them know what is going on and what to do next. Senior HR professionals must think ahead and anticipate some ways that operations might be impacted in these situations.

Electronic Media

In today's digital environment, companies must be able to assess the risk that is posed by the World Wide Web. User agreements are a means to inform employees about policies governing access to data systems and appropriate use for work and leisure purposes. Most companies allow some reasonable personal use of organizational computers and equipment. These agreements or policies specify the limitations and restrictions of their use. Senior HR professionals are instrumental in helping an organization develop effective policies and ensuring that proper training is conducted to prevent abuse of company email, social media, and appropriate website access.

Virtually every organization will have email as a means of communicating official business and personal information between employees, management, and the outside world. Companies, in some cases such as government entities, are required to maintain any official correspondence, and this includes email. Senior HR professionals are responsible for ensuring that employees understand their rights concerning email access as well as the duties of the company to maintain this information if requested. Criminals and data hackers have discovered that to gain access to company information, one of the easiest means is the use of social engineering through fake phishing emails. These are designed to get the employee to click a link or download a file in the body of the message that unwittingly helps the criminal gain unauthorized access. Because of this risk, the company must take steps to help employees recognize these tactics and encourage proactive measures to prevent loss. Senior HR professionals can assist in this process by developing policies that limit the use of official email to only those items necessary for business. Restricting personal use of company email reduces the likelihood that spam or other high-risk emails will be sent to employees.

In that same manner, HR professionals must have strong policies that define appropriate website access. Pornography, hate groups, and extremist websites that are being "surfed" by employees on company time not only pose a risk in the loss of productivity but also can create potential harassment claims against the company if proactive steps are not taken to address the risk. If the appearance is that the company has a permissive attitude to these activities, it can be held responsible for actions that stem from this conduct by employees. The acceptable use policies are maintained by HR and must be communicated to all employees so that they understand what is considered to be the appropriate activity on Internet access. It is not practical to limit web use to work-only sites because it becomes harder and harder with the growing number of sites today. However, there are effective web tools that can block sites actively as needed. Senior HR professionals are responsible for establishing training that discusses appropriate office conduct and the websites that should be used in the conduct of business for the company.

Privacy Policy

Senior HR professionals are responsible for developing and implementing internal and external privacy policies. Privacy relates to the protection and proper use of personal information that has been collected by an organization as well as the internal controls that verify that policies and procedures are being followed. To protect against unauthorized release or disclosure of information that could adversely impact an employee, senior HR professionals must ensure that they collect only the minimum amount of information that is required to achieve an intended purpose. They must also control access to the information so that only the fewest number of people who need the information have it. Finally, they must inform an individual whose information has been collected, the intended purpose for collecting it, how it will be shared, and if there is an unauthorized disclosure with the measures being used to protect or recover the information.

Identity theft is a growing threat to businesses and their employees. When personally identifiable information, such as a social security number, is stolen, it can be used for a variety of purposes. Credit cards, bank accounts, or other financial instruments can be obtained using falsified information.

In a similar manner, data files on a network should be protected and restricted for use by authorized personnel with a need for such information also. Senior HR professionals are responsible for coordinating with the information technology specialists to determine the proper level of data classification. Data classification is a process by which the organization determines the required level of safeguarding and then assesses the risk or potential severity of loss should the data be breached. Most often, the greatest risk is through human error in the misuse of passwords and other access controls that were in place to safeguard data but are subverted by employees for expediency without realizing the increase in risk. It is not just employees' data that the company has a responsibility to safeguard. Clients and customers have an expectation that their information is also protected. Senior HR professionals are responsible for ensuring that the policies and procedures protect all personally identifiable information obtained by the organization, not just the data related to employees.

One other area that senior HR professionals are responsible for is the policies and procedures on workplace monitoring. In some organizations, there are security cameras that record activities to protect against loss. The company must clearly communicate with employees the purpose of the cameras, what data is collected, and how it can be used. For example, if the stated purpose is to protect against theft and the camera recording is used following a workplace accident to determine whether an employee was negligent, there is a possibility that the collected video could not be used legitimately for this purpose. This is especially true if disciplinary action resulted from the monitoring, as it would violate the employee's expectation of privacy. HR professionals therefore should communicate a wide use of policy and ensure that employees are notified as to the possibility of being recorded and what the information could be used for in the broadest sense.

Effective Labor Strategies

While the organized labor movement changes over time and may not be as strong as in the past, it is a significant part of the United States workforce and therefore an important responsibility for senior HR professionals. They must understand the collective bargaining process and the associated requirements and must be able to execute the task. It may be that the employees of a company never seek to organize; however, there is a responsibility to the organization that HR be prepared to participate in the election process, contract negotiations, and administration.

Maintaining a Union-Free Organization

Senior HR professionals are responsible for proactively managing employee relations so as to keep the company union-free. It is an important distinction that this does not explicitly or implicitly mean that they are not to fully follow all the rules and regulations in the conduct of labor practices. To maintain a union-free organization, the company may develop strategies that result in a lower interest in unionization by employees. In previous chapters, we discussed workforce planning, human resource development, and compensation and benefits, and in the conduct of these functions the company can create a strong culture in which the employee feels valued and their needs are met. However, in addition to these functions, at a senior level HR professionals can provide guidance in the development of strategies to remain union-free.

Senior HR professionals can work with executives to develop and articulate a message that makes an argument for the company to remain union-free. By listing the reasons that both employees and the company benefit, it is possible to persuade employees from choosing the path to unionization. They must also ensure that employee relations matters are handled effectively in a timely manner. The company's values must reflect the importance of the employees' contributions to its success. A company that keeps its employees in high regard with respect for their work will negate many of the reasons employees seek unionization. If employees feel that they have a voice in the direction of the company and are free to bring issues to management that are resolved promptly, they may feel that the need for collective bargaining is not high.

Senior HR professionals are in a position to evaluate the morale of the employees through surveys, interviews, and discussions. They can offer insight to management as to employee needs and offer information to employees about the direction of the company or insight into executive-level decisions. They should always strive to ensure that managers treat employees fairly and listen to their concerns.

🌐 **Real World Scenario**

Educating Employees on How a Union Is Formed

It is permissible for HR professionals to educate employees on the union process. They are free to point out facts that a union can be created with less than the majority of the employees actively wanting a union. If a union attempts to get employees to sign organizing cards, the employees should know that they are not agreeing to elections but are agreeing to pay dues and actively want representation.

If just 30 percent of the eligible employees (which could be far fewer than the total number of employees) sign cards, an election can be held. In the election, only a majority of those voting are required to certify a union. So even if a company has 1,000 employees and only 100 vote, the union requires only 51 votes to certify. If an election is held, it is just as important that employees who are not in support of organizing vote against the union instead of abstaining from voting as their choice may not be reflected otherwise.

Some employees may have a strong desire for union representation only to learn, after the certification of a union, that their positions are not covered by the collective bargaining agreement and not represented. Employees may also have misperceptions about what powers a union has with respect to keeping an employee from being terminated or in getting a salary increase. The normal conduct of business if done in compliance will continue even if the company unionizes.

The Collective Bargaining Process

A large responsibility for HR professionals is participating in the collective bargaining process. Contract negotiations are complex with many needs from both sides and can be contentious or adversarial. HR professionals should strive to approach these negotiations in an open, fair manner that respects the needs of the employees while balancing those needs against those of the company and its stakeholders. Figure 10.1 shows the formal negotiation process as would be followed under the National Labor Relations Act. HR professionals may not participate directly in the negotiations but will provide essential information to the negotiators representing management. They must work for the interests of the company.

The outcome of the negotiation will be the result of several factors, but a negotiation to be most effective should focus on the interests of the parties and where there is common ground. When discussing differences, a negotiator should not anchor to a position as to be intractable. There are some principles that should not be sacrificed if doing so would be fundamentally contrary to firmly held beliefs or values, but these should be few. If everything is a critical point of negotiating, then nothing is. As with any negotiation, ideally the win-win works best in a collaborative gain and so both parties should seek out these options. This process is called *interest-based bargaining*.

FIGURE 10.1 Contract negotiation

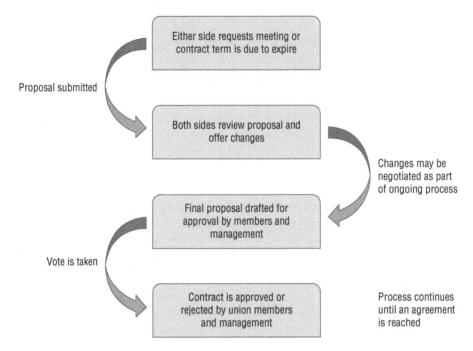

As part of the good-faith bargaining, senior HR professionals provide the negotiators with information as to be as transparent as possible when requested by union officials. There are certain exceptions that protect privileged or proprietary information about the company's operations or private information about employees that is protected from disclosure. Some examples of violating these principles are as follows:

- Not bargaining in earnest
- Not making any concession or considering valid proposals by the other side
- Not negotiating in a timely manner
- Circumventing the negotiators
- Unfair labor practices

Written intentions of contract negotiations are required at least 60 days in advance of contract expiration if a side wants to renegotiate and must include provisions for a time and place to meet.

Grievance Procedures

When resolving employee relations issues, senior HR professionals must be aware of and follow proper procedures. In the instances of an employee disputing actions taken by the company for disciplinary reasons, there should be a process to handle grievances. In union settings, an employee has a right to have another individual attend interviews during investigation processes that could result in disciplinary actions being taken. These rights are formally known as the Weingarten rights, named after a legal labor case ruling by the Supreme Court. Usually there are formal steps that are part of a grievance. Figure 10.2 shows a typical grievance process.

FIGURE 10.2   Formal grievance process

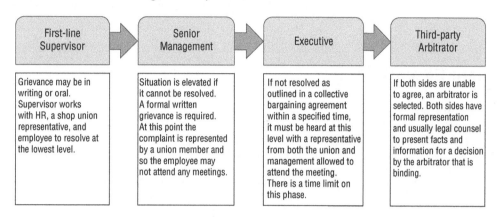

First-line Supervisor	Senior Management	Executive	Third-party Arbitrator
Grievance may be in writing or oral. Supervisor works with HR, a shop union representative, and employee to resolve at the lowest level.	Situation is elevated if it cannot be resolved. A formal written grievance is required. At this point the complaint is represented by a union member and so the employee may not attend any meetings.	If not resolved as outlined in a collective bargaining agreement within a specified time, it must be heard at this level with a representative from both the union and management allowed to attend the meeting. There is a time limit on this phase.	If both sides are unable to agree, an arbitrator is selected. Both sides have formal representation and usually legal counsel to present facts and information for a decision by the arbitrator that is binding.

In the grievance process, HR professionals have the responsibility to do the following:

- Investigate thoroughly and be prepared for any litigation or mediation that may result from a complaint.
- Work with union officials that represent the employee and determine any company obligations as the result of union agreements.
- Document all findings and maintain all notes, records, or other correspondence related to the investigation.
- Avoid making individual concessions that set a precedent or conflict with existing policy or agreements with a union.
- Settle a grievance if the company is, in fact, wrong on the merits of the case.
- Continually communicate with the executives and decision-makers of the company on the progress of the dispute, grievance, and resolution.

The other circumstance in a grievance process is with performance. Senior HR professionals must be responsible for ensuring that management has documented and truly performed the required steps in a performance improvement plan before dismissing an employee for failure to perform. This is certainly true in a union environment, as it is likely that the collective bargaining agreement will have provisions that protect employees for being terminated for performance if these measures have not been done. Senior HR professionals have the responsibility when developing performance policies to include the steps management must take to document employee performance deficiencies and corrective measures taken.

In situations where a manager has a poorly performing employee, they will often seek HR's help in "getting rid of the bad employee." Senior HR professionals must guard against this kind of action. This is because more often than not a manager has failed to document the deficiency properly and the failure has been going on for an extended period of time, but there is now a catalyst that makes the manager want to take action. Senior HR professionals must ensure that proper procedures are followed to avoid a grievance later.

Exam Essentials

Review strategies for employee satisfaction.   Be familiar with the variety of methods to improve employee satisfaction including recognition programs, career development models, and performance management. Review your company's practices in these areas and discuss their effectiveness with the individuals responsible for their design and execution.

Review union policies or practices.   This review is especially important for HR practitioners who do not have exposure or experience with unions or collective bargaining. Look at federal legislation and research decisions by the National Labor Relations Board.

Summary

The topic of employee relations and engagement examines how to effectively manage the expectations and relationships between employees and management. It creates a framework to handle and resolve conflicts that arise between members of the team and, in some cases, provides guidance on disciplinary action. The labor laws of the United States are intricate and attempt to balance the needs of the company with the rights of the workers to have a fair wage with safe and reasonable working conditions. It is vital that senior HR professionals understand the restrictions and limitations imposed by laws, including the National Labor Relations Act. The HR generalist taking the SPHR® exam may be located in a right-to-work state or in a company without organized labor representation. However, this topic is still required knowledge and remains relevant even in these circumstances. It is still possible to violate provisions discussed in this chapter if they do not properly understand the context and requirements.

Risk is a significant part of business, and great organizations take risks to ultimately succeed in their endeavors. However, unknown, unmitigated risks are unacceptable and will undoubtedly expose the organization to a great deal of potential litigation and liability. Senior HR professionals must be able to effectively identify risks, understand how those risks can potentially disrupt the business, and offer solutions on how to reduce risk profile.

They must champion safety practices and enforce standards that protect employees from illness and injury.

Test-Taking Tip

Don't overthink the questions in the exam. The test is very straightforward to practitioners of human resources. Most often, test takers try to think about a question in terms of their specific organization instead of a general principle. In those circumstances, they get the question wrong because their organizational practice may not conform to industry standards or are unknowingly not compliant.

Review Questions

1. A company is located in a right-to-work state. In what way will this impact the organization?

    A. The company is permitted to establish committees that can represent employees on employment matters.

    B. The company is not required to hold elections to unionize if requested by the employees.

    C. Employees are not required to pay union dues within a required time frame to remain employed by the company.

    D. A company can terminate an employee for any reason with or without notice.

2. A company is facing possible unionization and has decided to counter the efforts by offering $1,000 bonus to employees. This is an example of:

    A. A labor negotiation strategy

    B. A lockout provision

    C. A rewards and recognition program

    D. An unfair labor practice

3. Which of the following is considered not a mandatory subject of a collective bargaining agreement?

    A. The process for handling a ULP claim

    B. Overtime compensation

    C. The number of vacation days

    D. Safety practices

4. A company decides to conduct a climate assessment of the organization to gauge employee engagement. In conducting a survey, HR professionals should ensure which of the following?

    A. The employee responses are anonymous and free from retribution.

    B. The company discusses the results of the survey along with any plans to address the findings with employees.

    C. The survey is focused and asks specific questions to get answers to concerns by management.

    D. All of the above.

5. All of the following are legal arguments that a senior HR professional can use in communicating to employees reasons for remaining union free except which one?

    A. The company is in a better position to reward high performers if not restricted by a union agreement.

    B. The employees can provide input on committees formed by the company to represent their peers.

    C. Employees can have opportunities for cross-training and new responsibility without union negotiation.

    D. The company already has policies and provisions in place that benefit employees without them being required to pay dues.

6. It is important that HR professionals conduct investigations in the workplace in an unbiased manner. Which best describes actions they might take to ensure this?

   A. They interview only the supervisor in the course of the investigation.

   B. They investigate all past issues with an employee as part of the current problem or complaint.

   C. They do not require anyone to provide a written statement to allow them to speak freely.

   D. They attempt to resolve the issue in a timely manner and provide a written recommendation to the decision authority.

7. Employee relations programs are an important part of maintaining a positive, engaged workforce. Which of the following is *not* an example of these types of programs?

   A. An employee-of-the-month award

   B. A monthly history event that recognizes minority contributions to the company's history

   C. A safety program established by the company

   D. A suggestion box placed in the breakroom for the employees

8. A legal termination can be:

   A. Done only after consulting union officials if the employee is a covered employee

   B. For employees who are part of a protected class under the at-will doctrine

   C. Done without progressive discipline, if such a policy exists, if the offense is substantial

   D. Done without concern of litigation or arbitration

9. When employees believe that unsafe conditions exist in a company, one of their rights that they may exercise is to:

   A. File a formal complaint with the union

   B. Procure proper safety equipment or modify procedures as they see fit to address the conditions

   C. Notify their supervisor and demand that changes be made

   D. Request an independent inspection to determine compliance and provide recommendations

10. If an employee has a substance abuse problem and seeks assistance using a company EAP, they may be able to protect their job. This is an example of:

    A. Safe harbor

    B. Health intervention

    C. OSHA

    D. Hazard mitigation

11. Some topics that may be found in an emergency response plan include how to respond to:

   A. Fire

   B. Bomb threat

   C. Medical emergency

   D. All of the above

12. Managing risk is:

   A. Identifying hazards and implementing controls to reduce the likelihood of occurrence or the severity if it does

   B. Only done by executives in the organization at the end of operational planning for a new project

   C. Completely ineffective and should therefore focus on incident response

   D. An additional duty for identified employees on a risk committee

13. Security plans may be:

   A. Physical

   B. Electronic

   C. Both A and B

   D. Neither A nor B

Appendix

Answers to Review Questions

Chapter 1: Business Management

1. C. The fourth function is Directing. Implementation is not a management function but describes the process of instituting a new plan or directive. Someone who is directing as a management function may be directing the implementation phase of an operation.

2. D. Values describe how a company operates in the market and form the basis of decisions, policies, plans, programs, and actions.

3. A. Generally accepted accounting principles (GAAP) are commonly used financial rules and standards used by accounting and finance professionals for financial reporting. These agreed-upon standards provide a frame of reference to assess the financial status of an organization.

4. A. A competitive advantage is often an external factor that gives a company an ability to improve its market share or profitability and includes items such as geographic location, access to resources, availability of skilled labor, and limited regulatory constraints.

5. D. Frequency of occurrence or likelihood and the severity of loss or criticality are the two axes that determine the level of risk assumed in any course of action. Mitigation seeks to reduce one or both of these conditions.

6. A. As a confidant to many executives and leaders within an organization, the HR professional who is approachable will help them open up, and they will continually provide access if they feel that you are able to maintain confidentiality on sensitive matters.

7. B. The public comment period is when companies and private individuals may provide relevant information to the responsible regulatory agency on the impact of any regulatory changes.

8. B. It is essential that HR professionals be able to maintain flexibility and handle uncertainty internal and external to the organization. Oftentimes decisions will be required before all the facts can be gathered or analyzed fully.

9. D. The Sarbanes-Oxley Act (SOX) is a landmark legislation for corporate responsibility and outlines several provisions such as election of officers, conflict of interest, and financial disclosure.

10. D. Funding is determined by the finance department in conjunction with procurement and is generally beyond the scope of HR. However, the procurement department will require the technical expertise in developing a request for proposals, evaluating proposals for completeness, and monitoring the performance once a vendor has been awarded a contract.

11. D. By definition, audits are control measures that validate a company's programs and procedures. Along with management techniques designed to monitor output and measure performance, these techniques are part of the Controlling function.

12. A. Goals can be established at the lower levels of management because they do not require any additional input or support. The other choices have inherent impact beyond an operational group and could have monetary implications or similar effects.

Chapter 2: Talent Planning and Acquisition (PHR® Only)

1. B. Disparate impact is the unintentional discrimination of a protected class under Title VII of the Civil Rights Act. The impact to minorities who may be more likely to have a criminal record would violate the standards of equal opportunity.

2. B. Gender is one of the protected classes as well as race, religion, color, and national origin. The other answers are protected under other legislation including at the state level.

3. A. The federal form I-9 is the Employment Eligibility Verification form. Currently, the Department of Homeland Security is the cabinet agency responsible for the document.

4. A. Reliability is concerned with consistency of what the test is measuring. This is different from the validity of a test, which concerns what properties the test is supposed to measure.

5. C. A panel interview is composed of multiple people asking questions of the applicant in one setting. The intent is to draw upon the collective knowledge and assessment of the candidate compared to the required skills to perform the job successfully. A diverse panel also prevents bias of any one person making a hiring decision.

6. D. Successful organizations rely on everyone to be involved in the onboarding process of a new employee. The onboarding is not just the in-processing of an employee through forms and documents on the first day but a deliberate effort to assimilate someone into the organization's culture and business model.

7. A. Although the doctrine of "at-will employment" means that a company can terminate an employee with or without reason at any time, in the case of involuntary termination the reason (or reasons) should be clearly stated. This is a preventative measure for an employee claiming wrongful termination.

8. B. Third-party vendors to assess the skills of the workforce are often used to reduce costs to employers of finding qualified talent. Search engines through large résumé databases are made available to client employers to search for keywords related to their job openings.

9. C. Essential job functions are those duties performed by an individual that are unique to that position and are critical to the employee performing the job in a successful manner. In some cases, the functions may be highly specialized, which limits the available talent able to perform the functions.

10. D. Noncompete clauses are likely to be found in an employment contract, not an offer of employment. The offer letter should be in writing and provide the essential particulars about the conditions of employment (time, location, and compensation).

11. B. Among the myriad of tasks that HR might perform with new employees is to provide information on relocation or coordinate relocation services. This is done in the post-employment phase after an offer of employment has been made and accepted by the employee.

12. D. An organization's employment records are the key to demonstrate hiring practices and meeting the burden of proof for documentation for any audit of human resources. In most cases, official documentation has compliance requirements for the collection, storage, security, release, and destruction of information contained in the documents. In modern businesses, this information is no longer required to be maintained in physical form if digital records are readily available and serve the same purpose.

Chapter 3: Learning and Development (PHR® Only)

1. B. Existing copyright laws protect the author from unauthorized use of any materials that have not been properly credited or where the author hasn't been fairly compensated. Developed training must always comply with the law and any alteration, copy, or use of another author's material is usually in violation of the statute.

2. C. Though not clearly defined, fair use is most often determined by the negative impact an author will be subjected to by the work being used by another, especially in financial terms.

3. A. A needs assessment is usually the first step in the training development process to identify the issue and formulate a corrective action. Attempting to create a solution without first determining the problem may not achieve the desired results.

4. D. Return on investment (ROI) is determined after the training has taken place, when an assessment can be made on the overall effectiveness, rating the cost against any improvements that are attributed to the training. It is difficult to assess ROI before training is conducted. To build an effective training program, you must know the number of employees being trained, how long you will have to implement the training program to plan the development, and how the particular training will be delivered to the learners.

5. B. While determining how much employees enjoyed training and their ability to retain the information learned is important, what matters most are the overall changes and improvements to the organizational processes that the training was intended to affect. Surveys should be conducted after a short time to see whether changes resulting from the training are implemented and have an impact.

6. C. High-potential employees have shown their ability to perform at levels of increased responsibility and authority and should be developed by the organization as part of a succession plan to internally structure potential replacements for key positions throughout the company. These individuals may often be difficult to discover if their jobs and duties do not offer opportunities to demonstrate potential for further advancement.

7. A. Succession planning is a process to identify talent in the organization, assess their potential, and develop them over time. It does not preselect people for positions but ideally creates a pool that can be drawn from to fill roles that are vacated by senior employees who transition or separate from the company.

8. A. The change process describes the phases that an organization goes through when adjusting to organizational change. It transitions the group from their current system or structure through the change to a new period of stability. Implementation covers the major methods that HR professionals can use to help employees adapt to the change. Managing relationships, structure, or technology are the means by which change can be accomplished in the organization.

9. B. Classroom learning involves an instructor and direct interaction with the learners. E-learning is an instructional method using technology to deliver content online that is asynchronous. Blended learning is a combination of the two, usually involving pre- or post-work that can be done as e-learning and then discovery and more in-depth analysis conducted in a classroom setting.

10. C. A task or process analysis is the portion of a needs assessment that compares the underlying job requirement with the current knowledge, skills, and abilities of the employee to determine where shortfalls exist. When a task is discovered that the employee is underperforming, training can be developed and provided to make improvements.

11. A. Executive coaching requires HR professionals to teach and assist senior leaders of the organization to improve their skills at managing human capital. It may sometimes be referred to as "coaching up" as the relationship between executives and HR may often be a senior/subordinate one, so it requires trust and confidence that the HR professional is helping the executive improve their abilities.

Chapter 4: Total Rewards (PHR® Only)

1. B. The Wage and Hour Division (WHD) of the Department of Labor is the federal agency charged with the administration of regulations governed by the FLSA. It issues interpretations and guidance that helps employers maintain compliance with the law.

2. B. Even though the employee is not in a supervisory position, they are exercising independent judgment and discretion on matters of significance, are salaried and making more than the minimum required amount, and are in an administrative role.

3. A. Under USERRA the service member meets the criteria for return to their civilian employment after the military service call-up is concluded. The company must comply with the provisions of this law.

4. A. An employer will lag behind the market wage by comparison when they can afford to do so because of an abundance of available labor or if they have no choice because of the need to reduce costs. They must carefully balance this to ensure that they have sufficient workers who are qualified.

5. D. A job evaluation will result in determination regarding pay and ultimately can be combined with others to set a grade system that groups common jobs together for pay purposes.

6. D. In addition to the ones listed, responsibility and supervision are also compensable factors under these important laws.

7. D. A productivity-based pay system either has a relative amount percentage based on the units produced (such as $1 per widget) or is based on a tiered system where the more that is produced, the higher the pay ($1 for the first 50 units, $2 for the next 100. and so on).

8. D. Workers' compensation is paid for by the employer and is one of the mandatory benefits that a company must provide. Unemployment insurance, social security, and Medicare are other examples of mandatory benefits.

9. C. The needs assessment is truly the first step that an HR professional should undertake when determining what benefits to provide for the company that also align with the mission and resources available to commit.

10. D. There are serious legal consequences that may result in the interference or denial of the benefits associated with the Family and Medical Leave Act. As part of its compliance function, HR must ensure that policies and procedures are in place to facilitate the proper administration of this benefit and educate management as to their role.

11. C. Because the employee is making the changes, there is no requirement to inform. However, many companies will send a written confirmation of the change. The required notices all relate to actions initiated by the company, not the employee.

12. D. The period of open enrollment usually occurs once a year before the beginning of the new budget year or calendar year when benefits are initiated. The open enrollment season has sufficient time to make adjustments to payroll deductions and to inform all employees of pending changes. A qualifying event such as departing the job initiates another period of time in which changes can be made because the circumstances of the employee have changed.

Chapter 5: Employee and Labor Relations

1. C. Conducting business in a right-to-work state does not mean that the basic provisions of the National Labor Relations Act are voided. Unions can and do exist; however, there are limitations on their ability to collect dues from nonmembers, who are able to benefit without participating in the union.

2. B. The National Labor Relations Act of 1935 is also known as the Wagner Act and sets the provisions for the establishment of the oversight and enforcement to be within the National Labor Relations Board (NLRB).

3. D. Actions such as offering wages or benefits in exchange for a particular position toward unionization are prohibited and classified as an unfair labor practice. HR professionals should ensure that any adjustments that were planned in compensation and benefits not be put in effect in close proximity in time to any labor organization efforts.

4. C. The at-will doctrine allows employers to terminate employment at any time, with or without reason, of any employee provided that it is not otherwise illegal (such as a protected class). It also allows the employee to quit with or without cause with no notice. Even if a union exists, the at-will provision isn't negated unless specifically addressed in an employment contract or collective bargaining agreement. Therefore, employers must be aware how such agreements limit their ability to exercise at-will employment rights.

5. D. All of the answers are correct to assist the company in ensuring a strong response to a survey to assess the organizational climate.

6. C. A common confusion is the difference between job enrichment, which offers more depth to a position, and job enlargement, which results in new tasks and associated responsibilities. In this case, the responsibility for quality control requires the same skills and tasks but at a deeper level and therefore would be considered job enrichment.

7. A. Physical threats such as active shooters, fire, severe weather, and virtual threats such as cyberattacks and financial disruption are examples of security risks that require active steps to reduce exposure and liability.

8. B. Employees cannot represent any other employees in discussions with management about workplace conditions and other elements of employment.

9. D. When conducting investigations on employment or labor relations matters, HR professionals should seek to complete their work in a timely and accurate manner. They should keep a record and document all their actions should a review be required or in case of litigation.

10. D. The goal of progressive discipline is to use the lowest level required to correct employee behaviors and align them to company values and ethics. In this scenario, a minor infraction can be resolved with a verbal warning and review of the policies to correct tardiness before it becomes a significant pattern of behavior.

11. C. A safety program would be part of a collective bargaining agreement and is not considered an employee relations program.

12. B. The first step in this scenario should be to review the agreement with the union to understand what disciplinary actions are agreed to and the procedures that must be followed to comply with the collective bargaining agreement.

13. A. The Occupational Safety and Health Administration (OSHA) is mandated by the law to develop minimum standards for safety in four business categories. The practices establish guidelines for organizations to follow when developing and implementing safety programs.

14. D. Under OSHA, an employee has several rights including the expectation of working in a safe and secure environment. An employee has a right to request that OSHA inspect working conditions to determine whether they are in compliance with the law.

15. B. The decision to purchase new safety or health equipment does not prevent illness or injury without its use and training. However, completing accident reports and making them available for review allows employees to understand the cause of previous accidents and prevent reoccurrences in the future.

16. A. While an investigation may follow, it is important that the accident scene be secured for gathering evidence and preventing further injuries to co-workers. This also provides the best chance to determine a cause and develop prevention methods. To ensure that an employee receives benefits in a timely manner, HR professionals should notify the carrier that will be handling the claim that an incident has occurred after the company has determined no further hazard is present that can cause injury or illness.

17. B. While not all signs will be evident, it is possible to detect changes in behavior that can cause concern. Conflict is normal and part of everyday work operation, provided it is resolved effectively and challenges the group to constantly seek improvement. However, when one individual seems distant from the rest of the group with a radical change in personal behavior attributable to traumatic events in the employee's personal or professional life, it may be cause for concern.

Chapter 6: Leadership and Strategy

1. C. The fourth function is Directing. Implementation is not a management function but describes the process of instituting a new plan or directive. Someone who is directing as a management function may be directing the implementation phase of an operation.

2. D. Values describe how a company operates in the market and forms the basis of decisions, policies, plans, programs, and actions.

3. A. A company uses a cost-benefit analysis to compare courses of action when making a business decision. The evaluation usually considers as many factors as can be quantifiably and qualitatively determined beyond just a monetary consideration.

4. D. The Sarbanes-Oxley Act (SOX) is a landmark legislation for corporate responsibility and outlines several provisions such as election of officers, conflict of interest, and financial disclosure.

5. D. Funding is determined by the finance department in conjunction with procurement and is generally beyond the scope of HR. However, the procurement department will require technical expertise in developing a request for proposals, evaluating proposals for completeness, and monitoring performance once a vendor has been awarded a contract.

6. C. Companies will choose to outsource some nonessential business functions that burden the organization and limit their ability to focus on their core competencies. Often there are companies with capabilities that specialize in the associated tasks and can execute them more efficiently and effectively than a company could if they remained in-house.

7. D. By definition, audits are control measures that validate a company's programs and procedures. Along with management techniques designed to monitor output and measure performance, these techniques are part of the Controlling function.

8. C. Before any business case on shared services is approved, the company must determine what services are to be moved. Only once this is determined will roles and responsibilities and mitigation issues be addressed. Finally, a service level agreement will be put in place to formalize the process.

9. D. Metrics that are similar to the choices all represent performance expectations at the strategic level. Quantitative and qualitative measurements can be used to determine the effectiveness of decisions and, when needed, adjust actions going forward.

10. C. This is the best answer at the strategic level. In making a sound business decision, the impact of regulatory restrictions would have the greatest impact on the viability of the decision. Support services by definition do not remove core competencies.

11. C. Human capital projections must look at several factors including the available talent pool, turnover rates, and the types of separations. It allows senior HR professionals a complete look at the reasons people are leaving and how easy or difficult it will be to find a replacement in the talent market.

Chapter 7: Talent Planning and Acquisition (SPHR® Only)

1. C. Individuals who are working below market rate may be attracted to a job opportunity that is similar in the scope of responsibilities and duties to be performed but offers more compensation or better benefits. They may not be actively seeking employment but are drawn to apply when the offer presents itself.

2. A. Reliability is concerned with consistency of what the test is measuring. This is different from the validity of a test, which concerns what properties the test is supposed to measure.

3. C. A panel interview is composed of multiple people asking questions of the applicant in one setting. The intent is to draw upon the collective knowledge and assessment of the candidate compared to the required skills to perform the job successfully. A diverse panel also prevents bias of any one person making a hiring decision.

4. D. Successful organizations rely on everyone to be involved in the onboarding process of a new employee. The onboarding is not just the in-processing of an employee through forms and documents on the first day but a deliberate effort to assimilate someone into the organization's culture and business model.

5. C. Staffing effectiveness can be measured in a variety of ways to ensure that the cost of human capital is not excessive for what duties and tasks are to be performed. Turnover ratios, cost per hire, and number of applicants to number of qualified applicants are metrics that can be used.

6. A. As the economy improves, employees and job seekers enter the market believing that more jobs are becoming available and are more confident that opportunities exist to find meaningful work. This encourages employees who are less satisfied with their current employment to leave voluntarily.

7. B. Third-party vendors to assess the skills of the workforce are often used to reduce costs to employers of finding qualified talent. Search engines through large résumé databases are made available to client employers to search for keywords related to their job openings.

8. B. Succession planning is a subset of an organization's talent management strategy. It does not preselect talent but is developed after a gap analysis has been conducted for the company to see where succession is required to maintain continuity.

9. B. Among the myriad of tasks that HR might perform with new employees is to provide information on relocation or coordinate relocation services. This is done in the post-employment phase after an offer of employment has been made and accepted by the employee.

10. C. Companies that socialize and successfully onboard new employees integrate them into the culture of the organization. This builds brand loyalty and a shared sense of belonging and purpose, which strengthens an employee's commitment to the company based on values. These employees are more likely to be retained by a company in the future.

11. A. Exit interviews should be an unbiased collection of candid feedback and insights into the organizational culture and working conditions experienced by the employee. They should occur on all voluntary terminations when possible and others on a case-by-case basis.

Chapter 8: Learning and Development (SPHR® Only)

1. A. People, technology, and structure are the basic components that change within an organization. What is significant to remember is that when any one of these changes, it will have an impact on the other two. HR professionals must understand the relationship between them.

2. D. Return on investment (ROI) is determined after the training has taken place, when an assessment can be made on the overall effectiveness and the cost of any improvements that are attributed to the training. It is difficult to assess ROI before training is conducted. To build an effective training program, you must know the number of employees being trained, how long you will have to implement the training program to plan the development, and how the particular training will be delivered to the learners.

3. B. While determining how much employees enjoyed training and their ability to retain the information learned is important, what matters most are the overall changes and improvements to the organizational processes that the training was intended to affect. Surveys should be conducted after a short time to see whether changes resulting from the training are implemented and have an impact.

4. C. High-potential employees have shown their ability to perform at levels of increased responsibility and authority and should be developed by the organization as part of a succession plan to internally structure potential replacements for key positions throughout the company. These individuals may often be difficult to discover if their jobs and duties do not offer opportunities to demonstrate potential for further advancement.

5. A. Performance appraisal systems help supervisors, executives, and human resources professionals align employee performance to the corporate goals and objectives by assessing behaviors and results and matching them to the values of the company. By rewarding those employees who consistently demonstrate the desired behaviors, the company reinforces its commitment to promote those behaviors throughout the organization.

6. D. A forced ranking system is just one method of appraisal that is comparative in nature and allows an organization to rank employees from the strongest to the weakest in terms of performance. It is important to remember that this provides only one dimension of evaluating the team, and it is sometimes difficult to compare individuals who do not perform like duties or tasks.

7. D. HR professionals must ensure consistency in the evaluation process, and that is established through proper policy and training of those responsible for conducting the evaluations.

8. C. Senior HR professionals have the added responsibility to develop, implement, and evaluate programs to meet the changing needs of employees and the organization (for example, diversity initiatives).

9. A. Succession planning is a process to identify talent in the organization, assess their potential, and develop them over time. It does not preselect people for positions but ideally creates a pool that can be drawn from to fill roles that are vacated by senior employees who transition or separate from the company.

10. A. The change process describes the phases that an organization goes through when adjusting to organizational change. It transitions the group from their current system or structure through the change to a new period of stability. Implementation covers the major methods that HR professionals can use to help employees adapt to the change. Managing relationships, structure, or technology are the means by which change can be accomplished in the organization.

11. D. Specialized training is developed by the organization to meet the specific needs of the company that cannot be provided by commercial means. Usually this training involves proprietary processes and procedures or specialized equipment. This training is usually the priority to develop for HR professionals because it's not readily available outside the organization.

12. A. Executive coaching requires HR professionals to teach and assist senior leaders of the organization to improve their skills at managing human capital. It may sometimes be referred to as "coaching up" as the relationship between executives and HR may often be a senior/subordinate one, so it requires trust and confidence that the HR professional is helping the executive improve their abilities.

Chapter 9: Total Rewards (SPHR® Only)

1. C. The definition of a fiduciary is that they are solely concerned with the best interests of the participants of the plan and their beneficiaries, and this holds even if the interests do not coincide with the company's.

2. A. An employer will lag behind the market wage by comparison when they can afford to do so because of an abundance of available labor or if they have no choice because of the need to reduce costs. They must carefully balance this to ensure that they have sufficient workers who are qualified.

3. D. A job evaluation will result in determination regarding pay and ultimately can be combined with others to set a grade system that groups common jobs together for pay purposes.

4. D. In addition to the ones listed, responsibility and supervision are also compensable factors under these important laws.

5. A. Stock options, diversified stocks, and phantom and restricted stock plans are all examples of noncash compensation. Other perks provided beyond the salary portion are also noncash variants.

6. C. The needs assessment is truly the first step that an HR professional should undertake when determining what benefits to provide for the company that also align with the mission and resources available to commit.

7. A. Performance-based pay plans are dependent on having a fairly administered evaluation system that guards against bias and has clearly established metrics and evaluation criteria for success. HR professionals must ensure equal opportunity to pay based solely on merit and that institutional or historical discrimination does not prevent any employee from proper compensation.

8. B. A cost of living adjustment allows a company to take into account changes in the economy such as inflation and make onetime corrections that do not have lasting consequences to the annual budgets in future years.

9. D. Cost and coverage are essential elements of a plan design and must meet the needs of the organization. These factors and others will be discussed with a provider or broker service that can evaluate multiple offerings. Any broker decision or impact is decided before accepting any particular offer for services and therefore the reputation would not be part of the evaluation process for the plans themselves.

10. C. A defined benefit plan provides an amount that is consistent based solely on eligibility and will not change based on investment vehicles. This may, however, require changes to the amount of the contribution to offset any increased costs of the benefit and/or financial liability.

11. C. Work-life balance is achieved when companies recognize the need to improve the mental, social, and spiritual well-being of employees to maximize their performance potential for the company. They evaluate the whole employee beyond what is presented only during work hours.

Chapter 10: Employee Relations and Engagement

1. C. Conducting business in a right-to-work state does not mean that the basic provisions of the National Labor Relations Act are voided. Unions can and do exist; however, there are limitations on their ability to collect dues from nonmembers who are able to benefit without participating in the union.

2. D. Actions such as offering wages or benefits in exchange for a particular position toward unionization are prohibited and classified as an unfair labor practice. HR professionals should ensure that any adjustments that were planned in compensation and benefits not be put in effect in close proximity in time to any labor organization efforts.

3. A. Processes such as determining how to resolve unfair labor practices disputes are voluntary topics for a collective bargaining agreement. Another example would be discussions on retiree compensation.

4. D. All of the answers are correct to assist the company in ensuring a strong response to a survey to assess the organizational climate.

5. B. Employees cannot represent any other employees in discussions with management about workplace conditions and other elements of employment. This violates the National Labor Relations Act and is considered an unfair labor practice (ULP).

6. D. When conducting investigations on employment or labor relations matters, HR professionals should seek to complete their work in a timely and accurate manner. They should keep a record and document all their actions should a review be required or in case of litigation.

7. C. A safety program would be part of a collective bargaining agreement and is not considered an employee relations program.

8. C. Progressive discipline procedures should not limit a company's ability to terminate an employee for an egregious violation of policy or misconduct. It is not required that an employer seek lesser disciplinary action for high-level offenses.

9. D. Under OSHA, an employee has several rights, including the expectation of working in a safe and secure environment. An employee has a right to request that OSHA inspect working conditions to determine whether they are in compliance with the law.

10. A. The concept of safe harbor protects an employee from termination or disciplinary action if they are seeking medical help, counseling, or assistance for substance abuse and have sought help prior to being discovered in a random drug screen or other involuntary manner.

11. D. All three items are areas that may be included in an emergency response plan. Other areas may include active shooters, severe weather, and the responsibilities of marshals who are assigned as safety coordinators.

12. A. Managing risk is an integral part of a company's operation and a continual process that requires active attention and ongoing vigilance. As part of the process, the organization identifies hazards and implements controls in the process to be performed.

13. C. Security plans designate how information, infrastructure, and personnel are protected in the organization. This includes physical security such as access controls, cameras, and trained security personnel or electronic (digital) security such as passwords, off-site data storage locations, and file restrictions.

Index